PURSUIT OF ECSTASY

SUNY Series in New Social Studies on Alcohol and Drugs
Harry G. Levine and Craig Reinarman, Editors

PURSUIT OF ECSTASY

The MDMA Experience

JEROME BECK, Dr.P.H.
and
MARSHA ROSENBAUM, Ph.D.

State University
of New York
Press

Published by
State University of New York Press, Albany

For information, address State University of New York Press,
State University Plaza, Albany, N.Y., 12246

Production by Susan Geraghty
Marketing by Terry Swierzowski

Library of Congress Cataloging-in-Publication Data

Beck, Jerome. 1957–
    Pursuit of ecstasy : the MDMA experience / by Jerome Beck and
Marsha Rosenbaum.
        p.   cm. — (SUNY series in new social studies on alcohol and
drugs)
    Includes bibliographical references and index.
    ISBN 0-7914-1817-0 (hc : acid free). — ISBN 0-7914-1818-9 (pb :
acid free)
    1. MDMA (Drug). 2. Drug abuse—United States. I. Rosenbaum,
Marsha, 1948– . II. Title. III. Series.
HV5822.M38B43   1994
362.29'9—dc20
                                                                    93-3371
                                                                    CIP

10 9 8 7 6 5 4 3 2

This book is dedicated to
Alexander Shulgin, Ph.D., for rediscovering the Drug,
and (the late) Norman Zinberg, M.D., for explaining
the significance of Set and Setting

CONTENTS

ACKNOWLEDGMENTS

The authors would like to thank many people for their support. As we are two individuals, our acknowledgements are separate.

The completion of this book marks an important milestone in what has been a long and sometimes ardous journey of personal and professional discovery. Any attempt to convey my gratitude to the many individuals who provided support along the way seems hopelessly inadequate. Nevertheless, I will begin by thanking the logistical support provided by the staff at the Institute for Scientific Analysis. The generous financial support of the National Institute on Drug Abuse made the Exploring Ecstasy study a reality. A grant from the Stern Foundation helped in conducting further analysis following completion of our two-year grant.

Many thanks go out to the diversely talented co-members of our research team. In addition to the helpful assistance provided by Joel Brown, Jennifer Ham, and Sheigla Murphy, I want to acknowledge the substantial contributions made by each of the co-authors of our final report: Marsha Rosenbaum, Patricia Morgan, Deborah Harlow, Doug McDonnell, and Lynne Watson.

In addition to co-authoring this book, Marsha Rosenbaum's leadership from start to finish was vital to the successful completion of the Exploring Ecstasy study. I am particularly indebted to Patricia Morgan for many reasons. In addition to serving as co-principal investigator on the study, she also chaired my dissertation at U.C. Berkeley. My faithful mentor throughout graduate school, we continue to work together on a variety of intriguing research endeavors.

Deborah Harlow, Doug McDonnell, and Lynne Watson each brought unique and valued perspectives and research skills to the study. Their respective contributions and insights are amply reflected in the findings presented here. I am most grateful for the emotional and conceptual support they have given me over the past several years and look forward to many fruitful collaborations in the future.

In writing *Pursuit of Ecstasy,* I want to thank those individuals who patiently helped to ensure its eventual completion. With the assistance of Lynn Wenger, Sharon Michalske admirably endured the agonizingly painstaking process of ushering the manuscript through its many revisions. The considerable editorial guidance provided by Craig Reinarman was essential in transforming the book into a much more readable and engaging account of our findings. I learned a great deal about the art of writing from his insightful commentary and careful attention to detail.

I want to gratefully acknowledge the invaluable contribution provided by the 100 respondents who consented to formal, in-depth interviews for the study. Their generous gift of time and insight were essential in obtaining the depth and diversity revealed in our analysis. My appreciation also goes out to the many knowledgable users, professionals, and other "community consultants" who graciously shared their experiences and perspectives with us. I will begin with the other members of my dissertation committee at U.C. Berkeley: Troy Duster, David Matza, Pat Morgan, Robin Room, and Alexander Shulgin. I would like to particularly single out the scholarly wisdom and support provided by Sasha and Ann Shulgin, Tom and June Reidlinger, Laura Schmidt, Jean Farmer, Howard Kornfeld, Gary Bravo, Charlie Grob, Graham Potter, David Presti, and the irrepressible Rick Doblin, whose seemingly boundless enthusiasm and dedication to the just cause has been an inspiration for me. Finally, I want to express my deepest appreciation to the many wonderful folks who provided support on a more personal level during this lengthy learning process: Michael, Heidi, Rob, Maureen, Joel, Genevieve, Wayne, Jean, Deborah, Dale, Dominique, and Mom—thank you from the bottom of my heart.

Jerome Beck

I would like to thank Jerome E. Beck, who first introduced me to the MDMA phenomena. He inspired our grant proposal, which made our study possible. My continuing gratitude goes to Sheigla Murphy, who worked on the proposal and the study, and who remains my crime partner in drug research. Patricia Morgan was the co-principal investigator of the Exploring Ecstasy study, and provided a needed ear as well as methodological expertise. Lynne

Watson was project administrative assistant, editor, and writer, and did a wonderful job with all three tasks. Doug McDonnell was a great interviewer and writer, as well as a patient sounding board. Deborah Harlow conducted many interviews, contributed to the final report, and taught me a vast amount about the therapeutic and spiritual dimensions of MDMA, as well as about the history of its distribution. Jennifer Ham also conducted interviews for the study.

During the course of our research, many individuals helped us to complete the interviews. Jay Hopkins, in particular, put us in contact with individuals from one of our social worlds. Without his help, we would not have been able to procure these important interviews.

Several people were instrumental in helping to form my evolving perspective on Ecstasy. They are listed not in order of importance, but alphabetically: Patricia and Peter Adler, Diane Beeson, Rick Doblin, Lester Grinspoon, Deborah Harlow, Ethan Nadelmann, John Morgan, Ann and Sasha Shulgin, Andrew Weil, Kevin Zeese, and Lynn Zimmer.

The completion of this book was a monumental task in and of itself. Several individuals made important contributions. Craig Reinarman and Harry Levine, as series editors, first encouraged us to write this book. Howard Becker, Erich Goode, and David Nichols wrote helpful reviews. Professor Reinarman, in a most thorough way, spent a great deal of time editing the entire first draft. He then listened for six months while the book was revised. My debt to him as a friend and colleague is enormous. John Irwin read portions of the manuscript, as did Sheigla Murphy. Both listened endlessly as I expressed my frustrations during the eighteen-month course of revision upon revision upon revision. Lynn Wenger painstakingly worked on the bibliography, and proofed and edited the manuscript.

Finally, my administrative assistant, Sharon Michalske, worked closely with us on each stage, working long hours in the preparation of the book for publication. She was thorough and committed, and I thank her especially.

Marsha Rosenbaum

CHAPTER 1

Introduction:
Varieties of the MDMA Experience

THE DANCER

It was a fear of Dad and a fear of God for me. I was always—I was just a good kid. I didn't want to hurt my parents and I didn't want to disappoint my God. I was absolutely antidrug always. Antialcohol also. But my roommate came home one night saying, "I did that drug Ecstasy that Michael's always talking about." And she said, "You're gonna love it. You've gotta do it. You just want to dance. You want to dance, you want to dance, you want to dance." She was talking about it and how much fun it was, so a few days later, we were out with the guys, her friends that gave it to her, and they were selling it. And this is March of 1985, and it wasn't illegal 'til July. And so I tried it. And they gave us—we never took more than half, because a whole one is just too much for our body weight.

And I remember my first experience was that I just freaked out. We were at this place where they have live music, and we were watching Ray Wiley Hubbard. And they told me, "Now you may feel a little nauseous," and I freaked out. I got up and started walking around the room. You know, it was like (the drug was) following me around the room. I was just running almost. And then after a few minutes—all of a sudden you just feel great. So that was my first experience. We just had the best time of our lives on that stuff. I loved it. I thought it was a miracle drug. For someone who had never done drugs at all and didn't want to, it was wonderful! And I had heard all these good things about it and how it's not addictive and it's great for therapy. It's a very love, love, love kind of thing. And it was all true.

Oh, I loved it because that was one of the things that made it a miracle drug to me. With Ecstasy, you could go to sleep whenever you wanted to, as opposed to cocaine where you can't ever go to sleep. With X, I found that I could go to bed when I wanted to, which is usually after we'd been dancing. We'd dance for four or five hours. We'd get home about 3:00 A.M. I could go to sleep and I'd wake up feeling great. However, I came off of it about three in the afternoon the next day with a hangover, with a headache. And I lost a lot of weight 'cause I was dancing hard, hard, hard all the time and I wasn't eating that much.

We used to go to the Rio Room. The Rio Room was one of those clubs where you could buy cocaine from the maitre d' if you wanted to. It was in '84, '85. It was the biggest—it's a private club—and it was the biggest scene of anything and everything. Everyone that wanted to see or be seen was there. We all miss it like crazy. Well, we would tell people that you're going to feel the big D. Then you'll feel the big N, and then you'll feel the big O. Which means you're gonna feel a little dizzy at first. Then you'll get a little nauseous. And then you'll get orgasmic.

It's so funny, you can't wipe the stupid smile off your face when you do it. You just feel so great. And you just love everybody and everyone wants to dance. This was the main thing. We had to dance. We loved to dance so much. We were dancing all the time at Rio, and you have to dance. And I didn't mix alcohol with it because I always had a glass of water in my hands with it. The bartenders knew me. They had a glass of water when they saw me coming. They'd have it there ready for me. Even if I wasn't on Ecstasy, they figured I would be, I guess.

I don't think I ever did it more than twice a week. And the whole time, it was from March until July—April, May—just four months of it. Maybe once a week for about two months. If you did it two nights in a row, it wouldn't work the second night. You just never would get off on it, unless you took more, I guess. Also, if I eat—eat anything—it doesn't work for me. So it's a great diet pill, absolutely great diet pill, I thought, 'cause you didn't want to eat and you drink lots and lots and lots and lots of water.

Yeah. We partied. We danced our butts off when we were on it. To me, I used to call it my "gotta dance drug" because that's what it is. You gotta dance when you're on it. And also, it was fun because I always tell people if you have an enemy in the room, you will make up with that person. I don't care if you haven't spoken for ten years. You will make up with that person if you're on X because you can't not talk to them. You talk to everyone and you love everybody.

The only negative I can feel about it is the hangover you get—that I got afterwards. Not everyone gets a hangover. And it wasn't like a drunk, like a beer hangover or an alcohol hangover. It was a minor headache usually, and I'd be tired 'cause I would—well, if you dance four hours straight, you're gonna be tired the next day anyway.

And then once it became illegal, they wanted me to do it and I wouldn't do it anymore because I'm a chicken. I don't want to get caught at doing anything that's not right. I didn't want to do it anymore. I wouldn't take the chance. And also, I started fearing it because people were getting out of control with it. I heard a couple of horror stories about someone dropping dead using Ecstasy 'cause they took like ten of them, which no one would ever do. But still, this was a new drug to all of us, and I thought, "Well, we don't know what the side effects are going to be." We just quit. I quit clubbing. I quit partying. Dallas has changed a lot. You don't understand. The economy is so different now. People don't have the money to play with anymore. They don't go out and buy drugs like they used to. They don't party like they used to. (Lynn, a 25-year-old secretary)

THE SEEKER

I read about it in the newspaper. And what fascinated me about it is it said that one experience could be the equivalent of years of therapy. That's really how I learned about it—in the media. Then later I heard about it from my friend and she was kind of suggesting maybe I should try this. But I wasn't ready to, because I'm afraid of drugs. So I didn't, until maybe '87 when some other friends of mine, who are older and more experienced than my first friend, told me they had been taking quite a bit.

They were extremely well educated and they're total intellectuals—he's a scientist and she's a writer. So I heard a lot about their experience of it, and they're very cautious and sort of timid in life. They both had terrible, terrible family lives and terrible childhoods. A lot of the things they're most interested in have to do with the mind. So they've explored a lot . . . like Eastern religions and philosophies and various forms of psychiatry. Plus, I trust their common sense not to do something really dangerous.

What finally made me do it is that things were really getting pretty shitty in our relationship and we needed something positive to happen. We needed some relief and some good experiences, because we'd been through so many hassles with the kids and so many hassles with our house and working too hard and not having fun and just got sort of turned off to each other. So it was kind of a desperate move on both our parts. So I talked him [her husband] into doing it. I tried to get him to hear about it from different people because he just didn't want to do it. But I think he finally did it for the reason I did—that we weren't feeling like we were in love or anything anymore at all. And it was time to do something drastic about our relationship.

At 2:00, when we got where we were going, I said, "OK, let me take it first and then you see if I get violently ill or anything and you take me to the hospital." And so I took it and then he waited about twenty, thirty minutes. I still didn't feel anything happening, so he said finally, "Look, I don't want to be too far behind you, so I'm going to take mine now, too." So he took his in a surge of bravado or something.

So then, a few minutes later, I still didn't think I was feeling anything. I looked at him and he started complaining about his head. He felt like maybe his head was hurting and maybe his neck was getting stiff or something. I don't know, some complaint. But I looked at him and I said, "You know, you have all these complaints, which is very funny, because if you look at your face, it's got this huge grin on it." And that was when we both started smiling and then we turned up the heat and took off our clothes and got in bed and started talking. We realized we really were madly in love with each other, but I think you would feel that way about anybody you took it with.

There was something interesting that happened that first time. Toward the end of it, while we were still under the influence, I don't know if he went to the bathroom or what, but somehow my attention was away from him for a few minutes. And something real scary started to well up inside, like in my mind or something, something black and gloomy and frightening. It went away, except that I remembered it and I knew it was significant and I was particularly interested in it because of my conversation with my other two friends. And so I knew there was something there that I needed to look at that was frightening and scary. And then we knew we each wanted to do it alone the next time.

But you should know as background that several times I've been in therapy. I went into therapy when my marriages broke up, but a couple of times I've been in therapy when it wasn't a crisis to try to figure out why I have anxiety attacks a lot, especially when I'm successful. So when I felt this welling up that first time, this feeling of anxiety for those two minutes, I felt like there was something there that I hadn't really explored and understood and that if I could get to that and take a look at it, that would be like going through years of therapy and I would know what it was that was driving me. So I thought this MDMA would help me do that and there would be a lot of growth. And I thought that this could speed up the process and make me stronger and more aware of myself.

When I took it that second time, I got nauseated and I ran to the bathroom and threw up. But as soon as the nausea lifted and I went back into bed, up suddenly came exactly that same feeling . . . that black thing, that black feeling, that dark, ominous, scary feeling that I had felt for a moment. And all of a sudden I knew what it was, and I can't believe what it was!!!

I was being BORN! It was the birth process. And my breathing started. My respiration started like what was probably mine and my mother's. I guess we were connected by an umbilical cord. And it was horribly frightening because something was wrong. It wasn't going right. . . . And later I asked her what happened and she told me that the birth had been horrible for her. It never occurred to me it was also horrible for me. And they finally gave her ether and she passed out and I think it must have affected me, too, because the next thing I knew, all that had passed and I was being held in her arms. It was some time later. And so the next experience was of being an infant with her holding me and again feeling really safe and secure and feeling connected to her, bonded to her in a way that is really strange. The most important thing about the experience was what I had discovered. And this is why I can't wait to do it again, to see if it's still true or it's an hallucination or what. . . .

I had the distinct feeling when I was on MDMA that in all these other things, whether my mother was abusive at some times, and she clearly was, that I understood her pain somehow, and I understood that I had an awareness and a form of consciousness as an infant that's way beyond anything that I thought human beings could have, and that I wasn't as traumatized by those later things as I thought I was, because my existence and my survival was in fact that initial trauma. And so all the other things that happened . . . were somehow conditioned by my trauma at birth. That is, I was responding to these things in light of the fact that I had this severe trauma at birth which in a way made them less serious, made me wiser, more understanding, but in some ways also made me more threatened.

I think what happens is you remember things as you experienced them at the time. And the way you remember things most of the time is the way we have redefined them to fit in with our current understandings of things. So what you do when you take MDMA is you go back to how you experienced it at the time, and what that allows you to do is come up with different definitions of the situation and different definitions of what you are and what your life is about.

I was really exhausted after the second one [MDMA experience]. You experience the emotions, you go through the emotions that you weren't able to go through at that time or that you only went through partially. And then you're free. I feel totally convinced that I will never, ever have an anxiety attack again like I have had before. What MDMA does is that you have a slow leak guiding the balloon. And MDMA just pops it wide open and then seals it up and you can put it back together with no leak, and so the course is smoother. (Susan, a 46-year-old psychology professor)

THE HEDONIST

So I was reading *Newsweek*. I was sitting in my office reading this article in *Newsweek* and they were calling this drug Ecstasy. They said that it reduced anxiety, and it had been used by psychologists and that there were bars in Dallas where they were passing it out, and people felt wonderful, and they did some user quotes where they said. "This is a wonderful drug." And it was kind of in the psychedelic family, but it wasn't like Acid, and everybody thought it was great. And it was the new hip drug, and it only lasted four hours. It's like, when I read FOUR HOURS, hey, sounds great. I don't do coke anymore. And it was selling for $15 a hit. And I thought, "I can even afford that. This sounds wonderful. I want to do this."

So what happened was I sat there and I was reading this article and a person in my office turned around and said, "I have some, here it is." And he gave me two capsules. I said, "Well, thank you."

All right, so he gave it to me and I had this friend, the friend and I had done quite a bit of drugs together before. He was an old buddy. And he phoned up and I said, "I just was reading this article about this new drug, and you wouldn't believe it. It just fell into my lap." He said, "I read the same article, I want to do some." So he came and picked me up from work, and we were supposed to meet some other people at this bar. So he said, "What do you know about it?" And I said, "I don't know anything. It's supposed to last for four hours." And we had just four hours, so we took it at about 4:00 in the afternoon. We dropped it at the office. By the time we got to the Embarcadero about 45 minutes went by, and we both went, "Oh my God!" It felt like Acid. I remember turning to him and saying, "This is fucking Acid, man. I know what this is. Twelve hours, son of a bitch." I was pissed. I started climbing, felt myself coming on. But fortunately I didn't go anywhere, kind of staying there with these rushes. That was kind of fun, it was nice. I kept waiting for the hallucinations and they didn't come, and I was pleased. I mean, its not that I don't like hallucinations, but that wasn't what I paid for, and I've never been one for surprise highs. They're not fun. And I only had four hours.

So it turned out to be wonderful. We walked into this bar and had a really good time. We grinned a lot. Talking was OK, but I did have a tendency to space out and get quiet. We'd gone and told all our friends, "Hey, we just took this new drug, its great." And they were watching and saying, "How do you feel?" So they got to see us be high. And then everybody wanted some, because it looked so fun.

So that was the first time I did it. I remember the next day. I got up in the morning and went out to breakfast. I remember I ran into some other people and I was still feeling the afterglow. I felt good, but I certainly wouldn't have wanted to be anybody's neurosurgeon the next day. I just kind of had a real nice day. I had a bunch of stuff I was supposed to do, which I didn't do because it was all stuff I didn't want to do. It was nice, it was fun. And I still . . . even into the next day, kind of felt, not really loaded but kind of a little feeling, like the drug was still there. It was a pretty excellent first experience.

I think the next time I did it was right before it became illegal, on June 30, 1985. So maybe it was three or four months after that first time. And then we had a "picnic" with Ecstasy for food, at the beach. And that was very fun. It was just a bunch of us laying around and being high, enjoying ourselves.

I like how it makes your body feel. It makes me feel pretty calm and spacey and drugged. This is one drug where you know for sure that you're high, and I like that. I know that some people see it as the new salvation. I don't see that. I think you can tell bold-faced lies on it if you wanted to.

I don't think it makes you any more . . . I think if you are open, an open person, it enhances that. I think if you're a little socially reticent, which I think I am, it would be easier to meet people while I'm on that drug. But I don't think that it makes you anything that you're not already. There's no magic. You have to have some kind of substance there to start with. So that if you give this drug to shallow assholes, they will continue to be shallow assholes. They're not going to get any better.

If I was a couple with somebody, I could see how you could cut through a lot of bullshit. I could see where if you were having a difference that you could have a really good discussion about whatever the difference was about . . . because the one thing the drug does is to take away suspicion. You're trusting, you're more trusting and you're more open and accepting. I think it does lower your defenses and make you trust that the other person is coming from a good place and the other person cares about you, and that they're trying to work it out and that there's no ulterior motive. I could see where in a couple situation it would be real good for that. I could also see where you could get very close to somebody.

I feel like it's something that's probably going to be a part of my life. It's a fun thing. I can see where it would be a therapeutic tool. But I've never taken the drug for a specific purpose. I want to do the one where you cover your ears and your eyes and just lay there. I want to try that one out. I'd last about 25 seconds. But I'd like to see what that's like. It's also just fun to take some and do it with friends. I can't see doing it alone.

I think we're going to see more drugs like MDMA. They can make anything now. It's great. And if they would make some more—like with a nice "down" that you could drive on, and only lasted a couple of hours—that would be nice. I'm putting in my order.

The short duration is important to me because I just don't have that much time to devote to drugs anymore. I'm very busy doing all this stuff. I could give it a Saturday, but not a Sunday, too. It's like, you can't give up two days. But it's got to be strong, an experience, too. I don't have as much time to be high as I used to. I'm in the "I took it to get high" crowd. I value getting high for getting high's sake, like a hedonist, exactly. Kind of a controlled hedonist. I don't do it to garner any insights. Not that they're not great, but that's not my motivation for doing drugs. I don't have any agenda. To me this is "time-out" behavior. I have lots of responsibility, I've got a lot of work that I need to do. I have a lot of deadlines. So to me it's like time out. It's a way to . . . it's like taking a vacation to Mexico for a week, only I'm going to do it in a day because that's all I've got. (Gail, a 37-year-old lawyer)

Three different people, three markedly different perspectives, three very different experiences, and *one* drug. There is nothing new about diversity of users, perspectives, and experience relative to a particular substance. Nevertheless, as revealed through respondent accounts in the pages that follow, MDMA provides a unique illustration of this phenomenon and the importance of contextual factors in shaping the experience. Those who have used MDMA generally have at least one thing in common—a very strong feeling about the drug and vivid memories of their experiences under its influence.

Less than a decade ago, few people had even heard of MDMA. But suddenly, in 1985, Ecstasy became the object of extensive media coverage, highlighting what appeared to be dramatic increases in use. Much of this interest was sparked by the controversy that followed government attempts to criminalize its use. At center stage, two interest groups were squaring off in a courtroom to decide the fate of MDMA.

Representing one faction were various psychiatrists and other proponents who viewed "Adam" as a valuable therapeutic adjunct with minimal harm associated with carefully monitored use (Downing, 1985; Greer, 1985; Grinspoon, 1985; Lynch, 1985; Strassman, 1985; Wolfson, 1985). The opposing side was largely composed of drug enforcement officials, who viewed "Ecstasy" as a dangerous and abused "designer drug" without therapeutic value (Lawn, 1985; Holsten and Scheister, 1985; Sapienza, 1985; U.S. Department of Justice, 1985). Summing up the controversy, chemist Alexander Shulgin observed that "MDMA has been thrust upon the public awareness as a largely unknown drug which to some is a medical miracle and to others a social devil" (1985:3).

The uniqueness of MDMA (3,4-methylenedioxymethamphetamine) is exemplified by the confusion over the proper terminology to describe its actions. As an N-methyl analogue of MDA, MDMA is related to both the amphetamines and mescaline. Although often referred to as a psychedelic drug, MDMA possesses stimulant properties as well. Moreover, it is rarely hallucinogenic and seldom produces the sensory phenomena or mental confusion commonly associated with other psychedelic substances (Nichols, 1986; Shulgin, 1985).

In response to challenges made by therapeutic proponents, three federal administrative law hearings were held in 1985 to determine MDMA's fate. What emerged from these hearings was the lack of research assessing the potential benefits and/or harms of MDMA. Overall patterns of use were clearly a mystery as well. Consequently, proponents of both sides of the controversy were limited to offering testimony based largely on anecdotal data or extrapolations from preliminary animal studies. The most significant point of agreement between the two camps was the need for further research to better determine the potential benefits and risks of a substance used by increasing numbers of Americans (Beck, 1986).

We followed the scheduling controversy and were struck by the depth of feeling, opinion, and commitment expressed by MDMA's adversaries and allies alike. Moreover, we were amazed at the dearth of sociological information about the drug—despite what appeared to be the inevitability of its placement into an illegal status. Sparked by this interest, we applied for a grant from the National Institute on Drug Abuse and in June of 1987 began work on the first federally funded, sociological exploration of MDMA users.[1] Its recent emergence and popularization furnished a unique opportunity to examine gradually evolving use patterns among different user populations. We collected information through ethnographic fieldwork[2] and conducted formal interviews with one hundred MDMA users.[3] Our study, completed in 1989, provided a detailed look at the diverse user populations attracted to the therapeutic and/or recreational qualities ascribed to MDMA (Beck et al., 1989).

Building on the findings of our "Exploring Ecstasy" study, in this book we describe the MDMA experience and the roles played by user social worlds, government, and the media in shaping that experience. We look at problematic aspects as well as attractions of MDMA. Our presentation uses the words of the people we interviewed and strives to provide their perspective. We also look at views of MDMA emanating from other sources, primarily those of the media and government.

We were fortunate to begin our study less than two years after MDMA had become illegal. This meant that many of our interviewees had used the drug both before and after its criminalization. Therefore we were able to examine shifts in attitudes and behaviors among users throughout MDMA's transition from licit to illicit status. Since MDMA had become popular only two years prior to our research, we were able to explore its diffusion into a variety of groups. This allowed us to look at the various factors encouraging and/or discouraging the spread of Ecstasy.

A unique aspect of the study was that it gave us an opportunity to look at little-studied drug-using populations.[4] This included individuals generally regarded as conventional, such as middle-class professionals. These rarely studied user groups attached expectations and meanings to their drug use that were very different from more visible and researched illegal drug users. They also had unique motivations and expectations underlying their pursuits of ecstasy and/or insight from MDMA use. Contextual factors emerged as essential components in understanding the diversity of such pursuits as well as variations on the MDMA experience itself.

By the end of our study in the late 1980s, the media had turned its fickle attention to other drugs. MDMA remained virtually absent from drug problem indicators such as the Drug Abuse Warning Network (DAWN). The government had successfully criminalized Ecstasy and it had returned to relative obscurity. Many saw it as simply another faddish drug that had run its course. Yet far from fading away, this book shows how its reputed therapeutic and euphoric qualities and "user-friendly" nature account for MDMA's continued popularity among diverse user populations. Exemplified by the rapid expansion of the British "Rave" scene to the United States and elsewhere, these attributes underlie MDMA's spread to new user populations despite the current strong antidrug climate.

In addition to presenting the findings from our own study, we will be reviewing other sources of information about MDMA and its users. Particularly valuable for trend analysis and comparative purposes are the findings of recently published studies conducted overseas.

PURSUIT OF ECSTASY: PLAN OF THE BOOK

In Chapter 2, we set the stage by providing a chronological overview of MDMA's popularization and control. We look at the emergence and diffusion of Ecstasy as well as the process by which MDMA was placed into Schedule I of the Controlled Substances Act.

In Chapter 3, we describe the diverse social worlds and scenes that have evolved around MDMA use. As demonstrated throughout the remainder of the book, these social worlds are very influential in shaping respondent motivations, expectations, and perceptions of the MDMA experience itself.

In Chapter 4, we look at why people use MDMA, and the various attractions ascribed to the MDMA experience. Differences in perceived attributes are considered in light of respondents' diverse motivations and social worlds of use. After first examining the reasons that most users try MDMA, the chapter addresses those aspects of the experience they most appreciate. We conclude with an examination of different user perspectives regarding MDMA's long-term benefits and therapeutic potential.

In Chapter 5, we look at why individuals moderate or discontinue Ecstasy use. We assess the various factors responsible for tempering enthusiasm and use.

In Chapter 6, we examine adverse reactions and abuse in assessing the potential of Ecstasy to become agony. We include lessons respondents learned from attempts to accentuate or prolong the MDMA experience. Noting the problematic use encountered in the British Rave scene, we examine similar patterns among some of our population in assessing long-term abuse potential.

In Chapter 7, we attempt to answer the question "What should be done about Ecstasy?" We begin by summarizing the key findings and implications of our study. A number of recommendations are offered for developing harm reduction strategies and encouraging research on the therapeutic potential of MDMA. Acknowledging the likelihood of continued resistance, we discuss how and why it is important to overcome these obstacles.

CHAPTER 2

Emergence of Adam and Ecstasy: Distribution and Criminalization of MDMA

MDMA is not a new drug. It was first synthesized by the German pharmaceutical firm of Merck in 1912. Human experimentation, however, has only been traced back to the early 1970s (Eisner, 1989; Shulgin, 1990). Thus, in terms of time "on the street," MDMA has been around for less than two decades.

We were in the fortunate position of researching a drug that had become popular so recently that we could trace its emergence and trajectory of use. Through a series of patterns and events, it was possible to see how the intended use of MDMA influenced its distribution, which in turn affected its criminalization. Our ethnographic methodology and extensive contacts in the psychedelic "community" brought us close to those who were part of the efforts to retain MDMA's legal status for therapeutic use. We also interviewed longtime distributors and users, who provided a historical perspective on both the recreational and therapeutic use of MDMA. In this chapter, we analyze the complex, albeit brief, history of MDMA including the emergence of "Adam," subsequent marketing of "Ecstasy," and inevitable criminalization.

Preceding MDMA on the street and in the laboratory was its chemical cousin, MDA (3,4-methylenedioxyamphetamine).[1] MDA emerged in San Francisco's Haight-Ashbury drug subculture during the mid-1960s. It quickly gained a reputation for producing a sensual, easily managed euphoria alluded to by such nicknames as the "love drug" and the "mellow drug of America" (Meyers, Rose, and Smith, 1967–1968). MDA's reputed qualities piqued the interest of both therapists and recreational enthusiasts, who were also attracted by its legal status. This soon changed, however, when

MDA joined a host of other known or suspected street drugs listed in the newly created Controlled Substances Act of 1970.

A few studies had been conducted to evaluate MDA's therapeutic potential before the government imposed legal restrictions and halted human research with LSD and other "psychedelics" (Grinspoon and Bakalar, 1979). Each of the investigations reported favorable outcomes, with subjects describing facilitation of self-insight, heightened empathy, and other positive qualities associated with the MDA experience (Naranjo, Shulgin, and Sargent, 1967; Naranjo, 1973; Turek, Soskin, and Kurland, 1974; Yensen et al., 1976).

THE EMERGENCE OF ADAM

Beginning in 1976, a small number of therapists on both coasts began to utilize MDMA for similar purposes. They found "Adam" (the therapists' nickname for MDMA) to be even more beneficial than MDA as a therapeutic adjunct, particularly in facilitating communication, acceptance, and fear reduction. Shulgin and Shulgin, in *Pihkal: A Chemical Love Story*, tell the story of a psychologist they call "Adam," who was very likely the "father" of MDMA use as an adjunct to psychotherapy. He had been using various psychedelic substances in his practice and was about to retire when Shura, the chemist-hero of *Pihkal*, introduced him to MDMA:

> In 1977, age was sneaking up on Adam and he was allowing his patient load to dwindle by attrition. I knew that he was getting ready to gather in his shingle and let the lease lapse on his Oakland office. One day, he asked me to drop by to see if I wanted to accept some of the unusual mementos which he had acquired over the years.
>
> I had decided, on this occasion, to bring with me a small bottle of my "low-calorie martini," MDMA hydrochloride, to tempt him to try something new. Knowing his fondness for MDA, I assured him it had some of the virtues of MDA, without the "stoning" properties, and it had something extra, a special magic, which just might catch his attention. He told me that he might or might not try it, but that if he did, he would let me know what he thought of it.
>
> He phoned me a few days later to tell me that he had abandoned his plans for a quiet retirement. I know none of the details of the increasingly complex network which he proceeded

to develop over the following decade, but I do know that he traveled across the country, introducing MDMA to other therapists and teaching them how to use it in their therapy.

... Many of the psychologists and psychiatrists whom Adam instructed developed small groups or enclaves of professionals who had been similarly taught, and the information and techniques he had introduced spread widely and, in time, internationally.

It is impossible to ever know the true breadth of therapeutic MDMA usage achieved by Adam during the remaining years of his life, but at his memorial service, I asked an old friend of his whether she had a guess as to the number of people Adam had introduced to this incredible tool, either directly or indirectly. She was silent for a moment, then said, "Well, I've thought about that, and I think probably somewhere around four thousand, give or take a few." (Shulgin and Shulgin, 1991:73–74)

Despite their belief in MDMA's efficacy, therapists were reluctant to publish any preliminary findings, fearing that such efforts would only hasten the criminalization of this still-legal "psychedelic" and block further research (Eisner, 1989; Seymour, 1986). It was not until the late 1970s that the first pharmacological investigation of MDMA in humans was published (Shulgin and Nichols, 1978). The researchers described how MDMA evoked an easily controlled altered state of consciousness, with emotional and sensual overtones. Some years later, Dr. Alexander Shulgin summed up the significance of their findings: "These properties, the openness of emotional expression and the unusually short duration, established the unique character of MDMA, which made it so promising to therapists and tempting, eventually, to the curious public as well" (1990:6).

The ongoing therapeutic use of Adam remained unknown to much of the "curious public," with the exception of a slowly expanding population of recreationally oriented users who were turning on to MDMA beginning in the mid-1970s. When distribution patterns changed, coupled with the media's discovery of Ecstasy in the mid-1980s, the recreational market took off.

THE DISTRIBUTION OF ECSTASY[2]

The motivations and attitudes of those who supply a drug are extremely important in determining who gains access as well as how it is used (Blum, 1972; Lee and Shlain, 1985). Distribution networks also play a key role in shaping norms regarding appropriate and inappropriate use, overall expectations, and perceived benefits and harms. This is particularly true with the initial dissemination of little-known substances, when user folklore about proper doses, reducing risks, and enhancing effects remain largely undefined.[3]

Such was the case with MDMA prior to the media blitz which accompanied its criminalization in 1985. Until then, distributors were typically the sole or primary source of information for first-time users. With the exception of those who were given MDMA as part of their therapy, suppliers were often close friends. The absence of alternate sources of MDMA ensured that the beliefs of these individuals would have considerable influence on those they initiated into use.

In looking at the diffusion of MDMA, we were interested in the delivery of information and instruction as well as the distribution of the drug itself. In addition to the large-scale dealers in our study, since nearly all respondents had reportedly introduced at least one other person to MDMA, it seemed important to look at their motivations for use.[4] Most had purchased various amounts of MDMA (from one to several grams) to distribute to their friends and colleagues for little or no profit. Many respondents were eager to share their discovery with friends who had no other source for obtaining MDMA. As circles widened to "friends of friends," some respondents became distributors, adding on whatever charges they deemed appropriate.

Differential Motives for Distribution

Clearly, those who distributed MDMA, whether for money or as a favor to friends, felt very strongly about the drug. Among distributors and users there was a primary difference between those attracted to MDMA's alleged therapeutic and spiritual benefits and others more enamored with its euphoric and sensual properties. Although most acknowledged both qualities, they differed with regard to their relative importance. These differing motivations for distribution and use may be seen as forming a therapeutic and recreational continuum.

The labels or terminology employed in referring to MDMA reflected differing perspectives. Some saw Adam as a therapeutic and spiritual adjunct, often for purposes of insight enhancement. On the other extreme were those who sought the euphoria and sensuousness associated with Ecstasy. These individuals typically had used a wide variety of psychoactive drugs and found that MDMA provided many of the qualities previously sought in other substances (such as cocaine).

Although many individuals fell somewhere in between, there was often a sharp dichotomy between those who used, sold, or gave MDMA for personal growth or enlightenment and others who primarily used it to "party" or socialize. These differences in attitudes and motivations were often communicated from distributors to prospective users, and shaped diffusion and beliefs about Ecstasy.

Proselytizers Versus Elitists

All the distributors we interviewed fervently believed in the beneficial value of the MDMA experience and saw themselves as performing a valuable function in "making the world a better place." Whereas a couple of dealers described their vocation in evangelistic terms, others offered a more modest perspective: "I don't think that it's made overwhelming, drastic changes in the society, but my philosophy is that any beneficial act is a beneficial act. There are lots of places to chip at the great stone of uncaring and this is where I chose to do my chipping" (080:17).[5]

Distributors, like other respondents, differed markedly regarding who they believed should or should not use MDMA. The conflict among various advocates over whether MDMA should be "spread to the masses" or limited to "intelligent, educated, responsible users" was reminiscent of a similar dispute among LSD enthusiasts over two decades before. Although their reasons were often stated in terms of ethics or personal philosophy, their dilemma could also be summarized as follows: "How do we keep this drug safe and available to ourselves and our friends while still protecting our profits?"

In probing the motivations of distributors, we found that several factors contributed to proselytizing or elitism prior to MDMA's criminalization. The threat of (then) future legislation was, for many distributors, a deterrent to rapid expansion. Several dealers expressed criticism toward those who used the drug "irresponsibly." They believed that open sales (such as what eventually occurred in Texas bars and nightclubs) would quickly lead to prohibitive legislation. According to one distributor, "it was a strategic issue, the classic struggle between tortoise and hare: Do we turn on as many people as we can before the drug becomes illegal, thereby hastening its demise, or go slowly and choose carefully those who will most benefit and/or be most responsible in their use?"

In addition to distributor perspectives, there were the concerns of those who strongly believed in the therapeutic potential of MDMA and similar substances. After interviewing many of these "professional explorers of inner space," Stevens observed that the "neuroconsciousness frontier, circa 1983, reminded me a lot of the psychedelic movement, circa 1962: there was the same quality of excitement, the same mix of therapeutic and metaphysical interests, the same cautious optimism" (1987:366).

In order to understand proselytizing or elitist stances taken by distributors and users, we need to understand their attitudes toward the drug itself. Many believed that the power of an MDMA experience resided in the drug. Consequently, this group felt that almost anyone could benefit from MDMA use regardless of rationale or context of use. On the other end of the continuum were those who saw MDMA as a "facilitator" or "enabler." These people felt that the nature of the MDMA experience was largely dependent upon "user context" or "set and setting." This group saw themselves as educators and disseminators of an experience rather than drug distributors per se.

An extreme example of elitism was demonstrated by a small group of New Agers who had borrowed the theory of "morphogenetic fields" developed by biologist Rupert Sheldrake (1983). Applying this to MDMA, they conceived of a field of cumulative collective experience that all users somehow "tapped into" upon ingestion of the drug. They expressed concern that the field would become "polluted" or "muddied" by casual thrill seekers. For these users, MDMA was a religious sacrament or healing medicine. They did not want it to be trivialized or abused.

The Marketing of Ecstasy

The recreational market for MDMA underwent a slow expansion into the early 1980s. This was the period dominated by chemists in the Boston area, called the "Boston Group," which had commenced production in 1976. The chemists in this organization had a "therapeutic" perspective. They worked on their own timetable, often neglecting to meet the growing and changing demands of the market. As a consequence, "droughts" often occurred, particularly during the summer months and Christmas holidays, when consumer demand was highest.

The increasing monetary interests of some distributors in the network was reflected in the commercialization of MDMA as "Ecstasy" in 1981.[6] In anticipation of enjoying greater profits by expanding efforts to both create and meet demand for MDMA, the Southwest distributor for the Boston Group put together his own operation with the financial backing of Texas friends. He commenced production in 1983 and distribution reached its peak in 1985, just prior to (and having a lot to do with) emergency scheduling. The "Texas Group" quickly became the largest and most intrepid MDMA distribution network in the nation. Their mass production and promotion of Ecstasy quickly alarmed law enforcement, therapists, and fellow dealers alike. According to one respondent knowledgeable about their operation, the Texas Group produced and distributed more MDMA in eighteen months than all other networks combined over their entire history (007:61).

The Texas entrepreneurs used blatant promotional tactics that shocked therapeutically oriented users and more established dealer networks. They swiftly built a pyramid referral system rivaling that of Amway. Ecstasy was sold openly at bars in Austin and Dallas. Purchases could be charged to Visa cards and proprietors paid taxes on their sales. The Texas Group circulated posters announcing "Ecstasy parties" at bars and discos with MDMA billed as a "fun drug" that was "good to dance to."

In sum, the quiet use of Adam in limited therapeutic circles had been transformed into a phenomenon. Ecstasy was now the "drug of choice" among Texas yuppies, and their use was anything but quiet. And so began the process of the criminalization of Ecstasy.

THE CRIMINALIZATION OF ECSTASY

Although the Drug Enforcement Administration (DEA) had first learned of MDMA in the early 1970s, reports were infrequent

and a decade passed before the government began soliciting information. In 1982, one of the first media articles on "XTC" quoted
a DEA spokesman as stating, "If we can get enough evidence to
be sure there's potential for abuse, we'll ban it" (Dye, 1982:8).
Noting the use in Texas and elsewhere, the DEA moved in July of
1984 to recommend the placement of MDMA into Schedule I of
the Controlled Substances Act (CSA) (Mullen, 1984).[7] Justifying
this action, a DEA chemist contended that "MDMA has a high
potential for abuse based on its chemical and pharmacological
similarity to MDA, its self-administration without medical supervision, its clandestine synthesis and its distribution in the illicit
drug traffic" (Sapienza, 1985:11).

A "routine" scheduling process of a little-known drug was
quickly challenged by a fairly well organized group of psychiatrists and other individuals who fervently believed in MDMA's
therapeutic potential. Citing LSD as a case example, proponents
argued that a Schedule I status would severely hinder any research
into the drug's therapeutic potential (Beck, 1986). The government's surprise at the therapists' reaction was evidenced by a DEA
pharmacologist's statement that they "had no idea psychiatrists
were using it" (Adler, 1985:96). Commenting on this, one distributor proudly noted that

> one of the wonderful things is MDMA has been known as Adam
> and used therapeutically in thousands, tens of thousands of ses-
> sions for 10 years, since the early, early '70s, when the DEA
> moved to make it illegal, they had never even heard the name
> Adam. It wasn't listed at all. It was people who had learned of it
> from a therapeutic community, some of them who had gone on
> to mass market it under the name of Ecstasy. (007:65)

The Impact of the Proposed Criminalization

The *proposed* criminalization and ensuing reaction by therapists
soon brought MDMA to national attention. Within a short
period of time in mid-1985, almost the entire print and electronic
media had devoted stories to Ecstasy. Reminiscent of previous
drug "discoveries," early media accounts often sensationalized
the reputed euphoric and therapeutic qualities of MDMA (cf.
Adler, 1985; Dowling, 1985; Leavy, 1985; Toufexis, 1985).

> The popular media loved MDMA. They loved the name
> "Ecstasy"; they loved its users—a white, affluent contrast to the

popular stereotype; they loved the bar scene in which it was distributed in Texas. And they wrote glowing reports about it in nearly every popular publication, including *Newsweek*, *Time* and the *Washington Post*. This was not the first time the media helped to advertise a "new" drug. (Rosenbaum and Doblin, 1991:12)

The Texas Group responded to the proposed scheduling by attempting to manufacture and sell as much MDMA as possible before the drug was banned. Based on his own interviews with members of the Texas Group, MDMA proponent Rick Doblin estimates that the operation reached its peak in the month or two prior to scheduling. The group allegedly distributed over two million tablets during this short period, almost equal to the amount supplied by the network until that time (Beck, 1990a). As a result, a number of respondents reported "fire sales" in several metropolitan areas where large amounts of MDMA could be purchased at reduced prices. A college freshman (056) who was then attending an elite prep school outside Washington, D.C., noted that they originally paid $25 per tablet for MDMA. Four months later, as MDMA was dumped on the market, the price had dropped to $8.

In response to proponents' challenges, federal administrative law hearings were scheduled during the summer and fall of 1985 to determine the final scheduling of MDMA. However, blatant open marketing and distribution of Ecstasy in bars and nightclubs led the DEA to invoke the emergency scheduling powers recently granted by the Comprehensive Crime Control Act of 1984.[8] As a result, MDMA was temporarily placed into Schedule I on July 1, 1985 (Lawn, 1985).

The DEA provided a number of rationales for the necessity of emergency scheduling. They had to demonstrate that the substance in question posed "an imminent hazard to public safety." The primary justification centered on a then-unpublished study associating high-dosage administration of MDA in rats with damage to nerve terminals which use serotonin as a neurotransmitter (Ricaurte et al., 1985; Seiden, 1985).

However, probably the more significant reason underlying the emergency scheduling could be found in a fact sheet produced by the DEA noting the "open promotion of MDMA as a legal euphoriant through fliers, circulars and promotional parties." It went on to assert that "30,000 dosage units of MDMA are distributed each month" in Dallas (U.S. Department of Justice, 1985:1). The blatantly open sales of MDMA in numerous bars and nightclubs presented a very public and problematic drug use pattern to authorities.

The Administrative Law History

The DEA (together with the Food and Drug Administration) clearly believed that Ecstasy belonged in Schedule I. The DEA attorneys set out to prove that MDMA fit all three criteria necessary for such a placement: a high potential for abuse, no currently accepted medical use, and a lack of safety for use under medical supervision (Sapienza, 1986).

Many researchers and therapists feared that a Schedule I status would destroy any hope of evaluating MDMA's therapeutic potential. Therapists argued that their quiescence in publicizing any preliminary findings was justified in light of previous control efforts directed at LSD and other psychedelic drugs (Beck, 1986; Eisner, 1989; Greer, 1985). Despite minimal evidence of adverse effects after thousands of uses, and arguable efficacy, once-flourishing explorations into the therapeutic potential of these substances (including MDA) came to a virtual standstill following their criminalization in the late 1960s (Grinspoon and Bakalar, 1979; Lee and Shlain, 1985; Neill, 1987).

A number of psychiatrists testified on behalf of MDMA's therapeutic potential at the hearings (Downing, 1985; Greer, 1985; Lynch, 1985; Strassman, 1985; Wolfson, 1985). They asserted that MDMA's ability to enhance communication, increase empathy, and reduce fear made it an invaluable therapeutic adjunct for a wide range of problems. Proponents also believed in the safety of such use, given the small number of doses which would be administered to any one patient. In support of this contention, they cited a then-unpublished study examining the effects of a single exposure of MDMA on twenty-one healthy individuals (Downing, 1985, 1986). The researchers utilized blood chemistry, physiological measures, and neurological examinations, and concluded:

> This experimental situation produced no observed or reported psychological or physiological damage, either during the twenty-four hour study period, or during the three month follow-up period. . . . From the information presented here one can say only that MDMA, at the doses tested, has remarkably

consistent and predictable psychobiological effects which are transient and free of clinically apparent major toxicity. (Downing, 1985:5–6)

Psychiatrists also sought to differentiate MDMA from psychedelics such as LSD by arguing that it produces far less distortion of sensory perception and fewer unpleasant emotional reactions. As Harvard professor and psychiatrist Lester Grinspoon asserted: "MDMA appears to have some of the advantages of LSD-like drugs without most of the corresponding disadvantages" (1985:3).

In countering the therapeutic advocates of MDMA, DEA attorneys called upon various research experts to critique the anecdotal nature of the therapists' testimony (Docherty, 1985b; Kleinman, 1985; Shannon, 1985; Tocus, 1985). These government witnesses also gave little credence to what they regarded as inadequately controlled preliminary studies conducted by proponents (Downing, 1985; Greer, 1983). In general, their critique of the therapists' testimony could be summed up in Kleinman's conclusion that "although these reports make interesting reading, their lack of scientific design, methodology and controls makes them scientifically unsound" (1985:2).

Following completion of the hearings, the DEA administrative law judge issued his findings and recommendations, which largely concurred with proponents' contentions. Citing currently accepted medical use and safety and noting minimal evidence of significant abuse or problems, the judge recommended a Schedule III placement (Young, 1986). This would have substantially eased research requirements and allowed for continued therapeutic use of MDMA by physicians. However, the DEA administrator subsequently rejected the judge's recommendation and attempted to permanently place MDMA into Schedule I on November 13, 1986 (Lawn, 1986).

The validity of some of the DEA's actions was challenged successfully in subsequent appellate court cases. The rulings faulted the DEA's actions on various technical grounds. Although greatly aiding the defendants who had been charged with MDMA offenses until that time, the court decisions provided minimal support for proponents' contentions (Harbin, 1988).The DEA administrator once again ordered the permanent placement of MDMA into Schedule I as of March 23, 1988 (Lawn, 1988).[9]

The Impact of Criminalization

The marketing strategy of the Texas Group appears to have been primarily "going for the short dollar." This caused concern and antagonism in therapeutic circles, as well as among veteran chemists and distributors who had gradually built up a clientele over the previous decade. Reflecting their consternation, one dealer lamented, "Our perception of them was that they were just primarily capitalists and that it's too bad that they didn't take the drug more and a little longer before they embarked on their project."

In addition to humanitarian frustrations, dealers also expressed chagrin at the loss of a lucrative legal market following the inevitable crackdown on MDMA as a result of the Texas Group's actions: "If they hadn't been on the scene we probably could have sold it for another ten years before they [the government] would have been called upon to move against it."

Many distributors retired or significantly cut back production following MDMA's criminalization. This resulted in droughts throughout much of the nation, particularly in those parts of the country served by the Texas Group. According to one knowledgeable source, their exit resulted in a great undersupply in those areas they formerly served: "I know that there's been difficulty of many people around the country to find any. I think a lot of that has to do with the Texas Group. . . . They were always the largest and the most widespread, and now that they're out of commission I think that there's a great overdemand, undersupply" (007:82).

Other manufacturers and distributors followed suit in departing the field during this time. One large-scale distributor reported that his "guys were ready to quit anyway" and that this provided the final impetus. Considering himself "too old to risk jail" and financially comfortable, he joined other "old-time" distributors associated with the original Boston Group in retiring from the field.

As might be expected, new suppliers stepped in to take advantage of the profitable demand that had been created at least partially through the free publicity accompanying the controversy. In many cases, retiring manufacturers and distributors simply handed over the reins of already established networks to new entrepreneurs willing to take the risk.

In response to MDMA's scheduling, an offshoot of the Texas Group began manufacturing and distributing large amounts of the still licit MDE, another chemical "cousin" of MDMA, and tried to market it under the name "Eve." This strategy was largely unsuccessful, as indicated by our finding that none of our twenty respondents who had tried Eve, preferred it to the original "Adam." In addition to MDE, some therapists and manufacturers also experimented with other unscheduled analogues of MDMA. However, these were judged to be less effective and/or possessed too many undesirable side effects to be therapeutically useful or commercially desirable (Eisner, 1989).

Shortly after attempts to market Eve, Congress passed the Controlled Substances Analog Act ("Designer Drug" bill) outlawing all new analogues of illicit drugs.[10] This legislation, with its stiff penalties, encouraged chemists and manufacturers to abandon attempts to market analogues like the unpopular MDE. Many returned to making and selling MDMA, which they probably would have done anyway, given consumer preference for it.

Of all the groups using MDMA, the therapeutic contingent was probably hardest hit by the ban. The Emergency Scheduling of MDMA, invoked in the summer of 1985, effectively stopped all human research and deterred most therapeutic use. Many small dealer networks that had served various therapeutic, New Age, and spiritual groups ceased to function. For one distributor who primarily supplied therapeutic populations, it was a difficult decision: "I felt really bad that they could no longer get it. . . . I'd seen a lot of good . . . but I had a family and a future to protect. It wasn't worth the risk."

To summarize, MDMA emerged in the mid-1970s as Adam— a drug with limited distribution and a therapeutically oriented clientele. This also marked the beginning of a period of several years of slowly expanding supply and demand for MDMA among recreational users. Careful, purposeful use dominated until the early 1980s, when a group of distributors saw an opportunity for expansion and profit. They renamed the drug "Ecstasy" and increased production. Visible promotion of MDMA caught the attention of government authorities and the process of criminalization began. Accompanying the scheduling controversy was extensive publicity and increased interest. However, when MDMA officially became illegal, many distributors quit rather than risk arrest and incarceration. Hence, since Ecstasy's criminalization in 1985, demand has generally exceeded supply for the various user groups throughout the country.

CHAPTER 3

Worlds of Ecstasy: Who Uses MDMA?

During the 1980s, Ecstasy found its way into a number of user populations. In fact, being a member of a particular "social world" or "scene" had significant bearing upon whether an individual knew about and experimented with MDMA. In this chapter, we journey through various MDMA-using groups, seeking to underscore the importance of context and social worlds in understanding drug use. As illustrated in this and subsequent chapters, these concepts play major roles in shaping motivations for, expectations about, and patterns of MDMA use. In this analysis, we intend to show how contextual factors may prove more satisfactory than pharmacology in accounting for the diversity of user experiences. In examining MDMA users, motives and expectations must be understood within the overall framework of environmental conditions surrounding use. The theoretical concepts of 'user context', 'social worlds', and 'scenes' are therefore essential in understanding the MDMA experience in a dialectical fashion. Membership in social worlds that "contain" MDMA is essential if an individual is going to experiment with Ecstasy in the first place. Also, identification with these social worlds includes perspectives that are conducive to experimentation. The social world itself establishes a context for use that shapes the user's expectations.

THE CONTEXT OF DRUG USE

Contextual perspectives are often neglected in favor of individualistic or pharmacological explanations. By simply assuming the predictability of pharmacology, professionals in the drug field frequently underestimate the potent combination of the human mind and the varying social contexts that continually shape the way we think and feel.

Environmental influences are important in shaping drug experience. An individual's *set* is his or her beliefs and attitudes as well as state of mind at the time of use. The *setting* is the physical and social environment within which drug use occurs. The essential contribution of these factors in understanding the varieties of the drug experience is amply documented in the literature (Becker, 1967; Harding and Zinberg, 1977; Maloff et al., 1982; Weil, 1972; Zinberg, 1984).

User set and setting are shaped by both prescriptions and proscriptions of an individual's culture and social group. One's values and rules of conduct influence the response one will have to the use of any drug. Social controls, sanctions, and expectations are the framework within which people decide whether and how a particular drug should be used (Zinberg, 1984). Such controls are operative within the variety of subcultures and social worlds of use.

SOCIAL WORLDS AND SCENES

Until the late 1960s, the stigma and threat of punishment associated with the use of illicit drugs were severe. As a result, those who chose to use them were generally members of well-insulated subcultures. Prior to this time, illicit drug use was largely associated with oppressed ethnic and racial minorities, as well as bohemians, jazz musicians, and other "deviants." Media attention and drug legislation often contained an underlying intent to control certain populations whose drug-induced escapades had aroused the fear and suspicion of the society at large (Duster, 1970; Helmer, 1975; Morgan, 1978; Musto, 1973; Reinarman and Levine, 1989). Repression and hysteria drove users into isolated and protective subcultures which developed their own social sanctions, rituals, and criteria for membership. Room describes how a particular subculture is likely to possess

> definite boundaries of membership and a normative structure to preserve the secrecy and privacy of its transactions and occasions. Both because of selective factors weeding out the less committed and because of the reinforcements of the "secondary deviance" process, its members will be strongly committed to it. (1975:365)

In describing an "amplification spiral" that frequently occurs between illicit drug users and society, Ray offers a similar conclusion: "Increased isolation of drug-using subcultures produces increased commitment to use as a means of maintaining identity, and so original stereotypes are further confirmed for all concerned" (1985:1227).

A new phenomenon took place during the 1960s with the rapid spread of illicit drug use across the nation. The new users were increasingly white middle-class youth. A gradual change in the status of some illicit drugs, especially marijuana, accompanied this shift to a more conventional, less threatening population. As the penalties and stigma associated with use became less severe, the need for highly protective subcultures diminished accordingly. In addition, users throughout the country were more and more informed and influenced by the substantial mass media coverage of drug issues.

Insulated, well-defined subcultures gave way to larger, more amorphous "social worlds" of illicit drug users. These new social worlds differed from traditional user subcultures in that they were not bound "by territory nor by formal group membership, but by the limits of effective communication" (Shibutani, 1961:130). We now had user populations whose identities were substantially shaped and informed by mass communication and the media.

The theoretical importance of social worlds in modern society was first noted by Shibutani (1955). Writing before the advent of the 1960s drug phenomenon, he argued that the voluminous information provided by the mass media led individuals to identify with "reference groups" or "social worlds" which were not necessarily tied to any particular collectivity or location. Mass communication made it possible for people to construct some perspective and identify with social worlds from a distance. In the process, he noted how individuals could identify simultaneously with many different social worlds with varying degrees of attachment or involvement (Shibutani, 1955, 1961).

Shibutani (1955) identified four interrelated aspects of social worlds. First, each social world is a universe of regularized *mutual response*; second, each is an *arena* in which some form of organization exists; third, social worlds can also be considered *cultural areas*; and finally, the boundaries of social worlds are set by the *limits of effective communication*.

Social worlds can be broken down into areas in which members from across the country may share a mutual response or attachment to a given phenomenon but organize their activities within different arenas. In a similar manner, Lindesmith and colleagues defined social worlds as "groupings of individuals bound together by networks of communication or universes of discourse. Whether the members are geographically proximate or not, they share symbolizations and hence, also share perspectives on 'reality'" (1977:174).

The above observations provide some insight into the rapid spread of drug use among white middle-class youth in the late 1960s and 1970s. Although some illicit drug users remain enmeshed in insulated subcultures (particularly heroin and crack users), most users in today's society identify to varying degrees with many diverse social worlds. An individual's positive attachment to and interest in drug use is significantly influenced by membership in social worlds in which such use is condoned or advocated. Conversely, the extent of one's involvement in social worlds that have minimal or no psychoactive drug use also contributes in limiting desire, availability, and/or use.

Irwin (1977) argues that the recent (and often rapid) evolution of particular "scenes" is one manifestation of social worlds. He describes a scene as "a central leisure activity, a set of special symbols and meanings, relative availability, and action . . . " (1977:30). Irwin attributes the popularization of particular scenes, such as surfing and hippies, to the increasing role played by various forms of mass communication (news media, film, music) in promoting them. He goes on to note that "scenes exist in a social context in which there are many social worlds known to many actors. Moreover, they are viewed as being at least somewhat available" (1977:229–230). This "availability" can be seen as continually increasing as a result of more efficient means of mass communication and transportation (Shibutani, 1961). According to Irwin,

> The power of the media to disseminate, and the tendency of segments of the public to adopt, lifestyles is demonstrated by the extreme cases in which a "fad" lifestyle appears in one location of the country, is given coverage by the media, and then spreads rapidly to other or all parts of the country. (1977:60)

In their examination of the European "Acid House" phenomenon, Kaplan and colleagues (1989) explain how the dissemination of such scenes into various populations (accompanied by MDMA use) calls into question pervasive models of drug diffusion:

> The consideration of the emergence of new drugs such as MDMA . . . involves the development of more general models of drug use epidemiology. The most widely used model in current use is the contagion model, which explains the spread of drugs in a community through personal contact of established peer group networks. While this model is indeed valid, it still remains to be seen how the first initiator comes into contact with a drug as well as how existing, established networks may be jumped and mixed in a mass media environment (e.g., concerts, performance, etc.) to produce new patterns of use. The role of the press seems critical in the initiation and diffusion of drug trends. . . . It can be suggested that drugs are *primarily* spread not through peer groups, but rather by certain cultural city centers that selectively transmit their fashions to other city centers which then, in turn, "invite" those individuals and subgroups who would first have awareness of the new drug. (1989:2)

Respondents in our study tended to fall into one or more social worlds or scenes of MDMA users. They included college students, gays, professionals/yuppies, New Age/spiritual seekers, and music/dance enthusiasts. This last category included Deadheads (aficionados of the Grateful Dead rock band); young professionals in Dallas, Austin, and nearby areas who used Ecstasy in nightclubs during the mid-1980s; and large groups of Ravers trance-dancing on "E" to "House" music in a movement which began in Britain and has since spread to America and other countries.

Some of these social worlds are more obvious than others. For example, although it is easy to see how Deadheads belong to a unique social grouping, it is much more difficult to see how college students around the country live in a common social world. Although this is an admittedly amorphous conception, it is important to recognize that students generally participate in many other social worlds on and off campus. Nevertheless, status as a college student (at least on certain campuses) often determines access to scarce and little-known drugs such as MDMA.

In the following paragraphs, we discuss the diverse worlds of Ecstasy users, beginning with college students and ending with dance/music scenes.

MDMA SOCIAL WORLDS

College Students

Government and media accounts typically portray college students as a primary MDMA user group (cf. Adler, 1985; Dowling, 1985; Dye, 1982; NIDA, 1985; Rae, 1989; Sapienza, 1985). Such observations are not surprising given the high prevalence of drug use among college students relative to other populations (Johnston, Bachman, and O'Malley, 1991). With some exceptions, it appears that MDMA first became popular in universities commonly associated with liberal values and psychedelic drug use (Beck, 1986). For example, a survey of University of Colorado undergraduates conducted in 1987 found that 20 percent reported trying MDMA (Accola, 1988). Two independent surveys of Stanford undergraduates found significant, but widely discrepant, levels of use. The first study, conducted in early 1986, found 8 percent of the students reporting MDMA use (Calvert, 1987). The second survey, conducted in mid-1987, found an astonishing 39 percent of 369 undergraduates to have tried MDMA (Peroutka, 1988). This discrepancy could be at least partially attributable to an apparently dramatic surge in use between implementation of the two surveys. However, the differences could also be explained by the "convenience"[1] samples employed in both surveys, as well as in the Colorado study. This raises reliability concerns in attempting to estimate the extent of MDMA use on those campuses. Nevertheless, these data lend support to anecdotal accounts suggesting significant levels of use on particular campuses by the mid-1980s.

Fortunately, much can be learned about overall extent of use and trends among college students and other young adults from the recent inclusion of MDMA questions in the national "Monitoring the Future" surveys (Johnston et al., 1991). Young college students (one to four years beyond high school) were more likely to have tried MDMA than their noncollege-age peers with a lifetime prevalence of 3.9 percent in 1990. Up from 3.8 percent in 1989, this admittedly small increase nevertheless stands in contrast to the declines seen with most drugs. Annual prevalence among this same population was 2.3 percent for both years. Although use in the last month remained tiny, it had doubled from 0.3 percent to 0.6 percent (Johnston et al., 1991).

Although only 13 percent of our respondents were students at the time of their interview, over twice as many were attending college when they first tried MDMA. For many of our respondents, their initial MDMA use came as college undergraduates in the late 1970s and early 1980s. Their experience differs from media and government accounts, which typically portray MDMA use among students as having begun in the mid-1980s (Adler, 1985; Dowling, 1985; Sapienza, 1985). This can be largely attributed to their enrollment at particular West Coast colleges where MDMA- first appeared.

By the mid-1980s, MDMA use had spread to increasing numbers of colleges throughout the country. On at least some campuses, MDMA attracted groups not traditionally associated with psychedelic drug use (Dowling, 1985; Smith, 1985). MDMA's perceived psychological safety (ease of control) and euphoric reputation helped to explain its increasing popularity among even fraternities and sororities on some college campuses (Beck, 1986). Although illicit drugs were becoming increasingly unfashionable among these populations, MDMA remained popular with at least some groups. Despite criminalization, a former fraternity member at the University of Oregon described in a pilot interview the changes he had observed:

> When I was first using MDMA about six years ago, only a few people in a couple of houses were into it. We were also pretty secretive about it since we weren't quite sure about the legality. Recently, I talked to my younger sister who is now in a sorority at the same school. From the way she describes it, its use has spread and is now much more out in the open. It certainly adds a whole new dimension to house functions.

Finally, it should be noted that college students were well represented in each of the three rock/dance scenes described later in this chapter. We anticipate that they may play significant roles in future Ecstasy trends as well, since they are consistently a group that is open to experimentation.

Gays

Gays have frequently been identified as a major MDMA user population in the United States (Dowling, 1985; Eisner, 1989; Prangnell, 1988; Seymour, 1986). This could be expected given the long-standing popularity of MDA among gays in San Francisco and other cities during the years preceding the emergence of MDMA. A study conducted by the Haight-Ashbury Free Medical Clinic found MDA to be more popular among both male and female homosexuals and bisexuals than among their straight counterparts. The authors also observed that "the evangelical eloquence of the proponents is noteworthy" (Gay et al., 1982).

In contrast to other MDMA users who possessed little or no experience with MDA, gay respondents were often uncertain or confused in distinguishing between the two drugs. Discussions with treatment providers, distributors, and respondents revealed that both MDA and MDMA have been extremely popular among gay populations in certain cities of America, Europe, and Australia. This is particularly true for enthusiasts of "clubbing" where gays appear to have played significant roles in the formative phases of the Dallas nightclub and Acid House scenes in Britain and elsewhere (Dorn, Murji, and South, 1991; Lewis and Ross, 1991; Solowij and Lee, 1991).

However, the AIDS epidemic has resulted in dramatic changes among the gay population. Social worlds previously associated with extensive drug use increasingly gave way to an expanding sobriety and fitness movement within the gay community. As a consequence, many gays have discontinued or sharply curtailed their use of MDMA and other drugs. At the time of our study, gays appeared to be one population (in the Bay Area at least) whose MDMA use had clearly declined in the last couple of years. Nevertheless, there appears to be a dramatic resurgence of interest and use among gay men at Rave clubs, particularly in New York City and other East Coast cities (Baldinger, 1992; Sullivan, 1992).

Young and Not-So-Young Professionals

A large proportion of the study population consisted of middle- and upper-middle-class professionals and/or "yuppies." Numerous media accounts described MDMA as a "yuppie psychedelic" whose popularity was spreading rapidly among educated professionals in their 30s and 40s (Klein, 1985; Mandel, 1984; Shafer, 1985). Psychiatrist Norman Zinberg, who had previously studied MDA users, characterized MDMA as "the psychedelic for the '80s. It's no big deal. It's mild. You've still got the taste of danger without the impact of LSD. It's a yuppie psychedelic" (quoted in Leavy, 1985:1).

In certain areas, MDMA's popularity among professionals

preceded the media blitz which accompanied the scheduling controversy. Describing MDMA's increasing popularity among this population in the San Francisco Bay Area, one of the earliest media articles quotes a drug abuse program director declaring that "some of these people haven't touched a psychedelic in ten or fifteen years, but cocaine is really scaring folks these days. They are turning elsewhere." The journalist then goes on to describe the attractive advantages of MDMA: "In contrast to the mind-bending hallucinogens of the 60s, Adam is reported to leave one's faculties fairly clear . . . " (Mandel, 1984:A2).

Sensing that Ecstasy was "their" drug, one respondent asserted that typical MDMA users are

> professional people like real estate brokers, nurses, doctors, lawyers, entrepreneurs in businesses; there is this group. . . . There is another group which is not professional. They're people who have been doing drugs and everything else on and off and they try everything that comes their way. But they're not the majority [of MDMA users]. Basically, the professional, young professional . . . class that I know are using it. (011:48)

Yuppies and professionals saw the MDMA experience as providing an opportunity to be open and relaxed within the context of an often stressful and rigid lifestyle. It presented a chance for such individuals to engage in what one respondent referred to as "controlled hedonism."

Many of the participants in the Dallas nightclub scene were professionals who "partied" hard on the weekends to relieve some of the pressures associated with their work. A 25-year-old public relations worker, who saw MDMA as "fun, fun, high fun," described her use as

> strictly recreational. Strictly to feel good. It's like taking a drink. . . . There would be weekends where you do it every weekend—every Saturday, every Saturday, every Saturday. And then it's like you gotta take a break for a few weeks. . . . When it would come to the weekends I would just really let it rip, because I felt there was so much pressure all week long, either at home, or at my job. (065:19,25)

Most professionals described much more infrequent MDMA use. Their Ecstasy experiences had become a part of the "good life" they had come to look forward to and enjoy:

It's like you haven't been to a ballgame for three or four months, or you haven't gone to a real fancy dinner in three or four months, or you haven't gone to a good movie in three or four months. This is part of those things outside of the workaday world that I look forward to. . . . I look forward to being around people that I'm with when I'm on it and it's like going to summer camp. (011:47)

For professionals who were more therapeutically oriented, MDMA was perceived as allowing an individual to "work through" a lot of material in a remarkably short period of time. They often complained that they did not seem to have the time necessary to allow friendships or relationships to slowly develop. A 30-year-old civil engineer described MDMA's tendency to accelerate interpersonal processes: "It (MDMA) seems to depress time. You have the ability to cover a lot of ground in this flurry of experience that you might take quite a long time to get to or may not get to without it. I think the world we live in right now seems too busy" (025:46).

Interesting parallels can be seen between the professionals in this sample and those found in the first exploratory study of non-medical LSD use (Blum, 1964). In explaining why they were among the first groups attracted to LSD, Sanford asserts in the forward to Blum's book that these professionals were reacting to the increasing depersonalization, loss of connectedness, and other ills associated with industrialized society. According to research conducted before the countercultural revolt, these professionals saw their use of LSD as a potent aid in helping them regain purpose and meaning (Blum, 1964). Although increasingly "wanting out" of the system, they dutifully carried on within it and few were likely to subscribe to Leary's later admonition to "tune in, turn on, drop out."

Three decades later, professionals are still searching for acceptable amounts of fulfilling "time-out" activities to fit into their busy schedules. No longer interested in the fearsome existential challenges posed by LSD, many professionals were delighted that Ecstasy enabled them to gain maximal enjoyment and needed "bonding" during these "minivacations" (Rosenbaum, Morgan, and Beck, 1989).

New Age/Spiritual Seekers[2]

As with other psychedelics, MDMA use has frequently been associated with individuals who have "New Age" philosophies and/or lifestyles. An early article in *Newsweek* referred to MDMA as "the drug of choice of those who identify with the global consciousness and romantic ecology of the 'New Age' movement" (Adler, 1985:96).

We operationally defined "New Agers" as a group that included many respondents who described their use of MDMA as primarily therapeutically and/or spiritually oriented. Many of these respondents did not necessarily conceive of themselves as New Agers. Nevertheless, the shared belief systems associated with New Age perspectives merits the following examination of the history and meaning underlying philosophies of this type.

Many respondents had studied Eastern religions, attended human potential seminars (such as est) and/or were following a wide variety of spiritual paths. Some had been doing so since the 1960s, when an explosion of consciousness movements, Buddhist and Hindu teachers, and psycho-spiritual practices appeared on the scene. Many combined these approaches with the use of psychedelics in their search for self-awareness and enlightenment.

Hippies of the 1960s often saw themselves as heralders of a "New Age." The new psychology was teaching people to love themselves, understand and communicate with others, and deal with their anger by getting it out into the open. These concepts were embraced by those who saw the New Age as a time of love, harmony, and total enlightenment in which people would transform a chaotic planet into a utopian paradise. In order to do this, individuals would need to prepare themselves by expanding their consciousnesses to unite with other enlightened ones and with the entire universe.

An article on the New Age movement in the *San Francisco Chronicle* defined its philosophy as "a new way of looking at the world that involves the mind, the body and the holistic way of seeing that everything is interconnected" (Fong-Torres, 1988). Marilyn Ferguson (1980) states that the purpose of the New Age movement is no less than to achieve total "personal and social transformation."

Spirituality—a "transmaterial world view," as New Age writer Mark Satin (1974) called it—is an essential part of New Age philosophy. New Agers and other spiritual seekers have used a wide variety of techniques to raise their consciousnesses in attempting to achieve oneness with God and/or the universe. Many have studied Eastern religions, which have been teaching such techniques for centuries. In the 1960s, psychedelic drug use increasingly became a part of New Age social worlds (Ferguson, 1980; Stafford, 1991; Stevens, 1987).

It is not surprising that after nearly thirty years of the association between psychedelics and spirituality, a strong belief that such drugs can serve as an adjunct has become firmly entrenched. Respondents who were engaged in New Age or other spiritual pursuits were particularly eager to try MDMA because of its reputed empathic, bonding, and psychedelic properties. One woman, who was the child of an alcoholic father and attended self-help groups to deal with childhood traumas, described her motivation: "I am very interested in spirituality. . . . I was studying Eastern religion, and I studied crystals, and I always looked at things outside myself . . . [MDMA] is almost like being close to God" (004:14). A 32-year-old writer emphasized the importance of using MDMA and other psychedelics as an adjunct to other spiritual practices:

> And I already had taken up the practice of meditation and spent time in a monastery and intensive meditation retreats and reading very thoroughly in Buddhism and Hinduism and stuff like that before for several years before I had taken any psychedelic drugs. . . . Psychedelic drugs are of inestimable importance for many people in breaking through, in kind of initiating one into another level of awareness. But for the most part, they are abused. In my life, I'm not so sure that I've had, you know, unbelievable experiences that have been incredibly important for me. But they go hand in hand with more disciplined kinds of spiritual [disciplines]—particularly in meditation, doing meditation. For me, they've enhanced things that I had begun to appreciate and become curious about. (002:16)

Many of these spiritual questers were also therapeutically oriented. Some were psychiatrists, psychologists, or counselors. Others counseled or guided people in their spiritual pursuits. For them, MDMA's benefits combined spiritual and more traditionally therapeutic aspects.

A 33-year-old man, who gave workshops "focusing on dealing with people in spiritual emergency," felt that the integration of the spiritual and the therapeutic was necessary for those in crisis. He explained how MDMA could help:

> I think that the preeminent aspect of MDMA is a sense of acceptance. That, I think, produces the timelessness—you just accept you're not going anywhere . . . that's why I've used it with

monks, rabbis, Zen Buddhist priests, as an aid to meditation in 25 to 50 mg. doses, some very preeminent and prominent. All the reports in the media that came about the spiritual use of it? Those are all people I'd turned on, and they were willing to speak out to the press because they respected the experiences they had. . . . Those people who are most distant from themselves need that the most. So people who [have] post-traumatic stress disorders, people who are psychotic, suicidal, schizophrenic. . . . Now, I'm assuming it's not psychoses of an organic nature. But if someone is that far gone, I think that's where it should be used first. (007:81)

A counselor explained how MDMA could be used as an adjunct in treating people who were depressed. She was a little embarrassed about using spiritual terminology to describe the MDMA experience, but she could find no other:

One of the experiences that people hesitate to talk about with MDMA, but which is actually the basic and most important experience that MDMA can give anybody, usually comes spontaneously. . . . It goes under many names, some of them very far-out spiritual sounding sort of nonsense, but those are the only names you can use. It's an experience of the core self or sometimes called the God-space or the peaceful center, or somebody once described it as experiencing themselves being held in the hands of God, this feeling that something in the universe is totally accepting of them as a whole, you know, bumps and warts and all, no matter what they have done or not or what they are or are not. It is a deeply spiritual experience, and it is perhaps most valuable for the person who is in a severe depression because it is the core of the experience of self-loving and self-acceptance. (077:30)

Finally, one New Age respondent argued that MDMA's therapeutic and spiritual potential could only be truly realized if people were taught how to properly use it. She recommended that a board of advisors and consultants be set up which would oversee the regulation and administration of the drug. When asked what type of people she would select to serve on such a board, she said:

Well, I would *not* look to traditional psychiatry because, as I understand it, their approach to altered states is that they are dysfunctional, and that's not what's happening, usually, with MDMA or LSD. I would be more inclined to ask the transpersonal psychologist; I'm gonna look in the psychology field. . . .

But then on the other hand, I think there's a need for spiritual guidance, and I would prefer to consult with yogis and people like that . . . or the shamans, sure. (014:62,63)

Of course, as in other social worlds, there were markedly varying degrees of identification with New Age philosophies. Whereas some respondents dabbled with New Age ideas or practices, others lived them in a much more consuming manner. The use of various psychedelics has frequently played a central role for many (Smith, 1988). Like psychedelic plants in indigenous cultures, LSD has been employed as a "sacrament" by certain groups since the 1960s (Lyttle, 1988). To a lesser extent, a similar phenomenon has occurred with MDMA. What follows is a brief description by one of our respondents of what may be the most prominent and well-organized spiritual group using MDMA for transcendental purposes.

Nan [037] is a 70-year-old artist and teacher who described the MDMA experience as "a eucharist, a communion." She took MDMA for the first time on the Inhuatana, the highest point in the ruins of Machu Picchu in Peru, and meditated for four hours. Later, she became involved in an occult spiritual system based on ancient mythology and astrology, which was formulated in the mid-1980s. The originator of the system introduced MDMA into the ritual of the group, at the same time giving up the use of all other drugs.

The purpose of this spiritual path, according to "Nan," is to "create your higher body so that you move into a state which is no longer death-interrupted." She estimated that several hundred people from all walks of life (including many professionals) were currently "making this journey," each attending a session on a day "ruled" by one's own particular planet. She described MDMA use at sessions:

"Well, for the first year one attends a session every three weeks. And people do their work individually—no sound. They just lie down, close their eyes and wait for the message that is uniquely theirs. [They're taking] different amounts [of MDMA]. It's graded in a resonance. . . . You start, for instance, with 50 [mgs.] and then you take 50 the next and then you go to 75 and then you go up to 100 and then you go down to 75. And there is a chart which, according to the powers of those particular times, they meet and provide you with what you are to learn at that particular time." (037:42)

People receive different personal messages and insights during their experiences, she claims, and no guidance or counseling as to the meaning of the sessions is provided. Among other changes, she had noticed remarkable physical and mental rejuvenation among participants as they proceed further down this spiritual path. Summing up her feelings about MDMA's contribution, she concluded that "it's not possible to say in a rational way what it is except that it feels good [and] it seems to be a system that is growth oriented. . . . I know that [MDMA] opens the gate, and I don't know why it is MDMA. I'm not a chemist. But it has a specific chemical basis that other substances do not have" (037:48).

MDMA SCENES

The three remaining social worlds of MDMA users are examples of "scenes" described earlier. Despite obvious differences in user demographics, contexts, and musical tastes, Dallas "clubbers," Deadheads, and Ravers share a devotion to particular leisure activities which encourage vigorous dancing with large numbers of like-minded enthusiasts to high-powered music. In the following paragraphs, we provide in-depth descriptions of the Dallas Nightclub and Grateful Dead scenes before closing with a brief overview of the Rave scene.

The Dallas Nightclub Scene

The explosion of Ecstasy use that occurred in Dallas and surrounding areas in the mid-1980s constituted a particularly significant episode in MDMA's history. Beginning in 1983, the widespread production and marketing of Ecstasy by the Texas Group played a pivotal role in its criminalization. The effectiveness of their promotional efforts was reflected in the diverse populations of gays, students, yuppies, and others who began using this *legal* drug (as opposed to marijuana and cocaine) which seemed to them not only remarkably fun but safe as well. These attributes combined with Ecstasy's growing reputation for enhancement of dancing, socializing, and even dieting to help fuel explosive growth in both demand and supply in the brief period of time prior to criminalization.

Among the more unlikely groups attracted to Ecstasy during

this time were students attending conservative Southern Methodist University (SMU) in Dallas (Dowling, 1985). In the midst of a war on illicit drugs and with alcohol banned from campus, SMU students gladly availed themselves of this legal option, buying tablets of Ecstasy at a fraternity house (Smith, 1985). Others frequented Dallas bars catering and often selling Ecstasy to users at a usual price of $20 per dose (plus tax).

Although use appeared to decline dramatically in the years following criminalization, we were nevertheless interested in understanding the motivations and experiences of participants in the Dallas nightclub scene. After meeting, by happenstance, a Dallas transplant, two members of our research team flew to Dallas in April 1988 to interview several of his friends who had participated in the MDMA scene there while the drug was still legal. We wanted to get a taste of what the "X" scene in Dallas was like at its height and to learn how its flavor had changed since MDMA's criminalization.

Rosenbaum and colleague Sheigla Murphy visited Ecstasy "venues," had many informal discussions, and conducted seven formal interviews. The respondents (three women and four men) had all been active participants in the MDMA bar and nightclub scene during the height of its popularity. Most were attractive, well-dressed yuppies in their thirties, wearing expensive jewelry and accessories, who were cautious but willing to talk about MDMA. What unfolded from their description of the Ecstasy years was a picture quite different from that of other user groups, even those possessing similar demographic characteristics in the Bay Area.

These respondents concurred about the types of people who became involved in the Ecstasy scene in Dallas. A 25-year-old public relations director, who described Dallas as "flash and trash," portrayed the typical MDMA user of the mid-1980s:

> Socially and economically they're all upper class people or middle upper class. . . . They might be called yuppies today. They might be more artistic and more forward in that way. They're certainly not conservative people—they're fairly liberal people. . . . Maybe they're in a group that's pressured to really succeed and be successful. And Dallas is . . . a very flashy type place. The businesses that most of them are in are maybe high profile positions, and they're with that kind of group of people. . . . They're moving, moving upwards, and constantly striving for that kind of lifestyle. (065:34)

A 30-year-old secretary described how people usually became involved in the scene through groups of friends:

> They were all just business people. . . . They had their jobs with various companies. Young, fun people. This apartment complex was very conducive to friendship and forming—we had this huge little clique, huge clique of people that we'd party together. We were together seven days a week. You know, it was like twelve, fifteen of us that were always together doing things and interrelating and dating. (067:16)

In addition to bars and nightclubs, private parties became settings for yuppie MDMA use in Dallas. According to a 32-year-old restaurant manager,

> People used to have X parties all the time, but everybody would come in . . . and they would have minimum alcohol. They would party with lots of juice, coffee, tea, mineral waters, things like that. It was very yuppie because it was so—I don't know, I'm not sure of the right word, adjective to describe it . . . but it was just so very yuppie. (064:50)

These individuals were aware of MDMA's popularity in the gay community as well. According to a 35-year-old advertising executive: "It seemed to be very prevalent in the gay community. The only time I think I've ever bought it direct from a place was a couple times when I couldn't get it through friends, and I would go to a gay bar" (063:29).

Men and women expressed different attitudes toward drug use when describing their reasons for becoming involved with MDMA. Male respondents typically had used many drugs, particularly cocaine, which had hit the Dallas nightclub scene prior to the introduction of MDMA. In the early 1980s, Dallas experienced an economic boom in the oil, airline, and real estate industries. Young professionals, dressed in the height of fashion and exhibiting as much of their wealth as they could, were out to "see and be seen." They had no problem finding or affording cocaine. Each of the four male respondents had used cocaine heavily at one time or another; three admitted to having had a problem with it. When asked why the men had switched from cocaine to MDMA use, a woman familiar with the scene told us:

> They didn't shift. They just did it, too. They did both, because back then everyone had so much money they always—all the

guys, they were so moneyed—they were so rich from real estate, 'cause all the guys here are in real estate—everyone was loaded and all the guys had coke. And they shared it with everybody. And X was a little harder to come by. You usually had to pay for your X for some reason. (067:34)

The women in Dallas had an interesting perspective on the use of Ecstasy. Two of the female respondents came from religious, "nice girl," backgrounds which frowned even on drinking. Drug use of any kind was not in the background of these women. A 30-year-old woman who is now a Sunday school teacher in Dallas described her upbringing:

And I'm sure there was a group in high school, where the kids would go at recess, and they had a smoking section. But I never hung around with those people. Those were like scums. Those were like yuckies. Like I was in drill team and I was a cheerleader. You're not allowed to smoke if you're in drill team, 'cause you are representing your school. So I was like All American, true blue. And I guess I tried to be that way because I wanted to make my mom proud of me . . . and I tried to be a good kid. . . . I'd never seen marijuana or anything. . . . I just always thought that is wrong. Drugs are wrong. I was still into my church group and Young Life and all that. (069:13)

Ecstasy's then-status as a legal drug cleared the way for its use by these otherwise conventional women. One of the male Dallas respondents, a 32-year-old restaurant manager, explained why women with such a background permitted themselves to use MDMA:

It was the kind of drug that SMU girls that would never even consider smoking marijuana would do because it was legal and it was . . . socially acceptable. . . . You weren't a drug addict if you used Ecstasy. You were normal people. And girls that would never do anything would do that—good little homey girls. (064:29)

The Sunday school teacher probably would not have tried MDMA if she had known it was a drug.

They said, "Here, just do this and have fun. Just do this," like it was a B-12. You know what, if somebody told me it was a drug, I probably would have put a negative . . . block, a mental block against it. In fact, I probably would not have done it if somebody had said, "This is a drug." But, "Oh, this is OK, it's B-

12." Then I did it, 'cause that's the way I was. I was always such a goody-goody. Really . . . it felt like I was being good. (069:40)

In sum, Ecstasy users in Dallas were primarily young professionals who were doing well economically (many were in real estate prior to the Texas decline) and fundamentally conventional if not conservative. The scene in which they partied was linked to their use of MDMA, and vice versa. As noted in our discussion of the distribution and diffusion of MDMA, it should be reiterated that the term "Ecstasy" was coined explicitly to attract the Texas market. And in Dallas, MDMA use was anything but a slowly evolving phenomenon. The man quoted above, whom we called "Mr. Dallas," described the rapid evolution of the scene:

[It was] '85, and I moved into a small apartment by myself. That's when I found some good X. It started becoming so much more available. All you had to do was get out in the street life— the night life. That's when it was all over the street life. I mean, suddenly it was like within one weekend, boom! It was everywhere and you could get it anywhere on the streets, in the bars, for 20 bucks a hit from anybody. (064:28)

It was the bars and nightclubs, as opposed to private homes and outdoor settings, that were the preferred settings for MDMA use. The bar scene in Dallas was already in place, and Ecstasy simply blended in. One woman stated: "It was just that the club life is real big at night, and especially when you're young and you hang out in Dallas, you hang out on Greenville Avenue all the time. . . . That's the biggest strip as far as clubs—it used to be—as far as clubbing and all that. It was just huge at that point" (069:45).

MDMA use in bars and nightclubs was open and unconcealed during the days when it was still legal. Again, "Mr. Dallas" described it: "They were selling it over the bars. You would order a couple of cocktails and two hits of X and put it on your Master Card" (064:45). He went on to explain that bar owners, who found their establishments crowded with people who weren't buying alcoholic beverages while doing MDMA, jumped on the Ecstasy bandwagon for economic reasons: "One of the reasons the bars started selling it is because it was drying up their alcohol sales. . . . It became a quickly understood practice that you didn't want to muddle it up, muddy the water (MDMA) with a lot of other things" (064:48).

MDMA use appeared to decline rapidly among this popula-

tion following its criminalization in 1985. In a manner characteristic of many scenes, Ecstasy had become "last year's fad." Illegality, reduced availability, increased price, the recession, and the
antidrug climate were variously cited by respondents who had
quit or sharply curtailed their use of MDMA. By the time we
arrived in Dallas to interview these users, over two years after it
became illegal, respondents were guarded about talking with us,
and over-the-counter sales were nonexistent (we checked).

The relative importance of various factors in decreasing use
among this population has important implications for understanding the natural history of other MDMA-fueled dance club
scenes. Despite considerable enthusiasm which often lasted over a
year, respondents eventually began to suffer from predictable
burnout and boredom with a scene that had remained remarkably
static. Similarly, some respondents had ingested MDMA almost
every weekend at the same nightclubs for up to two years. Perhaps
tired of the same predictable hedonism, one Dallas man believed
the scene would have died a natural death even without MDMA's
criminalization: "You come to a point of realizing you can't party
forever. You've got to take account of reality and plan for your
future. You can't just party, party, party forever" (064:58).

The criminalization of Ecstasy and the apparent demise of
much of the Dallas nightclub scene failed to deter many users,
who did not stop using the drug but simply exercised more caution in their affairs. When asked about perceived differences
between the situation before and after MDMA's criminalization,
"Mr. Dallas" replied: "Okay, it was rampant. It was everywhere.
And for a short time after that, it was still rampant and everywhere, just not as obvious to the eye. Oh, right before it became
illegal I think we may have just done it and said, 'Okay, tomorrow
it's illegal. Big heavy deal! Tomorrow we'll be careful'" (064:44).

The media's, hence the public's, fascination with the blatant
marketing of Ecstasy in Dallas nightclubs quickly faded following
criminalization and subsequent declining use. Although MDMA
was dismissed as yet another yuppie fad, DEA reports and informal interviews suggest otherwise. Despite problems of availability
and rip-offs, MDMA use, although nowhere near pre-1985 levels,
remains popular among young middle-class whites and in particular nightclub settings in a number of Texas cities (Texas Commission on Alcohol and Drug Abuse, 1991).[3]

Deadheads

The Grateful Dead is a rock band with a dedicated following. Despite the general demise and trivialization of much of the 1960s counterculture, the Grateful Dead has endured remarkably. As one critic recently observed:

> They are one of the only "through lines" in American culture, a living link with a past generation and a once-exuberantly alive culture. . . . By some priceless irony, the princes of acidhead anarchy, who remained true to their multicolored lights, have become an American institution, a musical legend. And they've earned it. (Kamiya, 1991:5)

The Grateful Dead formed in 1965 and served as the house band for the infamous Acid Tests and Trips Festival put on by Ken Kesey and the Merry Pranksters.[4] Looking back, one can see how these psychedelic tribal gatherings served as the forerunners for both the Deadhead phenomenon and more recent Rave gatherings. Conceived as an LSD-fueled group mind experience, the Acid Tests strived for sensory overload utilizing every means possible. Guitarist Jerry Garcia recalled that there were "thousands of people, all helplessly stoned, all finding themselves in a roomful of other thousands of people, none of whom any of them were afraid of. It was magic" (quoted in Stevens, 1987:249).

Although many of our respondents had attended Dead concerts, most would not be considered true Deadheads. Although we lacked clear-cut criteria for determining who qualifies for this appellation, at least 10 percent of our respondents were serious candidates by virtue of their considerable enthusiasm for and frequent attendance at Dead shows in many states. As one woman described the Dead caravans which follow the band on tour: "They're like a small community in themself. Every one of them knows each one, maybe not by name but by sight, and they all travel around the United States together to go to these concerts" (004:33).

Official Deadheads or not, many respondents had definite opinions regarding the Grateful Dead scene. A predominant perspective concerned the long-standing prevalence of psychedelic drug use among the band's followers. As one of the foremost and certainly last purveyors of "acid rock," much of the Grateful Dead's music is particularly appealing to the psychedelicized mind (Baumeister, 1984).

Citing the Dead's music and/or the friendly atmosphere supportive of such drug experimentation, a surprising number of respondents were introduced to LSD, mushrooms, and other psychedelics through friends at Dead concerts. Despite the potentially overwhelming crowds and sensory overload, most of these initial experiences were greatly enjoyed.

Based on our interviews and ethnographic fieldwork at concerts, it appears that MDMA's popularity slowly grew among enthusiasts of the Dead, who saw it as an addition to their psychedelic pharmacopeia. Ecstasy joined LSD, psilocybin, and marijuana as "drugs of choice" for experiencing the Grateful Dead. On the West Coast, MDMA use at Dead shows peaked in 1985–1986 because of increased availability and publicity.[5] MDMA use appears to have subsequently declined in many locations for a number of possible reasons related to low availability, higher costs, and physical burnout. Nevertheless, it has remained an option for many enthusiasts of the Grateful Dead.

Compared with its importance in the Dallas nightclub and Rave scenes, MDMA has played a much smaller role in the social world of Deadheads. Far from being essential to the scene, Ecstasy was simply a welcome latecomer to a time-tested menu of psychedelic options well suited to the acid rock and supportive atmosphere found at Dead concerts.

Nevertheless, many concertgoers greatly appreciated MDMA's smoothness and controllability, which made handling crowds much easier than with LSD or psilocybin. One respondent was a beautician (a skin-care specialist) who had a large clientele of Deadheads because, as she said, "my trip is sort of organic and natural" and appealed to "those types of people that don't fit in the 'normal' places." She surmised that Deadheads enjoy MDMA

> 'cause that music is very sensuous and that is a very sensuous drug . . . it's lighter than acid. They do acid, too . . . and also, MDMA is considered an organic drug, basically—like women prefer it rather than taking acid. . . . It really makes you feel sensual, your skin and how you see things. And they're into tie-dye and the colors are really bright. And when you look at things, your eyes are just—they hurt from seeing so much. So I could see where it would be a really cool music scene drug. . . . It's just fun to touch people. That's probably why the Deadheads like it. They're real touchy with each other. (004:33,34)

Some respondents, recognizing the advantages of each, combined MDMA with other psychedelics for maximal enjoyment of "acid rock" in an ecstatic frame of mind. Referred to as "L & M's" by some Deadheads, the combination of LSD and Ecstasy has become increasingly popular among Ravers who enjoy the user-friendly psychedelia of what is now called the "Candyflip" experience.

In a manner similar to their Raver counterparts, Deadheads thrive on the group spirit evident at concerts—the exhilarating sense of being a part of a supportive community. A 22-year-old student likened the experience of taking MDMA in such a context to group sex:

> It seems that the Grateful Dead, or a Grateful Dead concert, is such a community experience. I mean, it sounds a little silly, but it's just like this great big community orgasm, and everybody is like "Whoa!" and everybody's getting off all at once. And so when you put Ecstasy in the context of that experience, wow! It's really phenomenal, because then if you go and sit in the Henry J. Kaiser [auditorium] and there's 6,000, 7,000, maybe 8,000 other people, or if you go to the Oakland Coliseum for maybe a New Year show and there's maybe 25,000 people, it's really something else. (045:72)

Many Deadheads described how the empathic qualities of the MDMA experience, coupled with the supportive atmosphere found at Dead concerts, enhanced this sense of community. In such an uninhibited environment, several respondents said they enjoyed taking MDMA and experiencing the feeling of intimacy with strangers which they would have balked at in a different setting. A 33-year-old electrical engineer gave away Grateful Dead tickets "because they ought to be free":

> More than anything else, I think about the best experiences I've had with MDMA—it becomes incredibly wonderful to be with friends or to meet people you haven't known before. So there was a whole second stage level of experience that I had with MDMA when I took it at a Grateful Dead concert. . . . I used to go to the Greek Theatre and feel like a cell on the surface of someone's retina. But [at the Grateful Dead concert] I had this very powerful, overwhelmingly clear conception that we're all just like neurons. The thing about a neuron is it's no good by itself. It sounds really simple when you say it that way, but I suddenly just realized that the whole point of life is the synapse,

the connection of communication and the touching of hearts. It was just amazing. I was walking around like a goddam politician, shaking people's hands and just being completely unselfconscious about it. (021:23)

Many respondents commented on how the warm, accepting nature of fellow concertgoers created a supportive environment for positive psychedelic experiences. A 30-year-old civil engineer usually preferred to be in control during his infrequent drug-taking experiences, carefully choosing the environment and avoiding "any situations in which the impairment of my judgment might be a risk to myself." Nevertheless, he enjoyed taking MDMA at Grateful Dead concerts:

> Q: Do you feel like you try to have varied control of environments so that you can do what you want?
> A: The exception to that probably is doing it at certain Grateful Dead concerts in which—you could call that a controlled environment as well, by certain definitions.
> Q: Everyone's doing it.
> A: Yeah. It's sort of controlled chaos. And in that sense it is. It is a situation where you're not going to be called on to be straight. It's just not the environment for it. (025:34)

Acid House/Rave

Ecstasy served as an essential catalyst for the Acid House dance scene and continues to fuel the even more popular Rave phenomenon. Kaplan and colleagues have explored the origins and diffusion of Acid House and suggest that it may not have originated in England, as is commonly thought, but on the island of Ibiza:

> The first known specific fusion of MDMA in an intense public environment with a distinctive kind of music and dancing called "acid house" occurred on the Spanish island of Ibiza in 1985. This vacation island has been a haven for northern European (especially German) tourists who have been seeking hedonistic experience. Ibiza had been a popular resort for drug dealers, celebrities and new age cultists for a decade. By the summer of 1986 Ibiza became known as "XTC island." (1989:5)

When we were conducting our study, the seemingly trendy and faddish Acid House scene had just hit America. In a manner reminiscent of media portrayals of LSD two decades earlier, a *New York Times* article proclaimed that MDMA "has soared in popularity this year, occupying center stage in a wider social drama combining fashion, music and youthful restlessness" (Forderaro, 1988:26). In addition to illicit sales of MDMA, a profitable legal industry had evolved around the scene—catering to the unique music, clothes and identifying paraphernalia associated with "Acid House" (Cahr and Bashara, 1989). Possessing "its own music, dress code and language," Acid House was described this way by a London periodical: "Record and fashion industries have been rushing to catch up with the fad, and even commercial radio disk jockeys have drawn on the ecstatic commentary devised by their counterparts in nightclubs. What many appear to ignore is that the drug [MDMA] may not be so much a part of the cult, as the point of it" (*Illustrated London News*, 1988:29–30).

By the end of 1988, the only sizable Acid House scene in the United States appeared to be in Manhattan. However, following publication of the *New York Times* article, advertisements appeared in San Francisco Bay Area newspapers announcing "Acid House nights" at a number of local nightclubs.

We visited various clubs in the Bay Area in early 1989 to gauge both the popularity of Acid House music and the prevalence of Ecstasy use. We found that, unlike in London or New York, there was very little obvious MDMA use associated with Acid House nights at these clubs. An article in the *San Francisco Chronicle* arrived at a similar conclusion. It quoted a British expatriate who offered her rationale for MDMA's absence: "Ecstasy is a new drug in England. All the people in San Francisco who wanted to have already tried it" (Selvin, 1989:E1).

Sensationalistic media coverage of Acid House in England stimulated curiosity about and the use of Ecstasy just as it did in the United States in 1985 (Newcombe, 1988; O'Hagan, 1989). One researcher observed, "The advertising success was unprecedented, with night clubs throughout the country hosting Acid House nights" (Farrell, 1989:943). One newspaper article asserted that Acid House parties "attract up to tens of thousands of youngsters at a time, go on all night and can be heard miles away" (*Daily Express*, quoted in *International Journal of Drug Policy*, 1989).

The enormous popularity of Acid House led to increasingly harsh responses by law enforcement. The same article noted that "drug-busting police sealed off an entire town twice at the weekend to claim their first victory over the Acid House cult" (*Daily Express* quoted in *International Journal of Drug Policy, 1989*).

Police crackdowns forced Acid House underground, which only seemed to increase its notoriety. Despite law enforcement claims of victory, many observers tended to view this decline as inevitable for what they considered to be essentially a short-lived fad: "the threat to civilization will fade and be replaced by a hoola-hoop revival" (Jones, 1989).

Based on the limited information on hand in early 1990, Beck concluded that

> despite its recent decline in England, Acid House appears to remain popular in many European cities, particularly in The Netherlands and West Germany (Kaplan et al., 1989). A possible reason for this is that the scene, together with Ecstasy use, appears to have increasingly spread from more elite "trend setters" to working class populations (Haafkens, 1989). What effect this may have on MDMA use patterns or problems remains unknown at this time. Given the disparate scenes described above, MDMA's qualities evidently appeal to many diverse groups of nightclub enthusiasts. In attempting to ascertain whether a similar dance-oriented scene might develop again around MDMA or a similar substance, one should not underestimate the potent combination of marketing savvy and media sensationalism in piquing curiosity among potential user groups in different parts of the country. (1990a:114)

Indeed, the Rave scene, which had grown out of Acid House, was exploding across the British landscape. In a recent article about the Rave scene in England, Newcombe sheds some light on the transition that occurred there:

> Rather than fading away, between 1988 and 1989 the rave changed its status from a cliquey, mutating underground subculture to a more socially diverse, stable and consumerist popular leisure culture, blurring the boundaries between such previously disparate groups as football fans and various pop music 'tribes'. (1992:14)

The result has been the institution of the most popular venue for Ecstasy use. However, the Rave as a generic dance scene is not new. In what was arguably the first "Rave," the Family Dog dance was held at the Longshoreman's Hall in San Francisco on October 16, 1965. This lengthy extravaganza attracted a huge crowd of diverse celebrants decked out in weird costumes and dancing through the night to the music of Jefferson Airplane and other groups.

The Family Dog dance was a huge success, and soon these concerts became a staple of the hip community. Each weekend people converged at auditoriums such as the Avalon Ballroom for all-night festivals that combined the seemingly incongruous elements of spirituality and debauch . . . they rediscovered the crushing joy of the dance, pouring it all out in a frenzy that frequently bordered on the religious. . . . Attending such performances amounted to a total assault on the senses. . . . (Lee and Shlain, 1985:142)

Within a year, the Avalon Ballroom and Fillmore Auditorium (both in San Francisco) had already drawn about a million celebrants. Throughout San Francisco, smaller venues were competing with each other "to reproduce the hallucinogenic experience, with 'total environments', flashing lights, wild flowing colors, frenetic dances, and large signs proclaiming 'It's Happening'" (Marshall and Taylor, 1967:108). In January 1966, the "Trips Festival" staged by Ken Kesey and the Merry Pranksters turned into a wild three-day acid extravaganza in which "for the first time, all the elements of taped electronic sound, films, slides, psychedelic art, and dance combined in an explosive 10,000 person freakout. Since then, the formula has spread across North America and is now reaching Europe" (Marshall and Taylor, 1967:107).

Twenty-five years later, Europe reached back in the form of expatriate Brits bringing Rave culture to San Francisco in the winter of 1991. As in 1965, little time had passed before 7,200 people could be found celebrating New Year's Eve until 8:00 the next morning at a Rave venue called "ToonTown" (Robins, 1992). A veteran Raver described for us the dynamism of the scene:

And the dancing! Hundreds of people—male, female, young, younger, gay, straight, well-dressed, t-shirted, undressed—all grooving, spinning, and grinding to the relentless beat. The music never stops, though sometimes, just for a few bars, the high-tech percussion pauses, just long enough for a super keyboard solo to bring the energy level up to new heights. And the dancers never stop either. Some of them have been here since 9:00 this evening, and they'll still be out there on the floor, waving their arms in the air and blowing their whistles, at 7:00 in the morning when the Rave ends. Of course that's just a signal to go somewhere else - several local clubs host "afterparties" to keep the groove going all day. . . . You can rave all weekend long in San Francisco, and some people don't miss a single beat.

Within this "disco-inferno, psychedelic apocalypse," Robins observes that "if music is the magnet for ravers, drugs are the catalyst" (Robins, 1992:11). Although the same could be (and probably was) said in describing the psychedelic dance hall scene of the mid-1960s, the drugs and the music have changed. The same veteran talked about drugs and Rave: "Naturally, the psychedelics top the list. Half the crowd wanders around hugging everyone they see and glowing empathetically. Must be on Ecstacy, or "E" as it's now called. The other half is oblivious to everything except the music and their own internal dreamworld." Instead of dancing to the Grateful Dead on LSD as in 1965, the modern Raver is more likely to be dancing to "House" music on Ecstasy. According to our veteran informant:

> The centerpiece of the rave experience is a style of music called "techno-house," the latest link in a never ending evolution of dance music that stretches all the way back to the blues. Techno-house has the relentless rhythm of disco or 80s-style pop music, the speed of punk or speed-metal, the instrumental creativity of fusion, and the melodic beauty of baroque. Every moment seems to be more energetic, more exciting, and higher than the moment before.

The combination of Ecstasy and House music is considered ideal for prolonged trance-dancing. The importance of Ecstasy in this scene is reflected in various descriptors, which alternately refer to it as "the most essential catalyst" (Heley, 1991:125); the "ultimate rave drug" (McDonnell, 1992:13); and the "Ravers' cultural drug of choice" (Pearson et al., 1991:10). As Newcombe asserts, "Ecstasy, or 'E', is the prototypical drug of the rave scene, the mental state it produces being intimately related to the sounds, designs and concepts of house music culture" (1992:14).

Despite differences in musical preferences, McDonnell notes the many similarities between the psychedelic scenes of today and yesteryear. She goes on to assert that "Ravers are house music Deadheads" (McDonnell, 1992:13). Kaplan and colleagues argue similarly that the name and symbology associated with the Acid House/Rave scene

> suggest a living continuity between the counterculture of the 1960s and the post-modern cultures of the late 1980s. . . . On the surface it is 1988, yet underneath is the reconnection with

1968—back to the extravagances of the 1960s, not with LSD, but with a better psychedelic, XTC. . . . In the 1960s, LSD provided the experience of mind expansion which was defined as pharmacologically relevant by its users. In the changing socio-historical conditions of the 1980s, the relevance of MDMA lies in its ego-centering effect and in its fueling of a total dance experience. (1989:6)

In this chapter, we have attempted to answer the question: Who uses Ecstasy? We looked at MDMA users in sociological terms: where they came from and who they identified with as a backdrop for their drug use. We examined particular *social worlds* and *scenes* involving MDMA. As such, we were interested in how these shaped contextual factors (set and setting) which influenced the MDMA experience. We identified seven social worlds and/or scenes of MDMA use: college students, gays, professionals/yuppies, New Age/spiritual seekers, Dallas clubbers, Deadheads, and Ravers.

CHAPTER 4

Attractions of the MDMA Experience: Why People Use Ecstasy

In the previous chapter, we described the diverse social worlds of Ecstasy use. We now look at the various attributes users ascribe to the MDMA experience—why people like the high. We begin with an examination of first use, exploring factors underlying decisions to experiment with MDMA. We then segue into a discussion of people's motivations that account for their differential appreciation of the drug's effects. After addressing the question of *why* most respondents experiment with MDMA, the remainder of the chapter describes *what* they most appreciate about the experience.

We follow the trajectory of the MDMA experience itself, beginning with the initial "rush" often experienced when first "coming on," or feeling the effects of MDMA. This is soon followed by the two-to-four-hour "plateau" phase, which is generally regarded as the best part of the MDMA experience. We offer a considerable number of respondent perspectives to illustrate the variety of attributes associated with this phase of the MDMA high. In contrast, the "comedown" and aftereffects which follow are typically regarded as the most problematic parts of the experience. These aftereffects are only briefly addressed here because in the following chapter we examine their role in limiting use. Next we ask, "Is it really Ecstasy?" We conclude this chapter with an examination of differing user perspectives regarding MDMA's long-term benefits and therapeutic potential.

THE DECISION TO TRY MDMA

What influence, or series of influences, convinced individuals from various social worlds to try this new drug? The recreational and therapeutic qualities ascribed to MDMA appealed to a broad cross-section of potential users. For the recreationally minded, the promise of prolonged bliss was accompanied by references proclaiming Ecstasy to be the latest "love drug." Media accounts describing enhanced communication, empathy, and fear reduction were potent lures for others. For many veteran drug enthusiasts, the initial media coverage and/or friend's descriptions were enough to convince them to seek out what appeared to be an intriguing substance. As one 58-year-old professional told us:

> One of our summer crowd had read about Ecstasy and asked my wife about it. She thought maybe this was a drug she could enjoy from the description she'd read of it. She asked my wife if she could get some and they should try it. And my wife knew how to get some and said, "Of course, we'll get some and we'll all try it." (013:26)

By the 1980s, the War on Drugs and antidrug sentiment sweeping the nation had turned many people away from drug use. As a result, some of our respondents who were less experienced and willing than the man quoted above required more convincing to pique their curiosity. Given the reluctance to experiment, what influenced them to make an exception for MDMA?

Ecstasy's reputation as easily controllable or "user-friendly" (relative to psychedelics such as LSD) allayed the fears of many individuals. Reflecting these attributes, a recent article described how MDMA "became the drug of choice for yuppies and young hipsters—less overwhelming in its effects than acid, as sensuous as pot, emotionally warmer than coke" (Robins, 1992:11). An earlier article titled "Drugless in L.A." described how "for veterans of the 60s, it is interesting to note that the major new drug of the 80s, Ecstasy, has been hyped as a drug that is not really a drug" (Kaye, 1986:34).

The positive experiences typically seen with initial MDMA use led many respondents to become proselytizers who wanted to share this valuable experience with others. Since problematic availability has characterized Ecstasy since its popularization, a friend's access often constituted a crucial factor in initiating use. For many respondents, the most important dimension in their decision to actually try this new substance was the advice provided by trusted friends.

The trusted friend was particularly important for those who had doubts about using this or any other drug. A vivid example of this was provided by a married woman in her late fifties who had been strongly antidrug and claimed never to have been intoxicated on any substance in her life. She decided to try MDMA at the urging of a close and trusted friend who was also a therapist (012:19).

Another example was provided by a 34-year-old New Ager who, despite leading a nonconformist, nontraditional lifestyle, stated that she had a strong aversion to all drugs and "never experimented. . . . Didn't want to do drugs, ever." A close friend somehow convinced her that Ecstasy was the answer to her problems:

> She said that it opens you up and it makes you feel alive and, most of all, it makes you *feel*. . . . I would be in touch with nature. . . . It's almost like being close to God. . . . I didn't know how to feel. . . . There wasn't time for my feelings. . . . Why is the world like this? Why is it so painful? And she told me if I took this drug it wouldn't be painful. And she was right! It was great! (004:14–15)

After learning about MDMA through the media, a friend, or a therapist, and then deciding to try it, respondents described a wide range of beliefs and expectations about the anticipated experience. Those who were introduced to MDMA in the late 1970s in recreational settings, and those who impulsively tried it in clubs or at concerts, generally had minimal information to act on and consequently fewer expectations regarding effects. On the other hand, professionals and therapeutically or spiritually oriented types often received detailed information which led to more definite expectations as well as planning for the experience.

Respondents reported a potpourri of descriptions given to them by friends who had used MDMA: "a feel-good drug," "fun," "loving," "insightful," "empathic," "spiritual," "you'll dance all night," "deepens relationships," and so on. These cues typically correlated with their motivations for use as well as the orientation of friends or social worlds.

Those familiar with psychoactive drugs were often provided descriptions comparing MDMA to other substances. In attempting to account for its diverse qualities, people typically described MDMA's effects as a combination of a stimulant and a psychedelic, with the possible addition of marijuana or opium to account for one's ability to relax. For example, one respondent was told that "it's like a mild psychedelic mixed with a mellow speed" (008:11). Another respondent described the experience to others as a mixture of "LSD, hashish and crystal methedrine" (083:13).

Such descriptions were typically qualified as crude approximations which failed to adequately explain MDMA's unique effects.

The Importance of Recreational Versus Therapeutic Perspectives

As described earlier, the differences in respondent motivations for MDMA use can be viewed as occurring along a therapeutic-recreational continuum. On one end were those who cited various therapeutic and/or spiritual benefits as the most important reasons for using Adam. On the other end were respondents who placed a stronger emphasis on the euphoric and sensual properties they associated with Ecstasy. We found marked differences between those who ingested MDMA strictly for personal or spiritual growth and those who employed it exclusively for fun and partying.

With a few notable exceptions, however, the vast majority of MDMA users lie somewhere in between these two extremes. Even the most therapeutically inclined respondents reportedly experienced at least some euphoric or sensual enjoyment. Similarly, hard-core partiers often attributed their enhanced communication abilities or valuable long-term friendships to MDMA use. In general, most respondents felt their MDMA use had provided a varied mixture of therapeutic, spiritual, and recreational benefits. However, there were substantial differences of opinion regarding the relative importance of these diverse attractions.

The varied motivations, intentions, and expectations found among members of the diverse social worlds described in the previous chapter help explain the differences in MDMA experiences. Acknowledging these influences, a veteran user and former dealer described what he believed to be the three major types of MDMA reactions:

> Almost everyone really enjoys it and appreciates it. I would say maybe 30 percent of the people that take it have major insights about being alive and interacting in the world and trying to be fine human beings. 30 percent have those major insights. Another 30 percent really like it and have fun with it. And the last 30 percent, basically, probably feel fairly neutral about it. They're used to something much stronger or it disconcerts them in some way or it just doesn't move them at all. (080:16)

Respondent social worlds greatly influenced the particular qualities of the MDMA experience most sought after and valued by users. Differences in intentions and expectations help explain why positive attributes described by some respondents were devalued or not even recognized by others. As a consequence, the role played by a particular user's social world(s), combined with his or her own motivation, greatly shaped the actual MDMA experience itself. For example, a busy 58-year-old professional left little doubt where he stood regarding expectations of MDMA or other drug use:

> I take drugs to get high, and that's what I expected of Ecstasy. I expected a reduced, mellower form of the psychedelics which we had taken quite a bit of, and stopped taking for years. I never fully liked, but did like aspects of the psychedelics. It puts you through such mind exercises, who you are and what the Earth is about, etc., etc. And supposedly this [MDMA] was to have none of that. It was just pure ecstasy. And the name was the description of the phenomenon. (013:24)

A young New Age–oriented woman offered a markedly different point of view: "I never took the drug to get high, so the reason why I was taking it was to open myself up. And it did its job. It would be redundant if I took it now. . . . I don't need to take the drug with someone to talk about something. I have all the skills now. And it gave me the start" (004:28).

A 47-year-old businessman and former distributor offered a more complex appraisal. Describing the varied attractions of the MDMA experience, his account reflects shifts in motivations for use reported by other respondents as well as his own:

> I heard people since talking about the total recreational use of it, total therapeutic use of it. And I would say in the introduction of Ecstasy to my relatives, friends and loved ones, it was a combination of both therapeutic and recreational. It was fun to do. It was a wonderful, incredible mood elevator, a great time to be together. . . . But the therapeutic use here—the feeling that I want to save the world, seeing the incredible breakthroughs, the incredible opening and growth that has occurred since then, the immense benefit of the patching up of marriages or helping people see that their marriage was really over, has had such a positive effect on me, watching these things, that it made me very anxious to continue doing it. And that was probably the major motivation in introducing people to it. (040:15)

In sum, membership in social worlds that defined Ecstasy use as recreational versus those using it in more therapeutic ways had an impact on motivations for use. Those in the recreational camp saw an opportunity to take a minivacation—to get high. Those in the therapeutic camp saw MDMA as a tool for self-exploration and communication. Although each may go into the "trip" with a set of distinct motivations and expectations, the continuum is fluid, and there is a great deal of overlap in the actual experience of Ecstasy.

Planning and Preparation

MDMA's reputation as a fairly potent, long-lasting psychedelic often resulted in much greater planning and preparation than that typically associated with shorter-duration cocaine or marijuana use. Because they had experience with other psychedelics, many potential MDMA users recognized the importance of timing, place, companions, and state of mind in determining the outcome of their drug experience. Consequently, these individuals tended to give careful consideration from the start to creating what they perceived to be optimal contexts for MDMA use. Conversely, individuals with less previous psychedelic experience and/or more timorous dispositions often learned through a process of trial and error. There were marked differences in the actual extent of planning and preparation. Many therapeutically oriented users recalled being very cognizant and well informed about MDMA even before their initial experience. They often followed explicit instructions provided by therapists, close friends, or anonymously written "flight guides" (See appendix F).

A 72-year-old New Ager echoed other therapeutic accounts in explaining why he considered careful preparation necessary for ingesting MDMA: "It was like a sacrament. That's the best description. But if you are going to go into a Holy of Holies and present your body as a living sacrifice for something to happen, for healing to take place, you want to give it the best chance (078:45).

One therapist provided an extensive description of how she prepared her clients and attempted to allay any possible fears:

> First thing I try to set up is the general set and setting kind of thing. . . . And I make sure that what they see of me is obviously extremely comfortable, very relaxed. . . . It's obvious that I have no anxiety whatsoever about what's happening. . . . I tell them that the first effects—this is for the first time, again—are going to feel strange. It's a sensation they have never had before. . . . This is going to be, perhaps, a little anxiety-producing, and that

they can expect to feel a little anxious because it's a brand new feeling. (077:44–45)

Some experienced respondents recalled the more spiritual rationales and careful preparation associated with psychedelic use of a bygone era. As one veteran of the 1960s described it:

> I was very conscious of taking care of myself during the whole stage of experimentation. . . . You got high to expand your consciousness. That was the whole kind of idea of the thing was that you would do something new and adventuresome and explore yourself and your mind and your psyche. . . . I don't know if those ideas still circulate or not. (001:13)

Recreational users, particularly those young people in one of the dance scenes, tended to be more impulsive and less prepared for their initial MDMA experiences. The exceptions were professionals and other busy individuals who were often forced to rigidly schedule their MDMA use from the outset (Rosenbaum, Morgan, and Beck, 1989). Older respondents with families were forced to plan extensively for their trips.

THE TRIP

"Coming On" to Ecstasy (The "Rush")

The effects of MDMA usually become apparent twenty to sixty minutes following oral ingestion of an average dose (100-125 milligrams) on an empty stomach. The sudden and intense onset of the high experienced by many users is commonly referred to as the "rush" (also the "wave" or "weird period"). This phase was often described as a consummate euphoria, although some respondents (particularly during initial use) experienced a certain degree of trepidation, tension, stomach tightness, and/or a mild nausea. This discomfort was generally transitory and melted away into a more relaxed state of being. Although novice users occasionally experienced some apprehension during this initial onset, anxiety levels typically decreased with subsequent use, allowing for increased enjoyment.

The frequency and intensity of this initial phase were highly variable, with many respondents describing a much more gradual (and often delayed) ascent on at least some occasions. In addition to obvious factors such as dosage and recent food intake, this slower ascent was also attributed to differences in metabolism and subtle variations in quality resulting from different manufacturing techniques.

The most dramatic accounts of the rush typically came from respondents' first experiences. The intensity of these first effects frequently made an indelible impression which was easily remembered years later. For example, a 22-year-old graduate student recounted his initial experience this way:

> I was just sitting in the car and then all of a sudden, just boom! This terrific speed rush. It was just like whoa! And then I got this big smile on my face and I just started feeling great and I said, "You guys, I feel terrific! I love it! This is great! I'm so happy!" . . . It would start with this really intense speed rush. . . . It would be a little frightening because it would be like, "Oh, too much!" You know, . . . that on-edge feeling like, "Oh, I'm just about ready to explode!" And then three minutes later, you just, "Ahhh, OK, this is wonderful!" (045:64,85)

A 31-year-old man took his first MDMA with friends at a gay bar in Baton Rouge: "It was great 'cause it was our first time and I guess the waves were more intense. . . . Just like a wave, very physical chills over you, ten minutes of that, . . . Really intense. . . . Then it mellowed out. . . . It was classic" (047:15,16,17). An insurance salesman, who was a college student at the time, first thought he wasn't going to experience anything. However, to his surprise: "It hit! My heart opened up and exploded. . . . I had incredible feelings of joy and bliss" (001:20).

The power of this initial phase in shaping subsequent experiences can be seen in one woman's first MDMA use ten years previous to the time of the interview. She recalled literally "coming on" to the drug, experiencing a spontaneous, unaided orgasm during the rush: "The minute I did it, I was 'hooked' on MDM because it was the best experience I ever had. There wasn't any question about whether it was gonna be positive or not. It was positive. It is positive. It always has been" (094:17).

A 36-year-old Dallas man described the typical onset of his MDMA experiences:

> As the drug came on there was a sort of a sensation of warmth in my chest, right here. . . . My eyes seem to kind of open about ten or fifteen percent wider than they would. And I kind of look around. Ears and eyes and nose and smells, all my senses sort of light up. Everything is intensified. It's much the same way Acid

came on. . . . And there's a physical—there's a speedy rush that comes with it. So this all sort of happens at the same time. It's combined with the speedy rush. During that 45 minute period is when everything would go crazy. (068:74–74)

Although almost all experienced users enjoyed the "rush," this phase was generally more appreciated by recreationally oriented respondents, particularly those who liked the effects of other stimulants such as cocaine or methamphetamine. Many of them agreed with a physician's assessment that "in fact the rush on Adam is better than the rush on cocaine" (005:77).

Many respondents noted how certain batches of MDMA provided a more intense rush than others that had a smoother onset. A college student, who enjoyed binging with any stimulant, described the difference he perceived between batches received from the same source:

Quality. There is the kind that's really active that seems to be a lot speedier. The tinglies are much more intense. You have a lot more energy and you still have the euphoria. Then there is some kind of like introspective stuff, which you feel good, but it just doesn't give you the energy, and it's a lot more you thinking about things. You know, you still feel close to other people around you. It just doesn't have the kick to it. (084:52–53)

A contingent of longtime Oregon users fondly recalled the MDMA they obtained in the late 1970s as packing a more powerful and euphoric rush, a perception validated by several distributors. Although recreational users generally enjoyed this type of Ecstasy, therapeutically oriented respondents often preferred MDMA which had a smoother onset. Less enamored with the "rush," some even viewed the euphoria and/or intensity associated with it as a potential distraction to their intentions. Nevertheless, many had positive recollections of its power during their initial experience. A 57-year-old woman first took MDMA in an extremely controlled setting with her therapist in attendance. Having eschewed use of almost all drugs, she took the MDMA with considerable fear regarding loss of control. For her, the rush "hit me like a ton of bricks. . . . I released control for a microsecond and POW! . . . outer space . . . it was marvelous" (012:20).

A psychiatrist also described his first experience as occurring in an extremely controlled clinical environment. Wearing eyeshades and headphones and listening to soft, melodic piano music, he

began to feel "the rush . . . a sequence of waves of energy and pleasure and bliss . . . relaxation and energy. . . . It was scary the way it
came on . . . so profound and so powerful" (005:44,45,46).

The "Plateau Phase"

For those who experienced an initial rush, it leveled off to a
smooth "plateau" phase. It was this stable, long-lasting period
that was generally regarded as the most enjoyable and/or enrich-
ing part of the MDMA experience. For a few users (particularly
novices), the transition to this more comfortable state of being
came as a welcome relief to the anxiety experienced during the
initial rush. The Dallas yuppie who described a much longer 45-
minute rush phase or "weird period" compared the end of the
rush phase to a strong magnet whose intense power "started to
release. And as it released you start to relax a little bit" (068:75).

A young Baton Rouge woman, who had also taken her first
MDMA at a bar, described a dramatic transition: "I was a little
overwhelmed by it. . . . I sat in the chair and gripped the arms. . . .
I felt like I was tripping pretty hard. . . . Then I had this warm,
comfortable, loved feeling. . . . It was a very communal thing. . . .
Everybody felt real open toward each other" (082:9,10,11).

Despite many experiences, a 34-year-old veteran user described
the anticipation that typically accompanied this transition:

> I run through a quick adrenalin rush of, "Oh no, how high am I
> gonna get?" And then that will last for somewhere between
> twenty seconds and a minute and then usually by then I'm on
> the MDM and everything becomes absolutely relaxed and "Oh,
> boy!" "Oh, boy!" It's an "Oh, boy!" drug. "Oh, boy, here I am
> again!" (085:96)

This "plateau" phase generally lasts from two to three hours
before the first signs of "coming down" set in. With few exceptions, respondent accounts of this period were positive, with
descriptions ranging from "waves" of euphoria to more continuous feelings of "ecstasy." There is also a remarkable dearth of
problems reported during these two to three hours.

What do people do on Ecstasy? As detailed below, they may
dance, communicate, look inward, become sensual, or be creative.

Trance-Dancing   Many respondents, particularly those who
were under 30 and single, found various forms of movement to be

extremely pleasurable. This was particularly true of dancing. Accounts of the Acid House and Rave scene in Europe and informal interviews with their American counterparts frequently refer to long-lasting ecstatic states achieved through "trance-dancing." Noting the physical and mental intensity associated with this often all-night exertion, Pearson and colleagues assert that "this vigorous activity may well even interact chemically with the MDMA to produce experiences qualitatively different to those felt when the body is relaxed (and listening to Beethoven)" (Pearson et al., 1991:16).

Of course, trance-dancing (with or without drugs) is hardly a new phenomenon. What is new, however, is the popularization of Ecstasy as the all-purpose "dance drug" in remarkably different contexts. Preceding the popularization of Acid House and Rave gatherings, many of our respondents described the joys of MDMA-fueled dancing in such disparate settings as Dead shows and Dallas nightclubs.

In many ways, MDMA inspired the "dance fever" which took hold in nightclubs in Dallas, Austin, and nearby cities during the mid-1980s. Some nightclub owners installed hand grips and bars along the walls, enabling patrons high on MDMA to hold on when they became too tired but wanted to continue dancing.

More recently, MDMA has emerged as the primary catalyst behind the rapidly expanding Rave scene. Ecstasy's stimulant, disinhibitory, and empathic qualities make it, according to participants, the ideal drug for trance-dancing with thousands of fellow dervishes in modern-day versions of psychedelic gatherings held in the mid-1960s (Heley, 1991; McDonnell, 1992; Pearson et al., 1991; Robins, 1992). In those earlier all-night celebrations of "spirituality and debauch" held in auditoriums such as San Francisco's Avalon Ballroom, Lee and Shlain describe how the enthusiastic throngs

> rediscovered the crushing joy of the dance, pouring it all out in a frenzy that frequently bordered on the religious. When rock music was performed with all its potential fury, a special kind of delirium took hold. Attending such performances amounted to a total assault on the senses: the electric sound washed in visceral waves over the dancers, unleashing intense psychic energies and driving the audience further and further toward public trance. (1985:142–143)

Until recently, Grateful Dead concerts represented one of the last vestiges of these "techno-shamanic" tribal gatherings filled with music and dance and psychedelic substances. Although LSD, psilocybin, and marijuana remain the primary drugs, a 34-year-old respondent is certainly not alone in his assessment of MDMA use at Dead shows:

> I love to dance on it. It's spectacular for dancing. It's absolutely—you get the whole stimulation in the peripheral nervous system, so every nerve ending outside of your spine is just going, just bouncing to the music. And you're getting a perception of the many different mathematical chording patterns. (085:75)

The recent advent of Rave gatherings constitutes a somewhat different re-creation of the "Acid Tests" of yesteryear. Although once again people are striving for a "total assault on the senses," LSD and "acid rock" have been largely replaced by Ecstasy and "Acid House." It is this new drug/music combo which drives the nonstop tribal trance-dancing that often continues through dawn and beyond.

Communication and Introspection   Whether taking MDMA for therapeutic or more recreational reasons, almost all respondents mentioned enhanced closeness and communication with other people or their environment as a major benefit of the MDMA experience. However, respondents differed greatly when asked to describe which levels and kinds of "bonding" were most significant for them. Responses ranged from seeking a "oneness with the universe" to reaching an entirely intrapersonal reconnection with oneself. In most cases, "bonding" implied sharing intimacy and/or good times with a lover or group of friends in a variety of environments.

Almost all recreational users saw MDMA as a "people drug," a social lubricant to be shared with a lover or close friends. As did more therapeutically oriented users, they typically cited reduced inhibitions and enhanced communication and closeness with others as primary interpersonal attributes of MDMA. This 58-year-old professional, who took drugs exclusively to "get high," described his first experience which turned out to be more than that:

> We felt ebullience, talking, euphoria, warmth and friendship with the other couple, love and more tolerance of others. . . .

We were collectively, the four of us, settling on a very positive perspective on the world and friends. We talked about other people, which . . . all of us had some degree of hostility towards, and we mellowed out on that stuff, and we saw the good side of everybody. And it was a very gratifying experience that way, this whole bonding plus the development of a positive perspective on the world, and a very optimistic one. We felt at that time that we had worked through some things and we were going to go on in a much more positive way. Things . . . had been good and they were going to be better because of our feelings that we were experiencing. (013:49,62)

A 41-year-old professional's first experience was at an idyllic retreat. He described walking with eight friends down to a river: "We had a playful and enjoyable time, . . . a warm, loving experience. . . . I felt very warm and gooshy towards people. . . . You feel good about everyone" (010:43).

Although initially approaching MDMA as a recreational substance akin to cocaine or alcohol, many of the Dallas users came to regard its "bonding" actions as therapeutically valuable. As a 37-year-old Dallas real estate company owner described his underlying reason for use:

> It was in a party flavor, but it really was more than that. The reason we enjoyed getting together was not because there was somewhere where we could get lost. It was somewhere where we could get together and we could get down and talk to each other and get to know each other on more than just a superficial basis. (066:57)

Other Dallas respondents talked about an increase in sensitivity and emotional response in addition to increased communication. As one businessman described it:

> We'd be talking, and everybody would be so intense and so at a point of sensitivity and openness that the music, depending on what kind it was, could make you cry. You'd get the knot in your throat, and you'd be so emotionally like strings or very beautiful voices or water or natural sounds, mixed with very pretty, melodic music. You just feel so good! Oh, my! You just start crying. I'd be on the phone crying to my mother. We'd be talking and I'd feel this—I'd feel so close and so happy. You'd call people and just, "Hi, Mom. How are you doing? Just thinking about you." (064:38)

Although most respondents greatly enjoyed the interpersonal closeness experienced under the influence of MDMA, they voiced markedly different preferences regarding with whom and how that intimacy was best expressed. Whereas some respondents took MDMA only in the company of their lover and/or close friends, others were comfortable using it around strangers. A young college student/paralegal who took his new girlfriend to a Grateful Dead concert failed to convince her to try MDMA. Nevertheless, he felt that the drug and the densely populated setting contributed to a thoroughly enjoyable experience. In essence, he "bonded" with the entire group:

> Because I was very much in love with A. at that point. And that it was like a triumphant night and just too damn bad that she wasn't taking it [MDMA] that night also. But I was able to have a great time even so, which I think is one of the nice things about the drug is that it's great among many people. I think it's best among many people. But you don't necessarily have to have everyone doing it. (060:66)

MDMA was described as a therapeutically useful "truth serum" by some respondents. Noting this common conception, one businessman agreed that people are likely to tell the truth while on MDMA. Nevertheless, he argued that they are not necessarily compelled to do so:

> I believe it lowers incredibly your sense of fear and you fall in love with yourself. When you do that, you're more willing to take risks, and one of the risks is telling the truth. In that sense, it's a truth drug. You feel like telling the truth. You feel like being honest. And you know you can say some even very delicate things without hurting people, and therefore you can speak the truth. On the other hand, I would say . . . you can tell lies. You can withhold the truth if you need to. You're not *forced* to tell the truth. There's certain things that you know are just not appropriate for someone else to know, and it is possible not to tell the truth. . . . To even name it a truth drug, I think, does it a disservice. . . . It, again, makes you so loving and so in love with yourself, so open and trusting of other people . . . that you really do want to relate to others. . . . And so when you are feeling the most loving, the most beautiful, you want to be the most truthful as well. (040:32)

Several respondents, on the other hand, described occasions in which their honesty in communicating "delicate things" while high on MDMA had created schisms in particular relationships or friendships. As a consequence, they had reservations about taking the drug with certain people for fear of what might be said or done. The college student whose girlfriend was temporarily scared of MDMA, attributed her fear to having observed the "truth serum" effect with a friend of theirs. After taking his first dose of MDMA this friend "proceeded to tell us everything about his personal life. And he was very, very revealing. And it was stuff that, no way he would have told us under normal circumstances" (060:64).

Not all respondents agreed with MDMA's alleged power as a "truth serum." For example, a 39-year-old insurance salesman, who enjoyed partying with MDMA, was asked whether a guided MDMA session might be useful if he was having problems with his wife:

> It may make you more intimate, more vocal with her . . . not necessarily more intimate, but more vocal. . . . I think you might be spouting lies out there when you are saying certain things. But it does make you more vocal. And maybe with a counselor to advise you and channel that, it may work. And maybe you'd just tell him to fuck off, I don't know. I don't have any trouble with my wife. . . . I don't have any trouble talking either. (003:16)

Some respondents noted another pitfall associated with the enhanced communication and bonding commonly experienced on MDMA. The dangers of "falling in love" under the influence of MDMA (sometimes with a virtual stranger) was a frequent topic of discussion. This "problem" was often treated in a humorous vein, with respondents providing accounts of their own or a close friend's learning experiences. Many of these respondents were in general agreement with what Timothy Leary referred to as the "instant marriage syndrome":

> Lots of people who didn't know each other too well have shared the experience, activated the love-empathy circuits, and rushed off the next day to get married. In some cases, after rose-colored smoke clears, the couple realize that although they did, for a while, share the highest region of love, the practical aspects of their life were not in sync. You might say it's a cosmic summer romance. In fact, it got so bad in Boulder, Colorado that bumper stickers and T-shirts were printed saying, "Don't Get Married for Six Weeks After X-T-C!" (Leary, 1985:76)

Interestingly enough, Leary himself fell prey to this "syndrome," marrying Barbara Leary three days after their first experience. In contrast to the usual fate of such relationships, they have remained married for over ten years (Eisner, 1989). A similar exception was also described by a respondent who was a longtime Oregon user:

> My sister came to visit me, and I just had a strong compulsion for her to meet this friend of mine, and not for any other reason but I wanted her to meet him 'cause I knew she'd like him. . . . And so J. knew this guy had done MDM and had access to MDM, and the first thing she said was, "I want to do MDM with this man." And so they did MDM and she practically pushed me out the door because they were so into each other that they had to have this experience together. And that was the day they met, and they've been in love ever since. J. got a divorce, left her husband, and married this man. . . . She moved to Eugene with him, and it all worked out. (094:42)

She added that they had now been together over nine years and had remained very happy. When queried as to whether they continue to use MDMA, she said:

> Yes, whenever they can. And they still love to think about that night and how they did MDM and fell in love and how I had turned J., this friend of mine, on to MDM in the first place, and I had turned J. on to it. And so they still like to talk about how I got that going there. I introduced them, and the MDM just intensified it for them. (094:43)

Introspection is another "activity" engaged in by some of our respondents. For these individuals, the purpose of taking MDMA was to "go inward." The experience is set up in order to maximize the possibility of focusing on one's inner self. Earphones and blindfolds are often used for the purpose of eliminating outside, distracting stimuli, including other people. As this 38-year-old psychotherapist said:

> We would wear headphones and blindfolds. It was obviously not sensory deprivation, but was sort of sensory distraction. You have something to meditate on rather than having all the various kinds of things that could come to you—hearing other people, or buses going by. The blindfold was for us to be as much removed from visual input as possible. You do this for a total inward experience. It is like meditative visual. I have expe-

rienced myself as an Eagle, which I think is my totem animal but I don't know. When I did Yagé I didn't experience myself as an eagle. I experienced myself as a different self. With ADAM it can vary between, at times as flying, out of body experiences, and at the same time very much in the body experiences.

One woman, a 46-year-old professor, believed that the positive, warm, uninhibiting feelings that characterize MDMA make it possible for an individual to go inward, particularly if the material to be examined is not pleasant. In a personal communication, she said that MDMA enables one to take an inward journey because the usual fears that would prevent such an excursion are transformed into positive feelings. It is for this reason that introspective therapy is possible using MDMA (048, personal communication, October, 1992).

Sex and Sensuality   As with its predecessor, MDA (the "Love Drug"), MDMA has been frequently referred to as an aphrodisiac in the popular press (Nasmyth, 1986; Prangnell, 1988; Street, 1986). *Newsweek* noted that MDMA had become popular on college campuses, "where it is considered an aphrodisiac" (Adler, 1985:96). One respondent in our study became the lover of an MDMA chemist who introduced him to the drug at a gay disco bar when the respondent was 17 years old. In explaining why he agreed to try MDMA:

> R: I knew that it was a drug with sex. This was the drug you took if you wanted to have great sex. And that's all I knew about it. That was the big thing behind it. This is the stuff that you're gonna spend hours in bed and it's gonna be great.
> I: Was that more the straights saying that or everyone?
> R: Everybody was saying that. I heard it through them and I read articles in the papers and stuff about it. On Haight Street there were flyers. . . . (046:24,25)

Regardless of its reputation, most respondents described MDMA as providing a sensual rather than sexual experience. Ecstasy greatly enhanced the pleasure of touching and physical closeness but typically interfered with erections and generally inhibited orgasms for both men and women. These findings are in accord with those of earlier naturalistic studies of MDA users (Weil, 1976; Zinberg, 1976) as well as more recent explorations of MDMA (Buffum and Moser, 1986).

In many ways, respondent descriptions of MDMA's sensual effects resembled Zinberg's observations of MDA users:

> Sexual relationships were possible as the drug waned, but during the height of the high people described a greater interest in a general, diffuse sensualism than in specific sexuality. . . . This sensualism showed itself in a wish to touch others or to feel the sand, grass, water, flowers or the like. Again the desire to touch and pleasure in touching was specifically pan-sexual and often not connected to everyday closeness. (1976:70)

In explaining the increased sensuality associated with MDMA, most respondents also cited this augmented tactile feeling along with lowered inhibitions. A self-described "shy" 21-year-old gay college student noted how he "had like this incredible feeling in my fingers. It was like I just had to touch things. So I just was like holding his hand at times and didn't even feel anything like that was socially unacceptable or anything about that" (098:38). A former distributor described the enhanced tactile response associated with giving or getting a massage. He went on to note that

> a lot of body workers have used MDMA as part of MDMA massage. When it was legal in Texas you could sign up for MDMA massages. It was being used a lot because it releases your muscle tension, opens you up for touch. . . . Yeah, I think it's great for that. The whole tactile sense . . . you slow down, you touch slower and deeper and I think it's terrific on that (007:88).

Although enjoying sex after coming down from MDMA, a 34-year-old male respondent noted that "during peaking, there's definitely times of swoony feelings that you just can't focus long enough. You keep forgetting what you're doing and you'll lose your erection for sure" (085:94). A female therapist offered a similar appraisal:

> MDMA and sex do not go very well together. For most people, MDMA turns off the ability to function as a lover, to put it indelicately. It's called the love drug because it opens up the capacity to feel loving and affectionate and trusting. . . . I think I managed to have a lot of fun in bed with my husband once on MDMA, but we really both had to work awfully hard. . . . The particular organization and particular focusing of the body and the psychic energy necessary to achieve orgasm, it's very difficult. And most men find it almost impossible. . . . So it is a love drug but not a sex drug for most people. (077:58,61)

Some respondents (usually males) experienced occasional conflicts between feelings of intense sexual desire and difficulty in actual performance. One professional described how he would often think about sex, both with his wife alone and with members of the small group of friends with whom he typically took MDMA: "I would become overwhelmed with what I thought were sexual feelings . . . [but] when we did go back and fuck . . . I really had a hard time having a climax. . . . But the desire to immerse myself in a woman was very fucking strong" (013:56).

Despite what most perceived as more sensual qualities, a few respondents felt MDMA provided definite sexual benefits as well. This was particularly true among male respondents in the Dallas nightclub scene. They described frequent situations involving a great deal of sexual activity. As a young businessman reflected: "I'm sure that [MDMA] didn't do anything to help the different sexually transmitted disease problems we've got! Because people were like rabbits. I mean, all of them, as far as any people I was playing with, there were people running around just like bunnies" (064:30).

Many viewed the delayed orgasm on MDMA as an advantage, which, combined with some males' abilities to maintain erections for long durations, contributed to sexual marathons. The same respondent as above described the key to successful orgasm as simply a matter of timing:

> You don't want to get off on the first run on the slopes. You want to go to the top of the hill. So you pass it up and take it all at the top so you can take the big run down. Well, that's all well and good in sex. But if you have some MDMA in you, then you better take it the first shot. . . . The first time you feel it coming, don't suppress it. Let it go. And it's like nothing you ever waited for before in your life. It's ten times. And it's not in pulses. It's not like boom, boom, boom. It's like zooooooom, like for about a minute. You just—it's consistent, like somebody just jetplaned into you like that. It's wild! . . . I thought I was gonna bend the brass headboard. . . . And quite often, I think because I could do that in any situation with sexual partners, when one goes, quite often the other one follows. And my mate would always come right after that. (064:64)

However, another Dallas businessman argued that their obsession with sex occasionally got out of hand, resulting in emotional casualties. He described the case of a young woman who was repeatedly "taken advantage of" during Ecstasy parties:

> There was a girl that was involved in the group, . . . [a] gorgeous twenty-one-year-old girl who had been married and had a small child, . . . divorced, and ready to play, and was tied down, but was desperately trying to break out of the deal. . . . And she got involved in the drug in a dangerous, dangerous way and she was passed around the group, and it was just ugly . . . part of that period of time for her, because she was suicidal . . . and everything was tumultuous in her life. . . . And so she was constantly looking for any affection that she could get. And it was, "Oh, you looked at me kind of interested, come here. You know, let's take Ex and sleep together." It was horrible. It was just terrible. (068:45)

A few respondents commented on how the breakdown of inhibitions while on MDMA opened up new sexual possibilities for them. One male respondent described how some people experienced an increased acceptance of bisexuality: "I think it has effects in both men and women in moving them towards being comfortable with bisexuality, . . . kind of moving you back to the polymorphously perverse Freudian perspective" (007:111). A 24-year-old woman discovered this previously unacknowledged tendency while bathing with a woman friend during an MDMA experience:

> I tried it with my best girlfriend, and we discovered that we were bisexual, which it turned out not to be a mere drug effect, because as time went on, the perception remained the same, for which I'm very grateful, because I feel like it's a part of myself that I was not aware of before, and it's a very nice thing. . . . My girlfriend and I were tripping together. We had taken Acid together a lot and we heard, "Oh, there's this other drug, a psychedelic. Sounds interesting. Let's do it!" So we took a bath together and I gave her a back rub, and all of a sudden I was just struck by the beauty of her body and thinking how lovely it was and wanting to touch her. And I asked her if I could kiss her neck and she said yes. And then it was all over. (014:23,24)

Other respondents described how the reduced inhibitions and other effects of MDMA assisted them in their sexually oriented employment. Interviews of gay male prostitutes conducted by Waldorf and colleagues (1989) revealed that many found MDMA helpful in creating a beneficial atmosphere with their clients. Similarly, a respondent described a topless dancer who found that MDMA was really helpful in her work: "It's a crude emotional situation so you can be more loving, you can accept the more gross behavior and make more tips. . . . That was really, really true in Texas and the Texas bars—topless bars" (007:112).

Despite frequent erection difficulties during the peak of the high, some respondents described prolonged sexual encounters after coming down. As one woman described her experience with MDMA: "It made me really horny. Usually during the highest part of the drug I wouldn't want to make love, but when I came down I would definitely want to, and the reason being is that I was almost overly stimulated, to the point where it would be too much almost to have an orgasm during the rush" (094:34).

In general, however, most respondents felt the sexuality was secondary to the overall sensuality associated with MDMA use. One woman summed up the feelings of many respondents in describing the MDMA experience as

> definitely more sensual than sexual. I love to touch and be held, but I don't really feel as horny or a strong sexual urge. . . . It (sex) was very nice, but it's just not the main thing that comes to mind for me when I do it. I'm more of just wanting to hold someone and touch them. But sex was very nice on it. (095:29)

Creativity   Some respondents occasionally employed MDMA in their creative endeavors, such as music, art, or writing. For the graduate student/therapist who described it as a "flavor enhancer," MDMA provided a positive intensity to any situation or environment in which she chose to use it. In a manner uncharacteristic of other respondents, she described sticking her finger in a plastic bag and ingesting small amounts to augment studying as well as partying:

> I just use really small amounts. I think it's like caffeine or any small stimulant. . . . It's a good study aid. And just enough to stimulate your brain cells a little bit. It does, it keeps you a little more alert and a little more concentrated. I just would use it like speed or something like that. (096:87)

A therapist who employed MDMA with her patients also made personal use of the drug an adjunct for writing:

> I have one day when I can be completely alone and where I have actually twelve hours when I can be by myself and I get into a certain frame of mind which allows me to do a great deal of writing on the book I'm writing without any interference and with-

out any interruption. And it is a pure self-indulgence. I love doing it. I enjoy it thoroughly, and I produce a great deal. . . . Mostly I use it for the free flow of creative writing. . . . It's not that I don't write unless I have MDMA. That's not the case at all. That would be a dependence. But I enjoy the kind of writing I can do easier and more spontaneously. It just flows better with the MDMA. And if I did not have MDMA I would do perfectly well, but it's just enjoyable. . . . It seems to allow me to use what I have as a writer, to engross myself in the content, to allow it to flow more spontaneously than it does otherwise. I tend to censor a great deal of my intellect most of the time, and this cuts through a great deal of that. So that is why it's enjoyable. (077:56)

Comedown and Aftereffects

Approximately three to four hours after initial dosing, the first intimations of "coming down" strike the user. Respondents greatly differed as to their mood during this period. Some users would often counteract the comedown by taking a "booster" (generally much smaller than the initial dose) in attempting to regain "altitude." Other users eschewed this option, typically employing a variety of ways to ease the comedown. These included ingestion of alcohol, tranquilizers, or marijuana, or reliance on nondrug strategies such as a hot bath.

Five to seven hours after ingestion, most users had returned to a fairly normal, albeit fatigued, consciousness. Whereas some generally felt a "mellow glow" during this period with few problems going to sleep, others experienced a more jittery comedown often accompanied by insomnia.

Almost all respondents noted some aftereffects (mostly sluggishness) during the day or two following the experience, and most problems with MDMA are associated with this period. The gamut of emotional response was reflected in respondent descriptions ranging from a nasty hangover to a useful period of integration. As we describe in the next chapter, there were vast differences in the interpretation and perceived severity of these aftereffects and their impact on use patterns.

IS IT REALLY ECSTASY?

Did users actually believe that MDMA provided what they considered to be an ecstatic experience? Is its name appropriate?

Respondents provided a variety of opinions addressing both the semantics and political implications of the label.

Many therapeutically and spiritually oriented respondents expressed severe reservations regarding MDMA's nickname of "Ecstasy," in terms of either the accuracy or the highly charged implications associated with such a name. It was widely felt by early proponents that such a label helped determine its legal fate in the eyes of the government. In addition, many therapists argued that referring to MDMA as "Ecstasy" provided the wrong impression of what they perceived to be its valuable therapeutic properties. For example, some respondents argued that rape or other trauma victims taking MDMA in a therapeutic context were much less likely to experience "ecstasy" in their attempts to confront painful memories via the lessened fear and increased acceptance associated with MDMA.

With this in mind, therapeutically and spiritually oriented respondents frequently offered alternative names (such as "Adam") or descriptors (such as "entactogen," "empathogen") that better conveyed what they believed to be MDMA's most important qualities. One therapist we informally interviewed felt the term "entactogen," coined by pharmacologist David Nichols (1986), best described MDMA's role in the "opening-up" process:

> "Entactogen" is a word meaning "touching within." . . . The idea of a therapy using one of these drugs, which is a totally new class of drugs or psychotherapeutic adjuncts, . . . is using a drug which specifically allows for the opening of certain kinds of communication. Above all, a good entactogen, especially MDMA . . . appears in most cases to eliminate the very deep fear of remembering trauma, of bringing up things which are tremendously painful and very frightening and full of rage and grief. And in some way we have no way of understanding, MDMA makes it possible for a patient to stop being afraid of these things coming back to the conscious mind. They are able to elicit very buried memories of difficult and painful things which need to be unburied.

Reflecting the views of many, one New Ager explained her viewpoint regarding the most appropriate nickname for MDMA: "I prefer to call it 'Adam'. 'Ecstasy' is a beautiful word, but I think Ecstasy is a word more often used by people taking it for thrills. And since I'm not a part of that group, I don't like to use it" (014:27).

Nevertheless, many therapeutically and spiritually oriented respondents did admit to feeling "blissful" or "ecstatic" while under the influence of MDMA. According to one 41-year-old New Ager: "It's definitely of the heart. It is a very warming, heart-oriented drug. I can see why people say that and I can see why they call it Ecstasy. Cause you do, you just feel really good. It's a real positive thing" (028:21). As noted earlier, one of our respondents believed that it was the ecstatic part of MDMA that made the analysis of trauma possible.

Recreational users were often introduced to MDMA as "Ecstasy" and generally believed this to be a fairly accurate description of the high. A 23-year-old paralegal, whose first MDMA experience came at a Dead concert, described the "ecstatic feeling" that enveloped him: "I felt an overwhelming sense of the positive things in life, and an incredible need to touch people. . . . Great love. . . . I was very animated. . . . Embracing everyone" (060:63).

MDMA users in the Dallas nightclub scene were, as a group, perhaps the most recreationally oriented of our study population. They were not purposefully seeking spiritual enlightenment or personal insight. When describing their motivations for using Ecstasy, they used the word "fun" so often that one researcher commented on its frequency to a respondent, who replied:

> Mm hmm. I can see that, yes, 'cause it's young people doing it just to have a good time. No one here was doing it for anything serious. I don't know of anyone who was doing it for anything serious. . . . [They're doing MDMA] because it's fun. Because they escape, they have fun, and they just, you know, it's a fun drug. It's not like cocaine where it's fun for 20 minutes and you have to do more. I mean, you get hours of fun. (067:53)

Some respondents even conjectured that MDMA's pharmacological actions must somehow consistently stimulate the brain's pleasure centers for a few blissful hours. A college student who typically binged with MDMA described his experiences as a sort of mindless ecstasy:

> Everything's neat, especially other people that you know. You feel especially close to them. Your body feels real good. You feel strong. You want to stretch. You like climbing. And what especially my girlfriend and I came up with, you feel like a puppy. But everything's neat. You run around. Your tail's wagging. (084:51)

Whether taking MDMA for primarily therapeutic or recreational reasons, most respondents noted the remarkable ease with which the high itself was usually experienced, particularly when compared with other psychedelic drugs. This came as a surprise to many respondents, who expected a more intense experience comparable to that of LSD or mescaline. Even those individuals reporting minimal use of other drugs experienced little difficulty in handling their first MDMA experience.

This attribute helps to explain MDMA's popularity among individuals and groups who tended to avoid many substances (particularly psychedelics) for fear of being overwhelmed by the experience. Other respondents had used psychedelics in the past ("back in the sixties") but had discontinued use of such drugs until they discovered MDMA.

Unlike with other psychedelics, the diminished anxiety and disinhibition experienced on MDMA enabled many users to "lose control" without fear. This facet of MDMA was particularly appealing to professionals and others who craved the rare opportunity to engage in uninhibited "time-out" behavior. Reflecting the experiences of other young businesspeople in the Dallas nightclub scene, a 36-year-old executive described the needed "therapy" provided by MDMA: "Dancing, and getting crazy, and getting loud, and just being out of control. I never was out of control before this happened. I spent a year making a conscious effort to get out of control" (068:23).

A unique attraction that differentiates MDMA from other stimulants is its capacity to induce a strong paradoxical sense of relaxation and calmness. This effect often leads users to be largely oblivious to many of the stimulant side effects. Among those respondents who had tried both MDMA and cocaine, most expressed a clear preference for the longer, smoother euphoria provided by MDMA. According to a young psychiatrist, one reason that MDMA is superior to cocaine is that it "lasts a lot longer, it doesn't have quite the peak and valley" (005:77).

A perception shared by many recreationally oriented respondents was that MDMA's qualities made almost any environment conducive to good times. Given the virtual absence of "bad trips" on MDMA, the role of set and setting was considerably less crucial than with drugs such as LSD. A 29-year-old respondent illustrated the ability of most users to remain based in reality while still enjoying the MDMA euphoria. He recalled being at a residence where he and another friend (both former fraternity members) took MDMA while two other friends were present but not privy to their "altered state":

> It's hard when you're on LSD to talk to somebody who's not. With MDM, it's not necessarily hard to talk to the people, but they can't share the experience. And we did talk to them. What we'd do is sit with them and listen to music for a little while and act normal, and I guess we acted normal because they didn't figure it out. But then we'd go into the kitchen and hug . . . and talk. . . . I remember saying, "I feel like Superman, but I have the intelligence to know that I'm not." I felt that I could leap tall buildings, yet I realized that I could not. I could make proper decisions. (009:39)

The ease and smoothness of the experience led many respondents to describe the MDMA high as resembling an enjoyable intensification of everyday reality. Preferring to use frequent small doses, a 30-year-old graduate student/therapist referred to MDMA as the "MSG of the drug world"

> because it's a flavor enhancer. It makes things a little better. It's subtle. . . . You don't know it's in there. It's just adding a little extra sparkle to something that's going on, or maybe it's enhancing your feelings. It's enhancing your perceptions, as opposed to LSD, which is really bombarding your sensory system. . . . It enhances your emotional state. I think it enhances your emotional well-being. . . . It's just a real flavor enhancer for life, the spice of life. (096:83)

Therapeutically and spiritually oriented respondents also praised the gentleness of the MDMA high. As a 30-year-old Silicon Valley man described it:

> Well, MDMA is very smooth, especially if it's very pure. It's an incredibly smooth drug. There's no granularity. There's no— you're completely balanced when you're on MDMA, especially if it's MDMA by itself. . . . But my overall feeling is it's incredibly smooth. It feels like there's a wind blowing through you. There's a breeze of the universal stuff flowing through you. You feel just cleansed. (023:20)

The vast majority of our respondents, whatever their particular activity on MDMA, described the experience as ecstatic. Despite the array of settings and individual "sets," users expressed a decided appreciation for the feelings brought on by MDMA. These emotions in turn produced an interaction with other human beings, animals, and nature that was not to be found in people's everyday lives. The pursuit of ecstasy, then, was the search for a feeling of well-being, that everything was going to be all right, that one was forgiven and could forgive others.

It should be noted that most of our respondents could be defined as doing well in this society. They were neither down and out nor despondent. They had life options. The fact that they expressed such appreciation for this chemical is indicative of the kinds of stresses, worries, and obstacles to gratification we *all* endure in this culture. The feeling of ecstasy found in MDMA did indeed fill a void felt by these individuals—a void felt in general in modern American life.

LONG-TERM BENEFITS OF ECSTASY

Did the ecstasy found on MDMA endure? Was it just a good trip, or were there lasting benefits? The question of whether or not the MDMA experience is capable of providing any long-term significant therapeutic or spiritual benefits is important. Are the alleged therapeutic effects (e.g., enhanced insight, reduced fear, empathy) of MDMA illusory, short-lived, or potentially permanent? In the following paragraphs, we look at integration into everyday life, comparisons with other psychedelics, and therapeutic value.

Integration into Everyday Life

Therapeutically and spiritually oriented respondents believed that insights and other positive benefits gained from MDMA could be integrated into everyday life. In contrast, many recreationally oriented users viewed the benefits or enjoyment of MDMA as occurring almost entirely within the experience itself. Some respondents minimized the significance of any insights provided by the MDMA experience. For them, the fact that it was such a "fun" drug was reason enough for using MDMA. As a 39-year-old businessman put it: "I don't know if any new insights opened up. . . . We're all pretty sophisticated and as intimate as we're going to be with each other. It was Fun! It is a truly fun drug . . . because you feel so good and you're able to function, and you're glowing. And that's a fun thing to do" (003:16). Although acknowledging that "searching for enlightenment" is a "wonderful pursuit," a 38-year-old professional also insisted that MDMA (or other drugs) was not the answer: "It's for fun. It's not for anything else. . . . I get confused, I think, more than anything when people talk about it being, you know, integral to their life or having changed their life or when they get kind of even religious about it, sacramental about it" (019:91). A 41-year-old woman offered a similarly skeptical perspective regarding MDMA's therapeutic value: "being happy and laughing is real good therapy, but I don't know how objective it is" (028:23).

A similar point of view was offered by a 30-year-old musician and computer technician who had taken MDMA approximately five hundred times over an eleven year period. He was disappointed at his inability to incorporate the beneficial qualities he felt on MDMA into his everyday life: "I guess I tend to be skeptical of whether something like that can be permanent. In the early going it seemed like it was something to learn from, but I don't know" (092:56). Although acknowledging the potential value of MDMA-induced insights, other respondents expressed difficulties in applying them to their everyday lives. A young woman expressed her confusion regarding MDMA's real value: "I wish I knew how to use it for more benefit, for a positive thing, and not that it's just sort of like fun, party, great feelings and then you have to wake up Monday morning and go to work. . . . It's not the normal way to live, the way you feel on that. . . . I don't think it's reality" (097:59).

Despite similar reservations, many respondents believed that they had experienced long-lasting benefits from what had begun as recreational MDMA use. For many first-time users trying Ecstasy without any therapeutic intentions, the realization of MDMA's value came as a pleasant surprise. This "fortuitous therapy" contingent was exemplified by a 37-year-old realtor who was part of the Dallas nightclub scene and was simply looking to dance and party. In relating his first experience he alluded to "nirvana," and described the interpersonal benefits of MDMA: "It's like an encounter session. You get past the person's defenses . . . and to the essence of the person . . . and you remain sensitive" (066:54).

Although a recreational user, this 58-year-old professional gleaned long-term benefits from his experience:

We felt very good about the whole experience, the trip, the Ecstasy trip and our two days. It was just she and I, reviewing our life. That's another thing that I should mention. We did a lot of assaying what we had done and where we are. And felt very good about what we'd done and where we are, our kids. Very happy about our kids, very happy about where we were in life. We looked forward to great things because of what we had established, and so on. That lingered on.

I think that this overwhelming feeling of love and tolerance towards the other person eradicates a lot of the little irritations and hostilities that people have toward each other which are getting in the way of them working things out. I think, in my perception what really corrodes a relationship is not deep, profound things, but it's the buildup of little petty irritations between the two. I think Ecstasy has a way of melting those, and then after you remove those you can find some commonalities and some good aspects of a relationship and dwell on those and recreate bonds. (013:42)

The most frequently reported spiritual effect was a profound feeling of connectedness with all of nature and humankind. As this 40-year-old physician noted:

The first time was Sea Ranch. And then I did it in Jamaica. And Jamaica was kind of primordial, what I call a primordial experience of going into myself and experiencing myself on a cellular level and relating to organisms and beings and the seashore animals as sophisticated beings and having some kind of extrasensory communication and perception. Not really, it was more like a projection and appreciation of feeling of unity with them or something like that. That stayed with me. (091:41)

Several respondents described how their first experiences with MDMA had resulted in profound realizations and life changes. A 32-year-old woman who had been seeing psychiatrists for depression since she was 17 told us that her first experience with MDMA had "changed my life. . . . I'm able to be confident about myself. . . . I am valid, I have worth. . . . I never really believed that. . . . I realize that I'm pretty interesting, and talented. . . . I'm more confident in a great way in my everyday life" (082:18,19).

A 39-year-old mother of three who had almost no previous drug experience said she had no preconceptions about MDMA when she first took it on a secluded beach. She described both spiritual and therapeutic qualities in experiencing an incredible "bliss" while at the same time realizing she must end her marriage: "I experienced my essence. . . . I had only been experiencing a small part of me. I felt this tremendous love for myself. . . . I felt so happy, blissed-out, beautiful, and free, free, free. . . . I went for a walk and figured out my whole life. . . . I decided to get a divorce" (054:25-26).

In a similar manner, a 40-year-old woman was very ignorant and negative about drugs in general before trying MDMA. As a result of her experience, she went from being a traditional housewife to a self-professed (divorced) "New Ager":

> I was conscious of my body. . . . My heart got to swell out. . . . I moved into a space of consciousness where I experienced everything as one experience. . . . You never see things the same again. . . . A classic cosmic experience. . . . I felt warmth and flowing, . . . a release of those blocks in me. . . . I realized I was finished with my husband. . . . I love him . . . but I'm done. (039:20-21,47)

Both respondents reported that they were able to leave their spouses with a minimum of trauma in what the research team began to refer to as a "no fault break-up." This term described a tendency on the part of one or both spouses to accept the ending of a relationship with compassion instead of blame and acrimony.

Introduced to MDMA in a recreational context, a Dallas businessman attributed profound therapeutic changes that he ascribed to his MDMA:

> It came about at a time in my life where I. . . . really, really needed to look at myself closer. That my marriage had fallen apart and I had created this absolutely false life around myself. . . . Nothing was real. And it caused me to look close— real close. Closer than I'd ever looked in my life at myself. And it started a process going that is real healthy. And I say "is," because it's ongoing. (068:82)

Several recreational users believed that the long-term benefits they derived from MDMA use were primarily social ones. One respondent described her experiences as

> a lot of energy. A lot of dancing. A lot of all night parties and feeling real close with people, and I guess what happened was I got to the point where I could talk to people more easily and that kind of carried over to when I wasn't high. And it gave me

this sense of, I don't know, social ease that also carried over into when I wasn't high. (082:14)

Nearly all our respondents cited MDMA's effects of reducing fear, increasing self-acceptance, and/or enhancing communication as valuable therapeutic properties. Even hard-core recreational users generally thought that MDMA could be therapeutically useful for at least certain individuals or problems.

Comparisons with Other Psychedelics

Some respondents compared MDMA with other psychedelics vis-à-vis integration into everyday life. The vast majority who had used psychedelic drugs saw MDMA as possessing many advantages over more unpredictable substances such as LSD.

They cited the minimal distortion of sensory perception and comparatively fewer unpleasant emotional reactions with Ecstasy. The MDMA experience was frequently described as both personal and familiar, differing only in degree of intensity from that of everyday experience. This sharply contrasts with the effects of psychedelics such as LSD, where the experience is often perceived as radically unfamiliar and transpersonal. For these reasons, they argued that the relative ease associated with the MDMA experience would enable it to be safely used by most people without fear of psychological trauma.

For example, a 34-year-old Deadhead believed MDMA to be therapeutically superior to LSD because

> it's not cartoony on M. It ends up being cartoony and slithery on LSD, whereas you can get more focused and talk about things for longer periods of time and think about things for longer periods of time on MDM than on LSD. . . . You can clear things out and I imagine you can reprogram good things back in your head and have it stick. I have real good feelings about like the next day and the afterglow and like three days later still feeling good about myself. (085:92-93)

A recreationally oriented respondent noted this effect in describing the unexpected therapeutic benefits of MDMA:

> It wasn't the introspection of Acid. . . . You weren't so disturbed about it. . . . The overwhelming thing was you saw your life, but you were so accepting of it, you were so satisfied with it. You were rather smug with it. . . . You're really happy with the way things are going. You do make some plans for doing things

slightly differently in your relationships, particularly of not being down on certain people and being a little more tolerant. We did a lot of that. (013:54–55)

Therapeutic and Spiritual Value

Therapeutically or spiritually oriented respondents joined their more recreational counterparts in praising the ease and safety of the MDMA experience, but frequently used very different terms and emphasis in describing it. Whatever their reasons for taking MDMA, most respondents experienced a dramatic drop in defense mechanisms or fear responses as well as an increased empathy for others. Combined with MDMA's stimulant actions, this often led to an increase in intimate communication and potentially valuable insights. One counselor described how patients were able to freely communicate on MDMA without losing control or revealing things against their wishes,

and yet they're able to control themselves in the session. There is no threat of loss of control, which is the most frightening thing to anyone who is taking the drug. The thing that people project most readily onto any new drug that they haven't taken, especially something called psychoactive, is that they'll find themselves saying something they didn't want to say or they'll find themselves losing control of themselves, or in other words, losing their power, making fools of themselves. It's basically loss of power, is what they're afraid of. MDMA does not do this. It removes the fear barriers to remembering and to insight, but for some reason it does not remove caution. Just ordinary common sense, caution, remains completely intact and the person is not divorced from their ordinary judgment. In fact, the judgment seems to be to some extent clarified and sharpened. (077:8)

She went on to talk about what this means regarding the establishment of a trusting relationship between therapist and patient:

To trust is many different things, and it's almost like a kind of energy field, to use a very scientific phrase, that gets going between the patient and the therapist, a feeling on the part of the patient that they indeed can place themselves in the hands of this person that is trying to help them, and that their power is not going to be taken, their dignity is not going to be destroyed, and that they are basically safe. And again in a way that we do not understand, MDMA facilitates this to an extraordinary degree. (077:11)

Although spiritually oriented respondents were generally impressed with their MDMA experiences, they differed as to what they had actually experienced, how it had influenced their lives, and whether or not the insights gained during the experience had permanently enhanced their spiritual lives. A 24-year-old Bhakti yoga practitioner explained how MDMA helped guide her on a spiritual path:

> Bhakti is the yoga of devotion, and I'm trying to see every expe-rience in life as leading us closer to God and bringing out a more loving, harmonious way of being with other people and generally just having a devotional attitude. . . . MDMA's been very useful from a Bhakti yoga perspective, because it's very heart-opening and that's what you try to do in Bhakti yoga. So I think that it could have potential for people who want to learn to do that who don't already know how, especially. (014: 6,72)

Another respondent, who had studied Eastern religions while retaining some of his earlier Christian beliefs, offered similar remarks on MDMA's effect on his spirituality: "It certainly makes me feel a confirmation that there is sort of an equity in life, certain equity between the souls of people and equity in the balance of the life of man and the life of other forms on earth . . . certainly that man is a part of the web of life on earth" (025: 60).

Referring to MDMA as "penicillin for the psyche," another therapist went on to describe what such possibilities could mean to someone who was severely depressed:

> They can see something that would make no sense to them under any other circumstances, which is that it is up to them to choose to step out of there and that there is another place, a place with color in it and a place with life in it, that they can—they do—have the choice of life, if you want, over the death place. And just the ability to see that it is up to them to choose to step out, to struggle out, that there is another thing to strug-gle out for or to, is the beginning for recovery. And I've seen it happen over and over again. And in this way, I would call MDMA literally a lifesaver. (077:28)

In addition to being a "lifesaver," several respondents strongly believed in MDMA's value in dealing with terminal illness and a few knew of positive examples of such use. One respondent, a counselor and writer who uses hypnotic trance, provided a vivid account of her husband's decision to try MDMA near the end of his bout with cancer. She described the experience as overwhelmingly positive and strongly believes in its value in terminal illness:

> This drug can allow people to die well. They die well in the emotional arms of their families. They get reconciliation, they talk about things they normally would never talk about. . . . It's so benign. It doesn't toss you out and give you gibbering fits and all that stuff. It's not particularly addictive, and even a one-shot deal would be marvelous for these people to go home after Uncle Joe dies and say, "Gee, I at last told him I loved him" and things like that. I think it's so sad that we don't have this in every hospital, not for just cancer patients, though I think it allows people to rise above their pain, too. . . . My husband died at home in his bed. . . . But because the MDMA had opened his psychic door, I was able to put him in this deep, trance-like state so he was in great joy without the body. (012:77)

Contemplating her own death, she described her MDMA experience:

> Well, I can say two things about the drug that I think are very, very important. One is, the door opens to your psychic self, so you see what you could be. It doesn't force you. It doesn't do anything but allow you to see what you really could be and what your life could be and what your gift to the universe could be if you would be willing to work like hell. And the second thing is, for me at least, it is a taste of death. I was always afraid of death and now I'm not afraid of death. Because I tasted what death is—no body. I was all mind, in communication with every mind that ever lived. And that was an *extraordinary* experience and I'll never forget it. This was my number one gift of all my life. I'll never have anything as wonderful as this. . . . It told me what my deepest subconscious feelings were about life. . . . That's pretty profound! So for me it was the most profound experience of my life, absolutely. (012:22,44)

One therapist noted that a long-term benefit of MDMA has little to do with the drug's specific effects. Instead, Ecstasy simply brings out those aspects of one's personality that are already there. Referring to an experience she defined as awareness of "the core self" or "God space," she stated that each person has their own way of explaining what it is. But once experienced, it is a permanent part of their consciousness and their view of themselves. And this is something MDMA can open up. It has nothing to do with the drug. It is intrinsic in the human psyche, of that there is no question. But MDMA seems to be able to open that up, especially in an extremely depressed and stressed person. Now, that is one of its greatest values. (077:30)

Psychotherapists, of course, were particularly interested in long-term benefits of MDMA therapy. Some also believed that they could garner insights that could permanently improve on their ability to help their patients. The above psychotherapist said:

It's tremendously important for any good therapist to know his own trauma, his own dark side, his own fears. Otherwise, there will be entire areas in some of his patients that he can't get near because they are too close to his own hidden areas. And MDMA is a tremendous training material in that way. Whether they use MDMA with their own patients or not is something that is up to them when they've gone through the process. And I've seen some superb work done by good therapists who just became so much better from their use of MDMA. (077:23)

Those Ecstasy users who were spiritually oriented often had more expansive visions about MDMA's possibilities. Many saw it as a priceless tool in assisting spiritual evolution and New Age consciousness. A 72-year-old longtime New Age user echoed the views expressed by many respondents in arguing that MDMA is the ideal medicine for an ailing society:

It is empathizing. It is so reassuring and rewarding—allowing a renewed access to feeling which has been pretty much eroded out of our culture. Too much thinking, not enough access to feeling. And the feelings are so warm and so trusting that I think it's a precious gift and we're not learning how to use it. (078:64)

Attempting to sum up MDMA's long-term therapeutic potential, one veteran user explained how he saw it not as a "miracle drug," but rather as something beneficial for those responsible enough to utilize it in proper ways:

I think that at least MDM gives people a chance to see something that they might not otherwise have the opportunity to see. And I don't take it as a panacea for everything because Jeez, you can't be on the drug all the time, and unless people are going to be responsible for incorporating what it is that they've learned from that experience into their lives, then it would be a wasted opportunity. And that's like anything else, though. (001:71–72)

To conclude, it would seem that the benefits of MDMA must be subdivided. In our attempt to answer the question, "Is it really Ecstasy?" we noted that, referring to the actual "high" experienced during the "plateau" phase of the trip, the response was overwhelmingly affirmative. Our respondents felt that the MDMA experience itself, during the time they were feeling the effects of the drug, was extremely positive. Yes, this was ecstasy.

The question of the permanence of the feelings and insights garnered while on MDMA is another matter. Our respondents retained, for a short time, several aspects of the MDMA experience: interpersonal connections they made during the trip, feelings of self-esteem, and insights gleaned. Moreover, MDMA had the effect of adjusting individuals to their situation while allowing them to define this situation in a positive way. As with the women who realized that divorce was in order, individuals had the ability to see negative situations and relationships in their lives in light of positive insights into resolutions for these problems.

The positive feelings experienced by many of our respondents while on Ecstasy—those of tolerance, forgiveness, validation— filled a void, even in the short space of a minivacation. These were feelings, unanimously described as positive, that individuals did not experience in their everyday lives. But in order to experience *long-term* benefits, it was necessary for people to work at it. It is here that the importance of social worlds and the perspective provided by these worlds become evident. In order for individuals to carry MDMA-induced insights with them, they had to pay attention to these insights, as well as the lessons learned. This is part of the definition of the usefulness of psychedelic experiences—from the therapeutic perspective. As our therapeutically oriented respondents reported, although feelings experienced on MDMA were very real, unless they purposefully set out to *make* them permanent (however that might be accomplished), they would have to wait until the next trip to pursue ecstasy. Whereas the recreational user, by definition, might expect few long-term benefits, this would not be acceptable to individuals immersed in the world of therapy who take Ecstasy for instrumental reasons.

In sum, regarding the bottom line—whether Ecstasy has long-term benefits—it is membership in social worlds that is crucial. Respondents who used MDMA for spiritual or therapeutic reasons tended to retain benefits. Recreational users who were more interested in getting high got high and had fewer lasting benefits.

MDMA use was not static, however, regardless of benefits. In the next chapter, we examine reduction in the pursuit of ecstasy.

CHAPTER 5

Limits to Use:
Why People Moderate or Quit Ecstasy

In the previous chapter, we addressed respondent perceptions of MDMA's positive qualities. If respondents used superlatives such as "ecstasy" to describe the MDMA experience, why didn't they take it all the time, and forever? Here we examine problems associated with the experience as well as the diminished appreciation that accompanied continued use. We discuss the various factors responsible for tempering but rarely eliminating MDMA use.

At the time of interview, the vast majority (90 percent) of our respondents continued to value MDMA and looked forward to further use. Nevertheless, respondents generally described marked declines in their MDMA use over time.[1] Given adequate availability, *most* respondents typically described their greatest frequency of MDMA use as following initial experimentation. This was often remembered as a time of great enthusiasm and anticipation for the next available opportunity to use. Many initially used MDMA more than once a month, with some ingesting it once or twice a week. However, these levels of use had generally tapered off within a short period of time (two to twelve months).[2]

We begin by assessing the impact of various *external* factors (such as availability and criminalization) on respondent attitudes and use. We then focus on concerns about toxicity. Finally, we look at factors *intrinsic* to the MDMA experience itself, such as the perception of "diminishing returns" in an effort to explain changing use patterns.

EXTERNAL FACTORS INFLUENCING MDMA USE

The criminalization of Ecstasy was a major turning point for users. As it became more difficult to procure, price and purity were affected. Also, MDMA's illegal status and increasingly negative publicity affected respondent attitudes and behaviors.

The Impact of Criminalization

Problems with Availability   The scheduling of MDMA exacerbated a situation in which demand exceeded supply in most areas of the country. Many respondents recalled considerable fluctuations in availability even before MDMA was criminalized. They often experienced "dry" periods when their only source would run out of MDMA.

Of all the user groups, the therapeutic contingent was perhaps most affected by MDMA's scheduling. Many therapists reported that they had only one source for the drug and were not able to find another supplier. For those who still had access, the risks inherent in supplying an illegal substance to patients, especially to those not well known by the therapist, were weighed against MDMA's perceived value. Making this decision created an ethical conflict for those who believed that MDMA was a powerful tool for healing. As one therapist described the dilemma: "Therapists are not the kind of people who appreciate being made into criminals . . . but some were determined that no matter what, they would not stop using this with patients who could benefit from it" (077:25–26).

Many users who had first tried MDMA in a therapeutic context now found the drug difficult if not impossible to obtain. A 57-year-old woman who had witnessed her terminally ill husband's psychological transformation on MDMA tried in vain to obtain some for her daughter-in-law: "I couldn't *find* it; I couldn't *get* it. I was desperate! . . . I would have gone to prison . . . to get a source for therapeutic use of an illegal drug" (012:47, 71). She even tried flying across the country to Dallas, where she had read that it was being sold in nightclubs: "I'll tell you how desperate I was, . . . I actually canvassed bars in Dallas, Texas and found it" (012:47).[3]

Price and Purity After Criminalization   Even before criminalization, the cost of MDMA varied dramatically, often depending on the number of distributors between chemist and consumer. An initial drop in price noted throughout the country just prior to criminalization was followed by a significant rise. For those groups most affected by cost considerations (college students, Deadheads), prices doubling from $10 to $20 or more per dose undoubtedly contributed to declines in use.

Street drug analysis conducted by PharmChem Laboratories before 1985 revealed high levels of purity for most samples (Renfroe, 1986). Unfortunately, PharmChem's abandonment of street drug analysis in the mid-1980s made it difficult to ascertain what effect, if any, MDMA's criminalization had on quality. Nevertheless, confiscated samples of alleged MDMA tested by the DEA found that MDMA on the street had remained high in purity up until the end of the 1980s (Sager, 1989).

These findings were reflected in respondent perceptions of consistently high levels of quality before and after MDMA's criminalization. As discussed earlier, respondents often favored certain "batches" or forms of MDMA over others. However, relatively few felt that they had ever ingested anything toxic. Complaints typically referred to experiences that were too speedy or ones that didn't happen at all.

Given higher prices and less competition among dealers, some respondents worried about the increased possibility of adulteration and/or substitution. However, few respondents felt that their MDMA (unlike cocaine) had ever been cut. One exception, a former fraternity member, did "remember actually this one fellow cutting it and us taking it and us realizing that we were not getting . . . the same intensity of effects" (009:42).

Respondents were even more concerned about the possibility of "bad batches" (cut with other substances, weak, a totally different drug) hitting the street as amateur chemists entered a lucrative market vacated by more experienced manufacturers. Problems related to "bathtub chemistry" continue to be a major concern, as they were with the criminalization of other substances. Our informal interviews with San Francisco and Los Angeles Ravers suggest that similar quality control problems may be accompanying this rapidly expanding scene. As in Europe, there appear to be ample supplies of alleged Ecstasy tablets and capsules available to Ravers in both of these West Coast cities. At a average price of $25 per dose, substitution of cheaper stimulants or other substances is a strong temptation for entrepreneurs catering to the scene. Total rip-offs are also not surprising given the anonymity in buying from strangers in such crowded environments (*DrugLink*, 1992).[4]

Effect of Criminalization on Attitudes and Use   The criminalization of MDMA had little effect on respondent attitudes toward the drug. The few exceptions were women who were part of the Dallas nightclub scene. These respondents represented a minority opinion among this population in that they typically came from conservative backgrounds and had little previous drug experience. One Dallas woman said:

> I respect the legal system. And I feel like if something's illegal . . .
> there must be some reason for it. . . . When it became illegal I felt
> guilty doing it. . . . It had not changed, but I thought they must
> have found out it can hurt you. I still had as much fun on it but it
> made me worried that, am I hurting myself now? (069:43)

This perception was not shared by the vast majority of other respondents, even those who had also come from nondeviant lifestyles with little or no previous exposure to illicit drugs. After a profound initial experience, a 57-year-old woman from the Midwest was shocked to find MDMA placed in Schedule I, ready to become illegal. As a consequence, she purposely arranged to have her second experience on July 1, 1985, the day MDMA became illegal: "It was the most wonderful defiance I've ever done. Here I am, so law-abiding, so everything, and we did this because we knew better than the government. We knew this was the most fantastic tool that was ever discovered" (012:23).

Most respondents believed that illegality had little effect in deterring people from using drugs. A few even expressed the popular opinion that criminalization merely enticed some individuals (particularly younger folks) to sample "forbidden fruit." One college student asserted: "Making them illegal does not make them unavailable. Making them illegal, in fact, increases the attraction of them for certain groups of people, myself included. . . . I never would have started smoking pot if it wasn't a sneaky thing to do" (045:96). Although very few respondents quit as a result of its newly illicit status, many became much more cautious in obtaining MDMA for others or introducing new people to the drug. This was particularly true for therapists in our sample, most of whom had reluctantly decreased or discontinued using MDMA as a therapeutic adjunct.

MDMA Toxicity: Awareness and Concerns

Drug research findings and accompanying media coverage are influential factors affecting use, particularly those findings aggressively promoted by the government. Most concerns about MDMA's potential dangers have been fueled by neurotoxicity studies conducted with various animal species. At the time of our study a number of researchers found large doses of MDMA to be associated with degeneration of nerve terminals that produced the chemical messenger serotonin in certain areas of the brain (Ricaurte et al., 1988; Schmidt, 1987; McKenna and Peroutka, 1990). The implications of these findings for human MDMA users remain unknown (see discussion in Chapter 7).

Most of our respondents were at least somewhat aware of these studies. Some expressed considerable concern about potential long-term toxicity that they heard might be associated with continued MDMA use. Referring to fears about toxic potential, one young paralegal and student described why he and others had sharply cut down on their use of MDMA:

> But of late, it seems like the word on the street is to steer clear of MDMA until more is known about it. . . . Among the people I've known there's kind of like a plateau of usage. I don't know how much that has to do with availability, but I know a bunch of people that sort of, they get this sense that comes over them that I've taken enough of this for awhile and I'd better chill out. I think that's a pretty typical reaction. (060:120–121)

In contrast, other respondents expressed little concern. Some had become so skeptical of any information provided by government or media that they tended to disregard all such reports outright. A college freshman who had first tried MDMA in high school described his reaction to media accounts following its criminalization: "Then it became illegal and all these reports started coming out. But I really never listened to them . . . because, I know they just come out with the most ridiculous reports ever just as with any other drug" (056:30).

Even assuming the worst, some respondents felt that the perceived benefits still outweighed the potential risks: "Even if it turned out—let's say twenty years down the line—that everybody who took MDMA had some kind of damage from it, I would still feel that the benefits I received from it would justify that, because it's given me—or it's helped me to have a richer life than I would have had otherwise" (014:81).

One counselor argued that in attempting to assess the risk-benefit ratio for MDMA, researchers are in an untenable position because traditional animal experimentation does not work for psychedelic drugs: "The fact is that the benefit cannot be established because it is seeable only in human studies. . . . You cannot track empathy or insight or trust in a mouse or a rabbit or a monkey. You have to work with people" (077:24).

Among our respondents there were a number of physicians and other knowledgeable professionals who had carefully reviewed the available research regarding MDMA's putative toxicity. Levels of concern varied, with little consensus about overall significance. A couple of knowledgeable respondents pointed out that the same kind of alleged neurotoxicity in animals is also seen with fenfluramine, a loosely controlled drug prescribed for obesity. They observed that there was no increased regulation or concern over fenfluramine, in sharp contrast to the government's response to MDMA.

One respondent was a psychiatrist who had worked with brain-damaged individuals for many years. He doubted whether the findings of these repeated high-dose experiments involving animals were applicable to human users. He noted that much of his skepticism resulted from having known many "highly creative and intelligent people who have used MDMA for at least a decade" with "absolutely no signs of any mental deterioration in them" (079:40).

Others were somewhat more cautious in interpreting the research. A psychiatrist and neurochemist stated that although he thought the serotonin studies were still inconclusive, he was concerned about possible neurotoxicity—particularly with heavy use. As a consequence, he advised others to refrain from "binging" or "too frequent use" (005:86).

The research did have a powerful effect on one respondent, who became convinced of MDMA's serotonergic toxicity. This individual was a 35-year-old male who greatly enjoyed his first nine experiences. He approached the drug in a recreational manner, describing the aftereffects following these experiences as similar to having an off-day. In describing what was to be his tenth and final experience, he said: "Well, I didn't feel depressed before I took the drug the last time, and I didn't feel that I had a negative experience on the drug. I feel that just—I felt very spacy and unconnected afterwards, and it just took me a long time to get better. Nine months" (081:25).

This respondent's burnout following this experience felt to him "like I fried a circuit or something" (081:25). Familiar with the animal neurotoxicity research, he became convinced "that somehow I screwed up my serotonin neurons" (081:26). As a consequence, he attributed the chronic depression which followed his tenth experience to MDMA's neurotoxicity. With this one exception, awareness of MDMA's alleged neurotoxicity did not stop use among respondents, although it convinced some to be more prudent.[5]

Vicious Rumors: "Designer Drug" Confusion and Spinal Fluid Drainage

In addition to valid concerns regarding potential neurotoxicity or negative aftereffects, we have also seen the emergence of various myths spawned by erroneous media reports and hard-to-trace rumors of MDMA's toxic potential. At the time of our study there were two major misconceptions circulating about MDMA's toxicity. The first can be attributed to frequent references to MDMA as a "designer drug." This has occasionally resulted in media accounts confusing MDMA with more appropriately labeled designer drugs such as synthetic opiate analogues. The use of these substances has resulted in significant problems: MPTP with Parkinson's disease and the potent fentanyl analogues with a number of fatal overdoses (Beck and Morgan, 1986).

Although this problem was mentioned only a couple of times by respondents, in our informal interviews and ethnographic fieldwork we found various sorts of "designer drug confusion" among less knowledgeable user groups. These ranged from the surprisingly common belief that MDMA caused Alzheimer's (rather than Parkinson's) disease to one person's insistence that she had read that MDMA "fuses the corpus callosum."

The most common and surprising misconception among respondents is that MDMA somehow "drains the spinal fluid" or "fuses the spinal cord." Until recently, this persistent myth was largely found among college students. Although it originated on the West Coast, colleagues on the East Coast have reported the spread of this belief to college populations there as well. A good example of the pervasiveness of this myth was provided by a University of California Berkeley freshman. When asked why he thought MDMA use had decreased, he provided the two answers most commonly heard from this population: "Well, it's just not that available. And there are a lot of scary (stories), like it's bad, like it drains your back, like your spinal cord will be totally drained. Which I think is true, but you have to be quite a user" (056:80).

The student added that he had heard rumors that MDMA "drains you so you get like a zombie, no feeling" (056:80). Another Berkeley student commented:

> I've heard that it causes meningitis, spinal meningitis. I've heard that it drains your spinal fluid. . . . And I don't know. I've not heard of anyone. I don't know. For all we know some authorities are spreading these rumors about how bad all of these drugs are. And I don't know. . . . I've never read anything that said anything about that. (062:69)

What is perhaps most intriguing and unique about this rumor is that it cannot be traced to any media source. Whereas most drug myths originate from media or government misinformation, this one has apparently spread by word of mouth through the common social world shared by college students and their friends.[6]

INTRINSIC FACTORS INFLUENCING DECLINES IN USE

There were two factors which often interacted to lessen enthusiasm and use among our respondents: (1) decreased enjoyment and benefits and (2) increasingly negative short-term aftereffects. This discussion includes the painful learning process described by some respondents in testing the limits of MDMA use. However, their desire to continue at least occasional use produced various strategies for countering these factors.

Declining Appreciation of the MDMA Experience

Many respondents felt that the MDMA high closely resembled their desired state of mind. Depending on motivation, they stated that the feelings of euphoria, sensuousness, empathy, and reduced fear were qualities they normally would like to feel in everyday life. However, respondents differed greatly as to how realistic or desirable such a transformation (from "normal" to "ecstatic" state) would or could actually be.

There was also considerable disagreement regarding frequency of use as it related to "diminishing returns." Some felt that the more they used MDMA, the less "high" they got. The beliefs of respondents on these matters greatly influenced their overall patterns of use.

An oft-repeated sentiment was that "the first time was the best." This perception tended to change for some users as time went on, but others continued to feel that there was a special magic to the initial MDMA experience(s). An extreme example of this was provided by a young college student, who described how his subsequent nine experiences never came close to approximating his very enjoyable first time. This led him to conclude that "Ecstasy doesn't have much effect on me" (062:60). As a result, he planned to stick with more potent and reliable psychedelics like LSD and didn't "plan to waste too much more money on" MDMA (062:60).

Similar views regarding the unique power of the first experience(s) have been frequently expressed about other drugs as well—particularly psychedelics (Blum, 1964; Grinspoon and Bakalar, 1987; Zinberg, 1984). A persuasive explanation for this phenomenon is that the first experience is no longer repeatable because mind and body become cognizant of the drug's particular actions. This learning results in the development of behavioral tolerance which prepares the mind to anticipate and react to subsequent experiences. In short, the element of novelty vanishes after first use. This could also explain the common perception among respondents that use beyond a certain amount eventually transformed the sublime into the mundane.

Although overwhelmingly positive in describing their initial MDMA experiences, many respondents reported substantially less enjoyment and/or benefits with subsequent use. There were numerous differences of opinion regarding the onset, progression, and degree of reduced enjoyment or benefits. Some respondents described a fairly linear rate of diminishing positive effects, a process that was accelerated with overuse. In contrast, some claimed to have experienced little or no deterioration in quality over time, particularly if they had used MDMA infrequently. What follows are two different interpretations of diminishing returns associated by many respondents with continued use.

"Getting the Message"   Many therapeutically and spiritually oriented respondents attributed sharp reductions or cessation of MDMA use to "getting the message," not unlike accounts provided by psychedelic users in the 1960s (Blum, 1964; Grinspoon and Bakalar, 1979; Stevens, 1987). In essence, they felt that they had learned all that the MDMA experience could teach them and had integrated it into their everyday lives. Further use would therefore be unnecessary and potentially draining. There was considerable variation, however, as to the number of experiences necessary before "getting the message." Therapeutically oriented users were often provided MDMA with an underlying expectation of requiring only a few experiences. In explaining why such minimal use is often all that is necessary, a German chemist and former manufacturer argued that MDMA is a quick and efficient "learning tool that can be drawn into daily life because the drug does not lead very far away from daily life. . . . It's not something that has to be used over and over again, because if somebody has learned it once, he got it. And he doesn't need it for. that anymore" (006:48).

A psychiatrist who employed MDMA as an introspective psychological tool felt that he had successfully integrated the experience by simply "choosing to be happy" (005:60). As a consequence, he no longer felt a pressing need to take MDMA again. Nevertheless, he remained open to the possibility of another experience, viewing his MDMA use as analogous to going to a monastery: "great, but you wouldn't want to live in one. You want to be able to use and utilize what you learn from them and be able to retreat to them periodically" (005:88).

Some respondents believed that a few experiences were all that was needed to transfer the benefits of MDMA to their everyday lives. One woman described how she structured her last few MDMA experiences to learn what was necessary to feel that way naturally: "I remember when I'm on the drug how I say to myself, 'Why can't you feel like this in your everyday life?' And I decided that when I took the drug that was going to be one of the reasons why I took it the last couple of times" (004:20). As a result of her MDMA experiences, she declared: "I never took the drug to get high, so the reason why I was taking it was to open myself up. And it did its job. It would be redundant if I took it now . . . I don't need to take the drug with someone to talk about something. I have all the skills now. And it gave me the start" (004:28).

Decreased Enjoyment of the High   In contrast to those who "got the message," more recreationally oriented respondents (who were out for "fun") described how decreased enjoyment of the MDMA high ultimately tempered their enthusiasm and use. For many, the initial "ecstasy" becomes increasingly subdued with continued use. Here the notion of 'set' is crucial. Individuals who took MDMA for the purpose of expanding consciousness became less interested when they believed their inward journey had ended. Those who pursued Ecstasy to experience a high became less interested when the high was less intense than it had been originally.

Remembering what others had told them, some respondents believed that one could only have a certain number of good MDMA experiences before the drug "lost its magic." After having wonderful initial experiences, a 58-year-old professional felt gradually diminishing returns with continued use: "I think it's steadily diminishing. . . . That belief, incidentally, may have been planted on us, because other people have passed that around. We've heard one person say, for instance, that you've got ten good trips in you, and that's all" (013:91). A college student described why he and many of his friends had cut down or discontinued MDMA use: "I think they've gotten bored with it. I mean as I said, there are only so many times that you can have your same old trip before it becomes like doing the laundry" (045:95). The problem of lessened enjoyment was most prevalent among respondents who typically used MDMA with the same people in the same settings. This phenomenon was particularly true for couples. Although many couples report having used MDMA with continued enjoyment for many years, most describe eventual reductions in use from when they were single and/or first getting together. Some couples who had used MDMA exclusively with each other eventually found their enthusiasm dampened with continued use. Stated simply, the novelty had worn off, and as one veteran user said, "You can only say 'I love you' to the same people in the same setting so many times. Then it gets to be old hat."

A change in social context accounted for lessened use for some respondents. For example, one member of a couple decided to quit for various reasons (pregnancy, lessened enjoyment) and the partner didn't want to take MDMA with anyone else. Also common were respondents whose use dropped dramatically or ceased when they got involved with partners who didn't want to use MDMA. Others described a kind of "maturing out" phase similar to their changing outlook on many other drugs as well. Having settled down with a partner, they no longer needed MDMA as a social lubricant or intimacy enhancer. Couples were not, however, the only respondents to cite changing social contexts as responsible for decreased use and/or lessened enjoyment. Many respondents felt that MDMA use was limited to certain groups or social settings that they no longer identified with (such as college parties, Dallas nightclubs).

Increasingly Negative Aftereffects

Most respondents who cut back or quit use cited increasingly problematic aftereffects as the primary reason. This was especially true for more recreationally oriented users, who saw little therapeutic value in the post-MDMA recovery period. Heavy users in particular often saw the day(s) after as a time of survival, the discomfort justified only by the continued pleasures of the experience itself. Most respondents complained of mildly problematic aftereffects (fatigue, malaise, headaches) that often persisted for a day or two (and in rare cases longer) after taking MDMA. However, there was wide variability in responses regarding the origin, progression, and perceived severity of MDMA aftereffects. Whereas some individuals stated that they were able to use MDMA frequently with only minimal problems, a few quickly decided to discontinue use.

There appear to be substantial differences in physiological response to the same dose of MDMA. Taking too much MDMA too often, overindulging in alcohol or other drugs, and overall physical condition explain much of the perceived severity of negative aftereffects. However, psychological interpretations of the recovery period must also be taken into account. One respondent's uncomfortable "burnout" was perceived as a less negative "spaceout" or a necessary "period of integration" by another. These differences in perception were illustrated by a 34-year-old longtime user who noted an increase in aftereffects in recent years, but was not disturbed by them: "But I do have to say that I generally just interpret it as feeling mellow. A lot of people interpret those things as being burned out, and I often just say, 'Well, now, this isn't physically burned out. This is just being calm and clear'" (085:39).

Once again, the set of the individual—the expectations she or he brought to the experience (before, during, and after)—had much to do with perceived effects. These beliefs are heavily influenced by the respective social worlds found in our study. Recreationally oriented respondents had few positive words about the hangovers which often followed and limited their MDMA use. In contrast, those respondents who were more therapeutically or spiritually inclined often claimed that the days and weeks following their MDMA experiences were equally if not more important than the actual high for integration and personal growth. They saw the positive benefits as outweighing any physical discomfort they might be experiencing. In order to best integrate the experience into their everyday lives, many of these respondents purposely set aside a few days following MDMA use for relaxation and contemplation. One therapist encouraged her clients to phone her the day after MDMA use because she found that "anytime they felt like it and usually within 24 hours after, there is a tendency to want to phone back and report what the feelings are. And as I said before, a great deal of the assimilation of the experience and a great deal of the insight often comes in the 24 hours after the experience" (077:52).

Many respondents described a kind of "honeymoon" period with MDMA, experiencing very few negative aftereffects the first few times. As a young psychiatrist described the aftereffects following what he saw as a very therapeutic first experience: "The first time I took it there was a real afterglow. . . . I was real benign and real mellow and real loving and real open and had a grin on my face. . . . I was just sort of on Cloud 9" (005:102).

Although many respondents recalled feeling somewhat fatigued the following day, they were much less likely to perceive the aftereffects following their initial use as negative. Perhaps the most common physical problem was a painful jaw resulting from bruxism (teeth grinding) during the experience. MDMA's euphoric and analgesic effects generally rendered respondents oblivious to this reaction or any pain associated with it until the following day(s).

In addition to chronic jaw soreness caused by teeth grinding, some respondents complained of mouth and tongue sores caused by chewing. As one longtime user lamented: "Well, what I've noticed is a lot of times I will chew the sides of my cheeks and that hurts for days sometimes. That's a really bad side effect" (007:97).

For many respondents, it appears that the perceived severity of aftereffects increased as the enjoyment or benefits associated with the MDMA experience lessened. For example, a college user described how his initial enthusiasm and enjoyment of MDMA declined with continued use. Following a progression similar to others, his aftereffects were "not particularly intense the first few times, but by the last three times, the day after was always a bad day, and I would have a headache, be in a bad mood all day and just be grumpy and grouchy and a real pain, I'm sure" (045:68). He finally decided to discontinue use when the perceived benefits no longer outweighed the burnout.

Other respondents attributed their increasingly negative aftereffects to MDMA's toxicity and/or the body's progressive intolerance of this new, foreign substance. Many voiced concerns about the long-term implications. Despite the "user-friendly" nature of the high itself, MDMA was increasingly seen as a drug that was hard on the body. One young college student and paralegal (060) cited jaw clenching, lower back and joint pains, and vision problems as the most troublesome aftereffects. The increasing severity of these problems led many of his college and Deadhead friends to cut down or curtail their MDMA use: "Just almost everyone I know who has done this has said, 'I don't know what it is but this shit's bad for you'" (060:121)..

Some respondents noted that, at least occasionally, the MDMA burnout was equally (or even more) severe on the second day following the experience: "I was a little lingering—a little more tired the second day after than I was the first day after" (013:82). This "delayed hangover" was most frequently associated with ingestion of large amounts late at night. As a consequence, users still felt somewhat high the first day after, which they had typically reserved for relaxation anyway. The fact that the respondents frequently had to go back to work or school on the second day probably made them more aware of lingering aftereffects.

Advancing age was also cited as a contributory factor in explaining increased burnout following use. Older users tended not to bounce back as well as their younger counterparts. This problem was more often noted by veteran users. Individuals who first used MDMA in their 20s with few problems started to suffer more aches in their 30s. A 34-year-old former dealer described this transition:

> At least for the first couple years or three years that I did it on and off, that was one of the things—one of my sales points or whatever you want to say—that you don't get burned out the next day. Like I wasn't physically wiped out like after a good

LSD trip. . . . Lately, I'd have to say, I'm getting older and I do feel some physical things the next day, whether I get sleep or not. (085:39)

Acknowledging slower recovery times, older respondents tended to do more planning and take MDMA less frequently than their younger counterparts.

In addition to health concerns, there were other problematic aftereffects. For example, a Dallas woman could no longer bear the spiritual dissonance of doing Ecstasy on Saturday night and teaching Sunday school the next morning:

I mean, when you get older and stuff your body can't handle it anymore. At least mine can't. I just can't handle it. And pretty much I was getting off all that kind of stuff, 'cause I am really getting my life in order; you know, spiritual development and all of that. I mean I can't do Ex one night and then teach Sunday school the next day. My conscience won't let me do that. (069:31)

Participants in our study were primarily middle-class individuals who used MDMA as a recreational "time-out" or more instrumentally as a therapeutic tool. They were busy and productive, and certainly had a "stake in conventional life" (Waldorf, Reinarman, and Murphy, 1991). As a result, necessary allowances for next-day recovery underlay the infrequent use reported by many of the respondents in our study. This was particularly true for professionals, who frequently stated that job, school, and family demands rarely allowed for what they considered to be a "two-day experience." As a consequence, professionals and other busy individuals in our sample were much more likely to rigidly schedule their MDMA use at infrequent intervals. As one 39-year-old Ph.D. described it:

If you want to do it it's gotta be a full-day trip. We always do it with this couple. There's a lot of preparation and juggling of schedules. . . . a weekend trip with another couple; there's so much thinking and work that needs to go into it. Because it is . . . it's like a two-day experience. There's the day of the drug and then the day after. (011:40)

Some of the respondents (particularly older professionals) described how they planned their experience in three-day increments. The day before was spent resting and eating well, the sec-

ond day was the actual trip, and the third (and fourth, if necessary) was slated for a relaxed recovery. As a 51-year-old airline
pilot explained: "I'll try and plan . . . ideally to have three days, a
day before to come down—in other words, to sort of slow down
so you don't just rush into it, a day before it actually happens and
a day to sort of relax and see what happens if there's any secondary effects. So three days to me is ideal" (072:51).

The differences in perceived severity of aftereffects can be partially explained by examining the contexts of use which contribute to (or perhaps ameliorate) the inevitable comedown. Alcohol and other drugs were frequently mentioned as contributing
factors to MDMA hangovers. Many respondents stated that
when they had ingested large quantities of alcohol to counteract
dehydration or the stimulant effects of MDMA, they suffered few
immediate effects but had a killer hangover the next day. As a
young "new-wave" user put it: "I can drink like a fish on 'X'. . . .
Yeah, I think that's a lot of where my 'X' hangovers come in is
just from drinking so much" (082:13). Another respondent
recalled the role played by other drug use in accounting for post-
MDMA hangovers back in his college days:

> I recounted incidents of drinking incredible amounts of alcohol,
> . . . I mean, deadly amounts of alcohol, and I'm sure that con-
> tributed to most of my burnout. . . . If I was burnt the next day
> I truly think that it was typically not the MDMA. It was the
> alcohol, cigarettes, marijuana associated with it. One of the
> problems, and until I had more information, that I would have
> with MDMA was I would drink a tremendous amount—you
> could. And I would smoke cigarettes, too, and I don't smoke
> cigarettes. (009:41–42)

Recounting often painful hangovers following such experiences,
he considered himself "more conscious" of his current drug use:

> I don't smoke cigarettes anymore when I do MDM. And I don't
> drink anymore when I do it, either. It's much more responsible
> now, certainly, or not necessarily so much more responsible, but
> more caring about what I'm doing to my body and a lot of that
> is because of the information that's been provided to me and
> also my own feeling. I mean, there was a point there where I did
> not want to do MDM ever again. My body was saying, "Hey,
> Buckwheat, I'm gonna fuck with you if you keep doing this."
> (009:51)

In sum, although few respondents in our study had totally discontinued their use of Ecstasy, most had reduced their consumption to relatively infrequent levels for a number of reasons. The criminalization of MDMA reduced availability and increased cost and concerns about purity. The increasingly negative publicity about potential toxicity caused many to be concerned about the health aspects of taking MDMA.

On a more subjective level, individuals began to experience MDMA somewhat differently than they had initially. Many no longer experienced the "high" so intensely or euphorically. Increasingly negative aftereffects also influenced respondent use patterns. As the high became less enjoyable or productive, and the next day(s) more painful, respondents' enthusiasm declined accordingly. Since the ability to function the next day(s) was crucial to this largely employed, middle-class population, drug use that interfered with their lives was eliminated. Just as most controlled their use of other intoxicants in order to continue to participate in conventional life, they also limited their pursuit of ecstasy.

CHAPTER 6

Adverse Reactions and Abuse: When Ecstasy Becomes Agony

Negative aftereffects played a significant role in tempering MDMA use among many respondents in our study. Although the aftereffects described earlier were enough to deter or lessen Ecstasy use, they were not defined by respondents as exceptionally problematic. By contrast, in this chapter we examine more extreme adverse reactions associated with MDMA use. We then look at the experiences of those respondents who have tested the limits of MDMA use in their pursuit of Ecstasy. We compare our findings with those of other studies in the United States and abroad, particularly the problematic use seen among Rave enthusiasts in Britain. Finally, we offer an overall assessment of the abuse potential of MDMA.

ADVERSE REACTIONS

We have divided adverse reactions associated with MDMA use into four separate categories. The first occurs during the onset of the "trip." The next has to do with life-threatening reactions and deaths. The final two regard chronic physiological and psychological problems ascribed to MDMA use.

Problems with the Onset of the MDMA High

Despite MDMA's "user-friendly" reputation, infrequent panic reactions and/or hyperventilatory episodes have been noted during the initial "rush" phase (Beck, 1986; Peroutka, 1990b; Seymour, 1986; Siegel, 1985b; Whitaker-Azmitia and Aronson, 1989; Winstock, 1991). Although none of our respondents had experienced a full-blown panic attack, several had seen or heard of such episodes occurring with other users. It appears that the vast majority of severe anxiety reactions occur with novice users who become overwhelmed by the sudden power of the initial rush. Fearing that this is simply a portent of worse to come, they succumb to a generalized panic reaction, often with profuse sweating and breathing difficulties. Reassurance by friends that this "peak" experience is transitory generally lessens the problem (Beck, 1986; Seymour, 1986).

Some respondents reported suffering various forms of discomfort during the initial onset of the MDMA experience. Often dose related, the most frequently cited complaints were of anxiety, dizziness, and/or nausea. These side effects were typically seen as transient and rarely discouraged continued use. An exception was a 21-year-old college student who was able to enjoy the MDMA experience only after first getting through a problematic onset. Although his initial experiences were very positive, two of his subsequent "trips" were marred by long-lasting queasiness and nausea. The first occurred when he took MDMA with several friends at a bar. "I started to come on and it never—that queasy, that weird feeling never left. It just got more intense. I never reached the point of ecstasy. I just had reached a point of nausea, and I had to leave" (098:55). As a consequence, he avoided MDMA for almost a year and only took smaller doses when he started using it again. "I was afraid of that queasy feeling. I hated that feeling. Just thinking about it I could feel it, just thinking about it" (098:63).

Life-Threatening Reactions and Deaths Related to MDMA

Less than one-quarter (21 percent) of our respondents had ingested single doses of at least 250 milligrams of MDMA. This is roughly double the amount taken normally. Although few had greatly exceeded this amount, some knew of friends or acquaintances who had taken exceptionally large doses (up to 900 milligrams in one sitting). Very few, however, had witnessed or suffered what they considered to be a potentially life-threatening overdose or severe adverse reaction.

This was not unexpected, given the infrequency of such mentions in American drug problem indicators. MDMA was associated with only eight emergency room admissions between 1977 and 1984. Although this number jumped to twenty-eight in 1985, and to thirty-nine in both 1986 and 1987, MDMA still represented only 0.03 percent of the total number of drug mentions for each of those years (DAWN, 1986, 1987, 1988).

Based on his review of the available data at the time, physician Graeme Dowling notes that "although minor side effects produced by MDMA are quite common, serious toxic reactions are exceptionally rare" (1990:67). He then goes on to conclude that "human deaths that can be attributed to MDMA or MDEA [MDE] appear to be exceedingly rare, especially when one considers the widespread use of these drugs in the United States" (Dowling, 1990:74). Pharmacologist John Fitzgerald (1991) arrived at similar conclusions after reviewing MDMA-related adverse reactions in the United States and other countries.

A notable exception has recently emerged in England with reports of at least fifteen MDMA-related fatalities among participants in the increasingly popular British Rave scene (Randall, 1992). Although some of these deaths could be explained in terms of other drug involvement overdose and/or underlying cardiovascular disease, most appeared to have occurred at seemingly normal doses in healthy young adults (Henry, 1992; Jones and Dickinson, 1992; Prentice, 1992). Dowling had previously noted what appeared to be idiosyncratic reactions in at least two of the American MDMA-related deaths (Dowling, McDonough, and Bost, 1987; Dowling, 1990).

Since deaths have almost invariably taken the form of hyperpyrexia followed by massive hemorrhage, a physician with the British National Poisons unit postulates that the fatalities result from a form of heatstroke (Henry, 1992). Although rare, this appears to be caused by the effects of MDMA intensified by dehydration and prolonged, vigorous dancing in hot, stifling environments commonly found in Rave settings (Jones, 1991).[1]

Chronic Physiological Problems

A small number of respondents complained of increasingly uncomfortable and prolonged "burnout" periods lasting more than the typical day or two. Some individuals noted an increased susceptibility to various ailments, particularly sore throats, colds, flu, herpes outbreaks, and bladder infections. These associations are supported by previous observations that MDA and MDMA may exert some type of adverse action on the immunological response of certain individuals (Weil, 1976; Beck, 1986).[2]

Such reactions appeared to be rare among novice or occasional users and individuals in good physical and mental health.

Nevertheless, some respondents noted health problems following relatively infrequent use. A psychiatrist described his most frequent period of use, during which he took MDMA twice a month for about four months. After each use he felt "run-down." He said he "got more colds . . . was sick a lot of the time" (005:31). He found that the colds decreased when he reduced his MDMA use.

In his observations of MDA users, Weil noted that "for unknown reasons it seems to be especially hard on women and will activate any latent infections or problems in the female genito-urinary tract" (1976:336). A 34-year-old longtime user in our study described how she would have taken MDMA more often had it not been for the bladder infections she associated with her use. Having a history of almost no previous bladder infections, this respondent recalled that "it wasn't the first few, but it seems like after I'd done it ten times or so it seemed as if I would often get really bad bladder infections. And some of them eventually got so bad to where I just couldn't get rid of them" (095:22).

At least two other respondents described somewhat less severe problems associated with use. A former distributor had also observed this problem in some of his women friends. He believed that it was primarily related to whether or not the user allowed proper time for recuperation and integration following the MDMA experience: "Well, there seems to be this sense of the urinary tract infections with women, sometimes . . . but I think that has a lot to do with that second day, whether you rest or not. If you rest, you'll come back stronger, but if you don't, you'll stress yourself" (007:96).

Despite these examples, the small number of such reports makes any interpretation regarding MDMA's health effects difficult and premature. It may well be that problems associated with MDMA are roughly comparable to other stimulants such as amphetamines and cocaine. It would be well to look at the conditions under which adverse physiological reactions occur in an effort to more fully understand these occurrences.

Chronic Psychological Problems

Although some respondents reported psychological difficulties of one form or another typically related to overuse, these were generally short-lived. Only two of our respondents described chronic psychological problems following their MDMA use. As described in the previous chapter, one user (081) attributed his chronic depression to MDMA-induced neurotoxicity. The other respondent (026) had been a frequent user for a number of years (having first tried MDMA while attending the University of Oregon in 1978). Whereas she occasionally experienced "loss of control" with LSD and psilocybin, her MDMA experiences for the first seven years had been positive. She typically took MDMA with a lover or at a Grateful Dead concert, and Ecstasy was her "drug of choice." Her psychological problems followed the time she ingested MDMA with eight other friends on June 30, 1985 (to celebrate MDMA's last day of legality). She took the drug at a park in the early afternoon and recalled that the experience was very pleasurable for all. Her problems started shortly after she returned alone to her apartment that night:

> Then as I was coming down, I decided that I wanted to be alone and I wanted to go home. And so I went home, which wasn't very far away, and I started to have a really interesting experience. I thought I saw spirits in my room. I was all by myself. There was nobody else in my room. I had just moved into a new house and I thought I saw spirits in my room. I thought I saw things in my room which were like wire mesh screening floating through the room. That's what I saw. And I was very much down off the drug, or so I thought.
>
> But then I got a feeling of loneliness and I felt that possibly one of the spirits was trying to communicate with me. And I started to feel extremely lonely. I started to cry. I just felt like crying. Then I stopped crying, and I remember listening because I thought I heard somebody else crying. And I realized that the other crying that I heard was myself or one of the spirits that was in my room. And then I just started to trip. "Why am I hearing this? I've heard this before. Am I sane or am I insane or what's going on here?" I remember just staying in my room pretty much for the rest of the night ... and I remember being extremely depressed the next day—not suicidal thoughts in the sense that I would kill myself, but suicidal thoughts in the sense that I couldn't remember what the purpose of my life was. And I became really concerned about doing MDMA again because of that. I had a really rough time for the next couple days. (026:52–54)

In retrospect, she believed that a combination of MDMA aftereffects, mounting personal problems, fasting, and PMS all contributed to this frightening experience. It took several days before she felt fully recovered. She subsequently vowed never to take MDMA again.

The apparent infrequency of chronic psychological problems related to MDMA use is also reflected in findings from other research in the United States and abroad (Fitzgerald, 1991; Korf et al., 1991; Seymour, 1986; Solowij and Lee, 1991). For example, out of a convenience sample of one hundred Stanford undergraduates who had used MDMA, Peroutka (1990b) found only two individuals reporting minor long-term problems (increased emotionality and increased anxiety and teeth clenching) related to their use of the drug. Nevertheless, a small number of cases of paranoid psychosis have been noted (Creighton, Black, and Hyde, 1991; Hayner and McKinney, 1986; McGuire and Fahy, 1991; Schifano, 1991).

ABUSE AND OVERUSE OF ECSTASY

Ecstasy can be abused. Our respondents who got into trouble with MDMA had attempted to use too much, or to prolong the experience. Some became heavy users. Context of use, as we document, plays a major role in abuse.

Our respondents often described how their enthusiasm for MDMA following initial use led them to test the limits of the experience. In attempting to accentuate or prolong the MDMA high, they quickly realized that more is not better. As a result, many ultimately subscribed to what the British Lifeline drug program refers to as the "Golden 'E' Rule:" "Less Is More" (Pearson et al., 1991:11). In the following discussion, we examine the often painful lessons learned from testing the limits and then look at the small number of respondents who continued to engage in heavy use.

Attempting to Go Higher

As with other drugs, many respondents described how they experimented with higher doses of MDMA to see if the high was even better than with the usual 100- 150-milligram amount. Thirty-six percent reported taking single doses of 200 or more milligrams on at least one occasion. With few exceptions (typically larger individuals), respondents found such doses to be "speedy" and uncomfortable with no perceived increase in benefits or enjoyment.

Among these respondents was a psychiatrist (005), who gave

himself and his petite girlfriend large initial doses (300 and 225 milligrams, respectively) in hopes of freeing her from an abusive relationship she had with another man. The attempt at therapy backfired when she became delirious and began hallucinating. He had been unaware of her prior speed use and sleep deprivation, which probably contributed to her delirium. A chemist (006) who manufactured MDMA claimed to have seen few problems among the hundreds of people he had observed under the influence of MDMA. Those he did witness were individuals who had consumed large doses of MDMA. Most notable was partial leg "paralysis" in a woman who had reportedly taken 300 milligrams. She was unable to walk for the entire evening, though she fully recovered the next day. This account fits our general observation that, although users often enjoy moving around or dancing at lower doses, much less movement is seen with higher doses. Decreased movement appears to be associated with lack of both desire and ability. At higher doses there is decreased coordination and increased involuntary movement of the eyes (nystagmus). These physiological effects make any attempt at skilled movement difficult.

In contrast to those seeking to go higher, a few spiritually and therapeutically oriented users decided to reduce their dose as the best way to "stay centered" and avoid becoming "too intoxicated." After taking larger doses on two separate occasions, a 27-year-old German woman reached a solution:

> I never took more than one hundred (mgs.) after this, and with 80 or 60 milligrams I am totally happy. Maybe 60 milligrams is the best. So I figured out this was unnecessary. . . . It was a good experience to know that the "mind speed" comes, and it's not necessary for me. I'm not interested in how the racing mind is. I just want to appreciate the real sensations and the feeling of being right now. (099:12)

Therapists differed regarding optimal doses. One woman described a significant difference between herself and another therapist, who believed in higher doses:

> The difference between that and the method I use is that also he tended to believe in the use of higher dosage levels for the first time. He had been known to use as high as 150, which—well, we had a very friendly disagreement on that. I think the first time is very important, and I just have seen too many extremely sensitive responses. (077:43)

Rather than increasing dosage, some respondents attempted to accentuate their high by turning to quicker, more powerful routes of administration. Although 33 percent had tried snorting MDMA, over half of these had done so only once, typically complaining of the "burn" and/or "speedy" effects. Five respondents had also experimented with intravenous use, but only two had done so more than once. With remarkably few exceptions, MDMA users strongly prefer the oral route of administration for its longer, smoother experience (Korf et al., 1991; Seymour, 1986; Solowij and Lee, 1991).

Prolonging the Experience

Most respondents (79 percent) reported having attempted at least once to fend off the comedown with one or more "booster" doses. This option was particularly prevalent during early stages of use. However, the increased harshness of the hangover made this a short-lived strategy for most. One respondent noted a strong association between jaw tension and her ingestion of supplementary doses:

> I have noted that in my own use of MDMA, I have almost no jaw tension whatsoever and haven't had for years and years, in fact since the second or third time I took it. But a few times when I have done the usual experimentation, which we all do at one point or another . . . taking more than one supplement, I have noticed extreme jaw tension. (077:37)

With continued use, many respondents were less inclined to employ "booster" doses to delay the comedown. As one respondent explained:

> I think generally that boosters are a bad idea because I find that what happens with people is that there's the initial rush and then they hit a plateau. And the instant they hit that plateau, the moment they come off the rush, they think they're coming down. And they're not coming down at all. They're just leveling out. And if they have a booster available, usually what they do is they take it then. And what it does for them, literally, is it only heightens the unpleasant side effects and it doesn't lengthen the experience by that much and they don't get any higher. (080:30)

Nevertheless, some respondents did permit themselves to regularly ingest a small booster (often about half the size of the original dose) two to three hours into the MDMA high. Although a third of respondents tried extending their high with multiple boosters on at least one occasion, such experiences were generally regarded as unpleasant or resulting in no improvement, and these became "lessons learned." One longtime user and former distributor described going through a gram by himself over a twenty-four-hour period:

> Well, it wasn't heroic. It was abuse. . . . I just continued to nip at it, essentially. I chipped at it over a 24 hour period until I'd done the whole gram. And I was totally physically depleted for three days after that, and I had a raging headache the next day. . . . It's not an experience I'd recommend to anyone. (080:30–31)

Another longtime user recalled a period of abuse following his enthusiastic discovery of MDMA in the late 1970s. A heavy user of other drugs as well, he once described taking MDMA "6 or 7 . . . maybe even 8 days in a row" (009:53). Surprisingly, he suffered little physical burnout from such a run: "I would have jaw cramps for a couple of days afterwards, certainly. The muscles were just too tense. But not much else, not really" (009:54). It was the mental burnout following such extensive MDMA use that most disturbed him:

> Typically not the next day, . . . not the day after, because I think you're still high, but I think the following day after that, life would get tough. Thinking processes were tough. And emotionally you were just on edge, . . . you could cut somebody, . . . especially with a reasonable vocabulary, to ribbons. You were a not a happy camper. And yet it wasn't necessarily physically oriented. It was upstairs certainly. (009:54–55)

Another extreme example of overuse was provided by a recreationally oriented respondent (083). Having taken MDMA over two hundred times, this respondent described various degrees of lethargy as the primary aftereffect. However, one time he ingested at least twenty-four MDMA tablets over a four-day period. Considering that the tablets he purchased tended to be about 110 milligrams, he probably took close to 3 grams during that time in an attempt to avoid coming down. This culminated in a prolonged and agonizing recovery period in which he suffered from chronic fatigue and a urinary tract infection.

Frequent Use over Long Periods of Time

We intentionally sought out veteran users who engaged in very frequent or binge use for prolonged periods of time. As a result, we were able to formally and informally interview a number of individuals who were arguably chronic abusers or overusers of MDMA.

Although fourteen of our one hundred respondents had taken MDMA over one hundred times, they generally did so over a long period of time (five to twelve years). With a few exceptions, most had gradually decreased their MDMA consumption over time. Of those respondents who crossed the one-hundred-episode mark in shorter periods of time, many were active participants in the Dallas and Baton Rouge nightclub scenes. These individuals often took MDMA once or twice a weekend for periods of a year or longer before burning out or becoming bored with the scene. A Dallas woman who had only recently decided to discontinue use described the general scene: "Starting two years ago I did it virtually every weekend, if not every other one. Sometimes Friday *and* Saturday. And then Sunday you would just be really, really, really trashed" (065:24). As with other respondents who cut down sooner, this increasingly negative "Sunday syndrome" became the primary reason she eventually stopped. Although greatly appreciating MDMA's positive qualities, most heavy users became increasingly disillusioned with the problem side of the equation.

Ecstasy use over a long period of time does not necessarily have adverse effects on users. Dose level at each trip, as well as the number of experiences packed into a short time period, seems more crucial. A 30-year-old musician and computer technician (092), for example, estimated that he had taken MDMA at least five hundred times over an eleven-year period. A shy, self-effacing individual, he usually ingested MDMA at least once a weekend, often taking it at parties or other gatherings. He believed that it temporarily made him more sociable and likable. Although initially optimistic, he had become disillusioned about his ability to incorporate these perceived benefits into his everyday life. Nonetheless, although he expressed some concern about potential long-term health risks, he had experienced no significant problems (other than hangovers) from MDMA. He so valued Ecstasy's ability to release him from his shyness that he did not foresee any major changes in his current pattern of use.

Another respondent quickly adopted MDMA as his drug of choice. Five years later, having used it well over two hundred times, he differed from the majority of respondents:

> The more I took it, the more I liked it. I found it to be . . . very refined . . . whereas Acid seemed to be kind of rough and clumsy. . . . I realized that this [MDMA] was a lot more relaxing, gave you the same—gave you similar highs without the side effects, a lot more in control, a lot more positive body feelings, a lot less aftereffects the next day or the next two or three days. So the more I did it, the more I kind of realized it was pretty ideal. (047:28)

In general, the above respondents were exceptional. It was often difficult for us to ascertain whether these frequent users actually experienced less burnout or were simply more tolerant of the aftereffects because they enjoyed the high and continually sought to reexperience it.

Binging with Ecstasy

In addition to doing a couple of formal interviews, we were able to informally interview a small contingent of bingers who had continued to use large amounts of MDMA on single occasions for long periods of time. They typically employed Ecstasy in a manner similar to their use of cocaine, starting with a normal 125–150-milligram dose and ingesting several boosters (either orally or intranasally) of varying sizes over the course of an evening or weekend. Like many cocaine users, they attributed such use to their desire to stay high and an inability to avoid using whatever amount was available. Although often experiencing excruciating hangovers, most did not perceive such use as particularly dangerous.

A young college student described how he had first discovered cocaine and was using about 2 grams a week before discovering MDMA. His strong preference for MDMA led to a significant reduction in his cocaine consumption. Although he used MDMA less frequently than cocaine, he described a similar pattern of use. He generally took MDMA about once a month with his girlfriend: "We'd start at 6:00, take an eighth, maybe a bit more than an eighth, come on, start to feel it coming down, took another tenth, another eighth, and then this'll go on 'til about 1 AM and we've gone through maybe three quarters of a gram, a gram each. And you just get so burned out" (084:32).

Like many cocaine users (Waldorf et al., 1991) he was unable to avoid exhausting his remaining supply of MDMA once he had taken his first dose. As a result, he would often go through $1/2$ gram or more in an evening:

> I've tried saving it and it just doesn't work. You know, we put it in the refrigerator and say, "We're not gonna touch that. We have a whole bunch right here we're gonna do." We go through all that, sit there, start coming down, feel a bit burnt, look at each other and say, "Yeah, go to the freezer and take it out." (084:33)

We conducted informal interviews with other binge users. Two of these individuals considered themselves to be the last remnants of a larger group of twenty fraternity members who first tried MDMA a decade before. For almost an entire school year (1979-1980), these "regulars" ingested MDMA at least once or twice a weekend. Like the other college student, these binge users were young stimulant enthusiasts who enjoyed MDMA's unique qualities. MDMA had replaced cocaine or methamphetamine as their "drug of choice." Although they generally ingested MDMA orally, their pattern was similar to that of cocaine—frequently going on all night or for weekend "runs."

Most of these students used MDMA much less often during the second year, leaving only a few who were still using MDMA with any regularity. By the third year only two remained. After graduating from college and moving to Southern California, one of these users described how his use had sharply declined, as a result of less availability and separation from his MDMA-using buddies. If it is available, he now takes Ecstasy about once a month, but still prefers to binge with it ("I binge with any drug"). Usually doing between $1/3$ and 1 gram, he said he consumed almost $1 1/2$ grams on one occasion. However, he has noted a much stronger burnout following such use than he experienced in his younger days and hopes to learn how to "just say no" to multiple boosters. He has also become an older, more responsible adult. Like many professionals and other respondents in the sample, this user sees his recreational drug use as a much-needed break from a stressful job. He works hard for five or six days a week with almost no drug use, saving himself for the seventh day (or occasional long weekend), when he often rewards himself by "getting blasted" on various intoxicants (alcohol and cocaine if nothing else is available).

Although these bingers acknowledged negative aftereffects, they were less deterred by them than other respondents. Most were employed or college students, appeared to be quite functional, and generally possessed an attitude of "work hard, play hard." Problematic consequences were generally limited to varying degrees of temporary "burnout." Ultimately, however, most such users eventually cut down their MDMA consumption for many of the same reasons as other respondents (reduced enjoyment, nagging aftereffects, increased life responsibilities). One college student who initially binged almost every weekend for the first couple of years explained why he had subsequently cut back to about once a month:

> I went through the stage of, "This is the best drug ever and I'd like to do it all the time," and then found out if you do that you just burn on it so much that you just experience the side effects more than the euphoria. So I think in that respect, it's actually a kind of good drug because it *regulates its own usage.* I've noticed absolutely no physical addiction to it at all, and nobody I've talked to has. Psychologically, you say it's a really great experience and you want more, especially when you're on it. But I haven't had the same desire as with coke to want it. (084:56–57)

Contexts of Abuse

Context is crucial in understanding the problematic potential of MDMA use. Certain contexts seem to be "safer" or "riskier" than others. In those social worlds in which Ecstasy use is carefully planned and controlled, few adverse reactions are reported by users. Dance club contexts, on the other hand, provide examples of scenes and settings conducive to overuse of MDMA. Our respondents from Dallas and Baton Rouge, for example, had often used MDMA at least once a weekend for over a year. Our fieldwork suggests that there were many others who had engaged in heavy weekend binges or ingested large amounts of Ecstasy almost daily for brief periods of time. One respondent described some of the casualties of overuse: "When I was in Baton Rouge, there was a pretty intense scene and there were people who would do it every day and start frying themselves. So I have seen that. And I have seen people who claim to have bad trips on it, but they were usually mixing it with other drugs, too" (082:28).

The problematic consequences increasingly seen in the British Rave scene suggest that dance club contexts may encourage overuse of MDMA. From his in-depth research with Ravers in the Liverpool area, Newcombe found that "a substantial minority get 'cabbaged' by taking anywhere between three and ten tablets at a single Rave ('stacking')" (Newcombe, 1992:15). He goes on to note that considerable use of other drugs in combination with Ecstasy, particularly amphetamine, helps to overcome the "jelly legs" which may occur in the quest to dance until dawn (Newcombe, 1992).

A recent study of eighty-nine primarily young MDMA users in London found twenty-three to have used Ecstasy over forty times (Winstock, 1991). One-third of the sample reported using MDMA at least once a week, with a small minority engaging in binge use consisting of up to ten to twenty tablets ingested over a weekend. The author goes on to state that "these patterns of use had been sustained for periods of six months to three years" (Winstock, 1991:6785).

Despite the much more significant levels of problematic use found in the British Rave scene, we would nevertheless speculate that pharmacological limiting factors will deter long-term abuse for the vast majority of this population.[3] The aftereffects will simply not compensate for the high, which will in turn become less and less euphoric and intense. Nevertheless, what seems to be a common pattern of at least short-term abuse of Ecstasy (often combined with other substances) still poses significant problems for Rave enthusiasts. The rapid expansion of this scene into other countries (including the United States) makes it essential to examine the ways Ravers experience problems from overuse and overexertion. As Newmeyer cautioned in his epidemiological review:

> It may well be that MDMA currently enjoys controlled, careful use by a number of cognoscenti, somewhat as LSD did around 1960. Perhaps in future years, a much larger number of less sophisticated individuals will be drawn into MDMA usage and will find ways to evince adverse reactions, police involvement and other unpleasant consequences from use of the drug. (1986:382)

OVERALL ASSESSMENT OF ABUSE POTENTIAL

Earlier we discussed the process by which MDMA became illegal. As noted, in order for a drug to be placed in Schedule I of the Controlled Substances Act, and therefore not available in any context, the substance must possess a "high potential for abuse." Although the DEA used preliminary animal studies and drug problem indicators to make their case, in actuality problems are reported very rarely.[4] Additional support for contentions of low abuse potential came from the findings of an early exploratory study of MDMA users. Ironically, in testimony submitted on the DEA's behalf, psychopharmacologist Ron Siegel (1985b) concluded that the most common patterns of MDMA use were "experimental" (ten times or less a lifetime) or "social-recreational" (one to four times per month). He went on to state that "compulsive patterns marked by escalating dose and frequency of use have not been reported with MDMA users" (Siegel, 1985b:2–3).

Although we found some adverse reactions and abuse of MDMA, our overall assessment is that Ecstasy has minimal abuse potential, and much of this can be accounted for by context of use. When overuse of Ecstasy occurred among our respondents, it generally declined within the first several months following initial use. Among social worlds such as professionals and New Agers, even brief periods of overindulgence were rare because most respondents strived to use MDMA sparingly regardless of their initial enthusiasm. A therapeutically oriented dealer concluded that those who attempt to abuse MDMA in their search for enlightenment are quickly disillusioned:

> For me, the drug abusers, the MDMA drug abusers have invariably been manic and have achieved these states that have been valuable to them but they don't want to come down after it. . . . It really is destructive of that feeling you were seeking in the first place. Which is one of the safeguards of MDMA, that within a relatively short period of time—I've seen it happen in a month and a half—it stops working at all. People get really exhausted. (007:52)

A young psychiatrist knew a few people who had (at least temporarily) binged with MDMA. He had difficulty understanding their compulsion:

> I think you got to be a nut to abuse MDMA because it's just so tiring. I know people who abuse it in that they take a lot when they trip. They just take it and take it and take it but then they start to get irritable and jittery and unpleasant and they're sort of like toxic on it. . . . That's the only abuse I've seen is people

who take too much in a day just to hang on to the memory or the experience of the rush. But all you do is get more side effects, the more you take. (005:77–78)

Although some respondents had engaged in frequent and/or binge use for short periods following their initial MDMA experiences, there was a general consensus that chronic abusive patterns were rare. Similar findings appeared in the only two other studies of American MDMA users (Peroutka, Pascoe, and Fuall, 1987; Siegel, 1985b), both of which found no evidence suggestive of long-term abuse. Among Peroutka's sample of one hundred Stanford undergraduate users, the maximum number of times MDMA had been taken was thirty-eight, and the vast majority had used it less than a total of ten times (Peroutka et al., 1987).[5] From these survey findings and informal discussions with approximately two hundred other students, Peroutka asserts that "the 'good effects' of the drug appear to diminish, while the 'negative' side-effects of the drug appear to increase, if the drug is taken too frequently" (1990a:xii).

These findings were also supported by recently published Dutch and Australian studies which observed infrequent use patterns and minimal abuse among MDMA users in those countries (Korf et al., 1991; Solowij and Lee, 1991). Solowij and Lee found little problematic use among their sample of one hundred MDMA users in Sydney. They conclude that "the existence of a 'chronic user' has yet to surface, and the number of reports of distressing residual effects and bad reactions are few indeed" (1991:37). Peroutka arrived at a similar conclusion in asserting that "there are simply no reports of individuals who take frequent and large amounts of MDMA for an extended period of time" (1990a: xii).

Although we were able to find some cases of adverse reactions and abuse, they were certainly the minority. Ecstasy, then, could not be characterized as a drug that has high abuse potential for the majority of users. When it does happen, overuse primarily occurs among individuals who test the limits in attempting to prolong or recapture the ecstasy they initially experienced with MDMA. For these people, the reduction of fear, combined with feelings of empathy and euphoria provides a confidence greatly desired in social interaction. Since most of our "abusers" were young, the negative effects were minimal and they could look back upon their abuse of Ecstasy as simply a phase in their life before going on to something else. This, we feel, is further testimony to the importance of context with regard to drug use or abuse. Individuals who possess life options (remember that 90 percent of our respondents had some college education and 30 percent had graduate degrees) tend to control their use of intoxicating substances so as not to threaten their "stake in conventional life." Likewise those who do fall prey to problematic use or abuse are more likely to reverse such a process to retain their societal position.

But what about the *potential* for abuse? We wondered why, with its pleasurable "rush," a long-lasting, controllable, euphoric experience, and multiple routes of administration, MDMA had *not* become popular with more populations. Why didn't people become addicted to it? As researchers who have completed extensive studies of opiate-using populations, we wondered why this group hadn't started using Ecstasy.[6] And if they were exposed to MDMA, might those prone to abusing other drugs be less deterred by problematic aftereffects in attempting to prolong or accentuate the MDMA high? Just as with other stimulants, might such users be more likely to experiment and prefer more potent and problematic routes of administration such as injection? The answers to our questions are negative.

Assuming increased availability (and this is a big assumption) to populations whose limited life options have made them most vulnerable to a drug *lifestyle,* our findings suggest that the rapid onset of diminishing and/or punishing returns associated with MDMA use would discourage long-term abuse. Ecstasy is not the kind of drug one can use on a daily basis to alleviate the pain and frustration of everyday life. Even among less conventional populations, it remains unlikely that significant numbers would rely on injection for an extended period of time. Oral use remains the almost unanimous preference among user populations, even those who have had a history of injecting drugs. If MDMA abuse has not occurred among the hard drug-using populations by now, it is highly unlikely that it will.

CHAPTER 7

What Should Be Done about Ecstasy? Findings and Recommendations

By the conclusion of our study, Ecstasy's "fifteen minutes of fame" had long since passed. Media interest waned as the controversy over its therapeutic value dragged on and MDMA failed to make a credible showing worthy of a "drug problem." As many had predicted, the criminalization of Ecstasy had seemingly hastened the demise of yet another trendy "designer drug." Far from being a passing fad however, MDMA has done anything but fade away.

A number of significant developments are now occurring in both therapeutic and recreational realms. In July of 1992, federal government meetings essentially reopened the door for human psychedelic research and, more specifically, the investigation of MDMA's potential as a therapeutic adjunct. In October of 1992, the FDA approved the first human study of MDMA.

On a more vocal note, the American media have rediscovered Ecstasy in its new persona as the chemical catalyst driving the popular Rave scene exported from Britain. The lighthearted tone characteristic of much of the early coverage of these youthful dance-till-dawn affairs is beginning to take an increasingly alarmist turn. Citing the mounting casualty count in Britain, media warnings that these Ecstasy-fueled "Dances of Death" have arrived in the United States will lead to increased crackdowns.

So what should be done about Ecstasy, its increasing popularity and potential problems? In this concluding chapter, we briefly summarize our key findings and their implications. We then offer a number of policy and research recommendations we see as essential for reducing the potential for harm with MDMA use, and for increasing the possibilities for therapeutic benefits. In the context of a war on drugs, such recommendations may sound utopian, even heretical. Nonetheless, we offer them and provide strategies for overcoming the formidable obstacles facing such efforts.

SUMMARY OF OUR FINDINGS

In summarizing our major findings, we concentrate on the highlights of our study. We begin with a discussion of the attractions of the experience. We then look at the influence of both pharmacology and social context as they relate to use and abuse.

Attractions of the Experience

MDMA's well-publicized therapeutic and euphoric properties, combined with its "user-friendly" reputation, accounted for initial interest and use among most of our respondents. For those individuals having a history of minimal or negative drug experiences (such as "bad trips"), reassurance was often needed in convincing them that they need not fear "losing control" under the influence of MDMA.

In looking at the diverse rationales offered for MDMA use, recreationally oriented respondents often viewed Ecstasy as a valuable addition to their hedonistic pharmacopeia. They saw MDMA as providing a euphoric experience filled with exuberant camaraderie and sensual enhancement. The MDMA high was typically perceived as smoother, more enjoyable, and more intimate than that of cocaine. In addition, respondents appreciated the sense of control and confidence of the MDMA experience compared with the ego annihilation associated with psychedelic drugs such as LSD.

Other respondents employed MDMA for more therapeutic and/or spiritual purposes. Almost all of these individuals claimed significant long-term benefits from such use. These therapeutically oriented users tended to view their use of Adam as a means to an end, promoting personal and spiritual growth through therapy, introspection, and/or bonding ("experiencing oneness"). Many of these respondents pursued New Age spiritual directions and reported minimal use of other mind-altering substances.

Although respondents often described their initial interest in MDMA primarily in recreational or therapeutic terms, many came to recognize and appreciate both recreation and therapy as benefits of the experience. Nevertheless, continued differences in respondent motivations were reflected in preferred contexts of use, which in turn shaped their overall experiences. Exemplifying these contrasts, significant numbers of respondents invariably took MDMA in private settings with lovers and/or close friends. On the other hand were those whose Ecstasy use almost always occurred in crowded nightclubs. The vigorous dancing to loud music preferred by these respondents sharply contrasted with the minimal movement and soft music typically favored by those using MDMA in more therapeutic or intimate settings.

The explosive growth of the Ecstasy-fueled Rave scene throughout Europe, Australia, and increasingly here as well underscores what has become a predominant view of MDMA as the ultimate dance drug. It has been argued that vigorous trance-dancing until dawn produces a qualitatively different MDMA experience when compared with lying in bed listening to classical music (Pearson et al., 1991). As evidenced by respondents who were Deadheads and Dallas nightclub enthusiasts, Ecstasy had demonstrated its versatility as a dance drug even before the advent of the Rave scene in catering to remarkably different musical tastes and contexts.

The Influence of Pharmacology and
Social Context on Use and Abuse

The diversity of our research team allowed us to gain entrance into both past and present worlds of MDMA use. We were able to interview distributors and longtime users who were involved when MDM first appeared on the streets and Adam was used in therapists' offices during the mid-1970s. From there, we were able to follow the diffusion of MDMA into new populations, with its evolving folklore. Through this broader sociohistorical perspective, we saw how variables such as time (for example, before or after criminalization) and place (such as Dallas or New York City) influenced the dynamic interplay of drug, set, and setting which contributes to the MDMA experience.

The large number of "veteran" users and distributors in our sample population provided a unique perspective for understanding long-term use patterns and problems among more recent MDMA social worlds or scenes both here and abroad. For example, in contrast with Ravers and other groups in Australia and England, where Ecstasy remained almost unknown until the mid-1980s (Nasmyth, 1986; Solowij and Lee, 1991), 19 percent of our respondents had first tried MDMA before 1980.

Although most of our respondents anticipated continued use, they also noted that their consumption had declined over time or had remained infrequent. At the time of interview, 81 percent of our respondents had used MDMA less than once a month during the past year, with 57 percent reporting three or fewer experiences during that time. In explaining their infrequent MDMA use, they often cited lack of availability, concerns about potential toxicity, and/or increasing career and family responsibilities. The importance of these factors varied between the different social worlds of use. However, the primary explanations for reduced consumption were perceived declines in enjoyment or benefits and increasingly uncomfortable short-term aftereffects commonly associated with continued use. Although divided as to which was more important, many respondents cited both factors as influential in tempering their enthusiasm for MDMA and in reducing use as perceived problems began to outweigh benefits.

To counter the above changes, many respondents described a more intensive planning process accompanying their occasional use. Informed by previous experience and user folklore, this preparation enabled them to maximize the "ecstasy" and minimize the "agony" which accompanied continued use.

Since the vast majority of our respondents described MDMA in glowing terms, one might assume that significant numbers of users would suffer problematic consequences as a result of overdoing Ecstasy. However, few respondents had experienced or witnessed serious physical or psychological problems associated with MDMA use. Although overenthusiasm inspired a few respondents to test the limits of MDMA, most quickly learned that "more is not better." Even among those who had a penchant for stimulants, Ecstasy binges were usually confined to the weeks or months following initial use. Experienced drug users often noted how increasingly unpleasant aftereffects, coupled with an almost total loss of desired effects, occurred with greater rapidity and intensity with MDMA than with other more commonly associated abused substances (such as cocaine). Pharmacological factors appear to play a significant role in limiting long-term abuse of MDMA.

Our findings of minimal abuse or problems concur with those of other studies of MDMA users conducted in the United States (Siegel, 1986; Peroutka, 1990b), Holland (Korf et al., 1991), and Australia (Fitzgerald and Reid, 1992; Solowij, Hall, and Lee, 1992). We were unique, however, in that we were able to locate a small number of respondents who had overused or binged with MDMA for periods greater than a year. Even these users were able to modulate or discontinue their MDMA use before suffering serious consequences or requiring treatment.

Given our experience with long-term use patterns, the Australian study conducted by Solowij and colleagues (1992) is of particular interest. Compared with our respondents, their sample of one hundred MDMA users in Sydney was considerably younger and less experienced both in total number of doses taken and in length of use. Lacking the "New Age Spiritualists" found in our study, the Sydney cohort was predominantly a recreationally oriented dance party crowd. Despite these demographic and motivational differences, the Australian researchers concluded that "motivations for use, patterns of use, mode and context of use, the nature of the experience itself (including effects, side-effects and residual effects), abuse potential and issues of tolerance" were "remarkably similar" to those found in our study (Solowij et al., 1992:1169).

Although the majority of the Sydney respondents intended to continue using MDMA on at least an occasional basis, their dampened enthusiasm led the researchers to conclude that "although controlled studies of long term users have not been undertaken, it is doubtful that the drug is being used on a long term basis . . . a reasonable prediction may be that Ecstasy use is a "fad" that will soon die out, to be superseded by the next trend" (Solowij et al., 1992:1171).

Our research suggests the opposite. Although various factors had tempered the enthusiasm of most of our respondents, only 9 percent had actually discontinued use at the time of interview. Of the 32 percent who had five or more years of experience with MDMA, the vast majority looked forward to continued use, with only 4 percent certain that they would not use again.

In sharp contrast, recent casualty counts coming out of the Rave scene in Britain and elsewhere are cause for concern (Henry, Jeffrey, and Dawling, 1992; Jones and Dickinson, 1992). Although we would anticipate that most MDMA users would be discouraged from long-term abuse, young Ravers are more likely to test the limits than any of the groups in our study, including Deadheads and nightclub enthusiasts. Expectations of trance-dancing until dawn in a continuous state of "ecstasy" encourage binging ("stacking") with MDMA because of its relatively brief duration of action. Within the Rave scene, both set and setting often result in substantial overuse of MDMA and other drugs (particularly longer-lasting amphetamines).

In addition to problems associated with overuse, there is the potential for heatstroke to occur at even normal doses of Ecstasy (Henry, 1992). As explained in the previous chapter, fifteen such deaths have occurred in Rave settings over the last two years (Randall, 1992). Each has been attributed to the combination of pharmacology and context. Apparently, the usual rise in body temperature caused by MDMA is synergized among these victims by dehydration and overexertion in hot, stuffy (Rave) settings. As Rave culture continues to grow in popularity, the following section looks at possible strategies to minimize harm among users together with the obstacles confronting them.

RECOMMENDATIONS

Toward a Philosophy of Harm Reduction

"Harm reduction" approaches strive to minimize or prevent problematic consequences associated with drug use. Acknowledging the inevitability of illicit drug use, such strategies represent what Strang and Farrell refer to as "the triumph of pragmatism over purism: the acceptance that second best may be best first" (1992: 1127). Rejecting abstinence-only approaches, Australian researcher Marion Watson describes the principles which guide such efforts:

> Harm reduction in relation to drug use is the philosophical and practical development of strategies so that the outcomes of drug use are as safe as is situationally possible. It involves the provision of factual information, resources, education, skills and the development of attitude change, in order that the consequences of drug use for the users, the community and the culture have minimal negative impact. (Watson, 1991:14)

The Dutch have led the way in establishing a successful drug policy framework guided by harm reduction logic. Rejecting what they view as a simplistic and harmful "War on Drugs," a Dutch Ministry of Justice bulletin asserts that

> within the Ministry of Public Health that carries the primary responsibility for national drug policy formulation there is no pledge of "solving the problem." Instead, policy efforts are

understood as pragmatic attempts to cope, meaning the management and if possible the minimalization of the risks and the damaging effects of the drug phenomenon and preparing society to optimally live with it. (Leuw, 1991:5)

Illustrating the harm reduction philosophy guiding their policy, the Dutch Ministry of Justice views illicit drug use as "a limited and manageable social problem rather than an alien threat forced upon an otherwise innocent society" (Leuw, 1991:2). In sharp contrast to the Dutch perspective, former U.S. Drug Czar William Bennett solemnly reminded American citizens of their moral duty as spelled out by the federal mandate stipulating "a drug-free America by 1995" (Bennett, 1989:9). Rejecting any deviation from "zero tolerance" (at least of *illicit* drugs), Bennett emphasized the need to seek out and punish the "highly contagious" casual user who "is likely still to 'enjoy' his drug for the pleasure it offers" (Bennett, 1989:11).

Until now, government hegemony over societal conceptions of drug problems has generated media and public support for increasingly punitive policies to combat the "drug menace" (Giordano, 1990; Morley, 1989; Reinarman and Levine, 1989). Opposition to the "united front" necessitated by the demands of "war" is seen as tantamount to desertion.[1]

Unfortunately, like the media, researchers and other professionals in the drug field are not immune from governmental pressure (Brecher, 1972; Trebach, 1987; Zinberg and Robertson, 1972). Psychiatrist Norman Zinberg (1984) described the obstacles facing researchers well before the arrival of Bennett and the intransigent dictates of the current drug war:

It is understandable that government agencies, already overwhelmed by the number of factors that must be considered before reaching a decision, and buttressed by the righteous sense that what they are doing is for the public good, would want to protect society from the confusion that might be engendered if still more controversial information were made public. In principle, a bureaucracy wants to get all the information possible, but once it has settled on a course or a value position, it believes that new information raising further doubts may lead to greater risks and therefore should be kept quiet. As our cultural belief in the disinterested scientist wanes and our disillusion with the omnipotent court decision as a righter of wrongs grows, bureaucratic paternalism becomes the obvious alternative. But unfortunately, when the governmental acceptance of responsibility for a decision shifts to the assumption that the belief that supports a decision (illicit drug use is bad) is more important than the decision itself, there is bound to be difficulty in achieving a flexible social policy. This is exactly what has happened to the policy on illicit drugs. (1984:202)

Public health considerations are all too often neglected in favor of social control concerns. In addition, an uninformed or misinformed public presents little challenge to governmental hegemony. Among other problematic connotations, the dictum of "just say no" increasingly pressures the media and other public educators to disregard mentioning anything that might be construed as positive about illicit substances. As a result, perhaps the most alarming casualty of the drug war has been the dissemination of objective information on the subject. (Riedlinger and Riedlinger, 1989)[2].

As a result of government pressure over the past decade, "responsible use" or "objective information" approaches have all but disappeared from the prevention field at most levels in the United States. Catalyzed by the AIDS epidemic, however, harm reduction strategies have become increasingly accepted in certain areas as programs and governments recognize the futility of "zero tolerance." The Dutch and Australians have established successful drug policy frameworks guided by harm reduction logic. In Great Britain, the influential Advisory Council on the Misuse of Drugs (ACMD) concluded that the potential spread of AIDS posed a much greater threat to both individuals and society than injection drug use itself.

By now, programs in other countries have increasingly extended such efforts to noninjecting populations of drug users. Unfortunately, America lags far behind in accepting the value of such harm reduction strategies. This is amply evidenced by governmental opposition to needle exchange programs. Although such efforts have been successful in combatting the spread of AIDS without increasing the number of intravenous drugs users, such programs, for the most part, remain illegal.

Outlining the goals of the Council on Illicit Drug Policy (affiliated with the National Association for Public Health Policy), University of California, Berkeley Professor Patricia Morgan contends that we must resist and offer alternatives to the coercive policies which now frame the approach to illicit drug use. Coercive policies operate to ensure that premises are not questioned and that deviations are punished accordingly. They rely on proscriptive norms, negative exhortations from above, rather than the promotion of positive internal values found in prescriptive norms. We should develop a normative response which revives, supports and enhances indigenous cultural customs for regulating drug use in general. (Morgan, 1991:1)

Harm Reduction for MDMA Users

Harm reduction efforts for those who use Ecstasy should be centered on education and improvement of contexts in which MDMA is used. In our discussion of such efforts, we look at Raves, the predominant Ecstasy scene in the United States today, as well as others in which people use MDMA more quietly.

The Rave scene has come to America in full force. The problematic nature of Ecstasy and other drug use within these contexts strongly suggests that this should be a primary focus for harm reduction efforts. The appropriate development and implementation of such strategies possess great potential for educating this young population and improving Rave environments.

The British response to Raves illustrates the best and worst ways of dealing with the scene. In forcing Raves to go underground through increasingly restrictive legislation, British authorities only served to exacerbate many of the problems associated with such contexts. As in Britain, there is an urgency in promoting harm reduction responses before an eventual tragedy catalyzes an overreaction by authorities. Fortunately, we have the examples provided by a number of enlightened British programs to help in developing and implementing approaches appropriate to the American Rave scene.

In contrast to MDMA users from social worlds commonly found in our study (such as professionals and New Agers), the youthful participants in the British Rave scene are often seriously uninformed and misinformed about Ecstasy and other drugs. Consequently, many are unaware of the potential risks associated with these substances and how to minimize them. Overuse ("stacking") and polydrug use are often done for the purpose of fueling marathon bouts of high-energy dancing by young people who feel invulnerable to problematic consequences such as dehydration and overexertion. Other contextual factors also contribute to problematic consequences. These include unfamiliar dealers selling suspect drugs; hot, poorly ventilated settings; alcohol promotion and the lack of readily available alternative beverages (including water) needed to combat dehydration. Much can and needs to be done to both educate users and work on altering environmental factors within the Rave scene that contribute to problematic consequences.

Recognizing this need and espousing a harm reduction philosophy, a number of British programs are striving to educate users and improve Rave environments. From his ongoing study of this scene, Russell Newcombe argues that "use of 'dance drugs' (or 'club drugs') has to be understood within the context of the 'rave' subculture" (Newcombe, 1992:14). He goes on to suggest appropriate strategies which take this into account:

> Trained outreach workers should be employed to offer advice and help at rave clubs and parties. The model of aggressive health promotion piloted by outreach workers in the field of HIV prevention among injectors can usefully be applied in the dance drugs scene, and has precedents in clubs in Liverpool, Manchester and Amsterdam. . . . Information of the kind discussed above could be provided on-site at entry points and inside clubs. Outreach workers can also directly intervene in drug-related problems, for example by counseling people experiencing unpleasant effects, giving first aid, and making referrals to helping agencies if appropriate. . . . Club based outreach teams could also provide free condoms to ravers, as is done by community outreach workers. Outreach teams could usefully have an office-base in large clubs, so that people seeking advice or help can make direct approaches, and to provide a quiet room for advice and counseling. Such projects could be partly or wholly funded by club owners and party organizers as a token of their wider responsibilities towards their customers. (Newcombe, 1992:16)

Recognizing the need to insure responsible management by club owners and staff, the Manchester City Council recently passed new laws regulating Rave clubs. Such clubs are now required to provide free water and a "cool" room.

Since 1990, The Lifeline Project in Manchester, England has been producing a wide range of informational materials which strive to both educate and entertain youthful Ravers. Building on their successful experience in reaching drug injectors with their "Smack in the Eye" adult comic series, they have now created the character "Peanut Pete" to convey safety tips to recreational users of "party drugs" (see Appendix G). Director Mark Gilman explains how Lifeline has responded to the demands of the Rave scene:

> Young ravers regularly engage in extensive use of powerful hallu-cinogenic and stimulant drugs. This is requiring our staff to become proficient in recognizing and assessing symptoms of mental health disorders that may or may not be drug-induced . . . dealing with bad trips, giving advice on how to avoid them, and how to reduce them are once again becoming bread and butter issues for drugs workers in the '90s. . . . Ongoing monitoring/ research allows us to record and respond to these needs. For example, the second Peanut Pete leaflet dealt specifically with drug-induced paranoia and we are currently responding to all the attendant physical problems of frequent stimulant use such as weight loss and depression. (Gilman, 1991:18)

In the same spirit of harm reduction, the Mersey Drug Training and Information Centre in Liverpool has designed "Chill Out: A Raver's Guide." Widely regarded for their innovative and comprehensive work with drug injectors, they have now targeted this new audience of clubgoers with a series of leaflets and calling cards. Focusing on "those already committed to using these drugs," the authors had the following goals:

> to provide basic information on the effects of the drugs; to enable clubgoers to identify potential problems and help them deal with them effectively; to alert them to the hazards of the set and setting in which the drug may be used; to establish standards for 'safer' drug use within the subculture; to give those experiencing problems a contact point for further information from a source they can trust. (McDermott, Matthews, and Bennett, 1992:12)

Unfortunately, comparable programs in the United States have all too often become casualties of the protracted drug war. Nonetheless, we also have a growing Rave scene replete with young enthusiasts whose "just say no" education provides little help when they decide to say yes instead. Since they lack the "flight guides" and information provided by the social worlds of more educated or experienced populations, we need to develop strategies for reaching this population. Ravers contacting the government for information about MDMA are likely to be disappointed when they read the obviously misleading and uninformative two-page pamphlet originally produced for the administrative law hearings in 1985 (see Appendix E).

Throughout this book, we have strived to delineate the significant roles played by MDMA social worlds and scenes in shaping attitudes, patterns of use, and overall experiences of our respondents. Within each of these social worlds, bodies of "user folklore" have evolved, instructing individuals as to appropriate and inappropriate use, overall expectations, and potential benefits and harms associated with the MDMA experience. Well-planned educational efforts should strive to build on this accepted folk knowledge. As Reinarman and Levine contend: "We must take more seriously the ways in which most users of most substances most of the time have developed self-regulatory strategies which work to minimize risk and abuse. Such informal social controls have always done more to reduce the harm of drug use than repressive laws" (1989:17).

Many researchers have arrived at similar conclusions in describing the variety of social controls which drug users and subcultures utilize in attempting to both maximize benefits and minimize problems (Fagan and Chin, 1991; Grob and Dobkin de Rios, 1992; Weil, 1972; Zinberg, 1984). In a prescient article written over a quarter of a century ago, sociologist Howard Becker provided perhaps the best illustration of the importance of an informed user subculture (Becker, 1967). He described how a continually evolving folklore educates psychedelic users just as it does for other drugs. Within this framework, individuals are increasingly able to identify and create a safe context favorable to their intentions. Writing in 1967, Becker predicted that the incidence of "bad trips" with LSD would decline as a result of evolving social rules and controls among LSD-using populations. As with the popularization of other substances, Becker described the appearance of a growing consensus among LSD users regarding appropriate set, settings, and expectations regarding LSD:

> Individuals accumulate experience with the drug and communicate their experiences to one another. Consensus develops about the drug's subjective effects, their duration, proper dosages, predictable dangers and how they may be avoided; all these points

become matters of common knowledge, validated by their acceptance in a world of users. (1967:171)

Becker argued that the initial availability of LSD was met with uncertainty about its effects. Sensationalistic media and government accounts repeatedly recounted horror stories about LSD before user social worlds had adequately evolved. Comparing these developments to that of cannabis in the late 1920s, Becker hypothesized that the increase in psychoses associated with marijuana use at that time was largely a product of secondary anxiety generated by unfamiliarity with the drug's effects and sparked by media hysteria.

LSD users in the mid-1960s lacked a well-developed subculture to adequately inform them. Consequently, as previously happened with marijuana, Becker argued that "psychotic episodes occur frequently" when there is "no authoritative alternative with which to counter the possible definition, when and if it comes to mind, of the drug experience as madness" (1967:171).

As with marijuana, Becker predicted that the inevitable development of psychedelic subcultures would minimize adverse reactions and redefine the drug experience as positive (as opposed to "going crazy"). The cultural assimilation of a new substance often changes user experiences as a result of altered expectations. As Becker argues in a later article,

> when a person ingests a drug his subsequent experience is influenced by his ideas and beliefs about the drug. What he knows about the drug influences the way he uses it, the way he interprets its manifold effects and responds to them, and the way he deals with the sequelae of the experience. Conversely, what he does not know affects his experience too, making certain interpretations impossible, as well as actions based on that missing knowledge. (1974:67)

Evolving psychedelic subcultures played a significant role in informing user experiences and perceived problems as well as shaping overall patterns of use. Zinberg explains how

> control over the use of psychedelics was not established until the counter-culture developed social sanctions and rituals like those surrounding alcohol use in the society at large. . . . The specific rituals that developed to express these sanctions—just when it was best to take the drug, how it should be used, with whom, what was the best way to come down, and so on—var-

ied from group to group, though some rituals spread between groups. (1984:14)

The ongoing American experiment involving Grateful Dead concerts is particularly instructive in surveying the emergent Rave scene. Both the ubiquity and relative safety of psychedelic drug use at Dead shows were noted by Newmeyer and Johnson (1979) in their review of rock concerts in the mid-1970s. They concluded that for those within this environment

> acid-tripping with the Grateful Dead may be an occasional weekend diversion in the time-honored tradition equivalent to tailgate, whiskey-lubricated parties at football games, or six-packs and hot dogs at baseball games. Such public drug use may correspond to what Harding and Zinberg (1977) have identified as rituals of controlled drug use, involving social sanctions which structure and limit the experience. (Newmeyer and Johnson, 1979:236)

Recently, many communities have cracked down on drug use and other problems at such concerts, often with tragic, violent consequences (Goodman, 1990). Although many of these cities have subsequently banished the Dead, the subterranean nature of Raves suggests that such efforts will only serve to exacerbate many of the health problems associated with drug use. When a scene goes underground, its members are more difficult to reach for educational purposes and crisis intervention. Consequently, it is important to examine the well-organized Grateful Dead and other concerts produced by the late Bill Graham's organization, Bill Graham Presents, Inc. According to Newmeyer and Johnson (1979), there have been surprisingly few casualties despite considerable psychedelic use at such concerts. This testifies to the essential contribution of good management and ancillary services such as Haight Ashbury's Rock Medicine, which is funded by Graham's organization.

Ravers are not the only group of Ecstasy users who could benefit from education and improvement of context. The early "flight guides" (see Appendix F) were a good start, as indicated by the lack of problematic reactions (such as panic attacks) seen among those in our study who had used them and/or actively sought "harm reduction" information prior to taking MDMA. Such information, though difficult to disseminate because of the illegal status of Ecstasy, would be useful in decreasing negative effects and aftereffects.

Research on Prevalence, Patterns, and Problems

Incidence and prevalence research should play a vital role in developing appropriate harm reduction strategies. In assessing the significance of toxicological findings, we need to gain an ethnographic understanding of user populations. In addition, we need a better assessment of actual numbers of users in order to predict the likelihood of problems or risk associated with MDMA use. Our current figures based on government seizures are grossly inaccurate. Unfortunately, continued reliance on estimates of use based on speculation frustrates an adequate assessment of the overall extent of MDMA use. Similarly, little is known about potentially significant patterns and trends among different populations.

This lack of valid data has a number of public health implications. Assuming that a particular physiological or psychological problem were associated with MDMA use, the overall significance and societal implications of such a finding would largely depend on a number of epidemiological factors of which we currently know little or nothing. For example, let us imagine that research establishes that MDMA does indeed cause some form of potentially harmful neurotoxicity, but only in cases involving high-dosage or binge use, as opposed to the more common pattern of infrequent ingestion of low to moderate doses. Good data would prove invaluable in providing some idea of the general prevalence of binge use among particular groups. As a result, appropriate health warnings or interventions could be quickly directed at target populations at risk.

The quality and quantity of MDMA taken by a user can have profound effects on his or her experience. Ecstasy generally comes to the consumer as a white or off-white powder or premeasured tablet. The user has no way of knowing whether the substance is actually MDMA, its level of purity, if it's adulterated, and the dose level. This lack of clarity opens the door for overconsumption and/or ingestion of unknown material, both having the potential to lead to significant health problems. Consequently, it is essential that street drug analysis (such as the now-defunct PharmChem Service) be revived and publicized in an effort to combat the dangers posed by the lack of any quality control. As with many other harm reduction strategies, we can learn much from the Dutch (Korf, Blanken, and Nabben, 1991). Of particular interest are recent outreach efforts that conduct on-site analysis of alleged Ecstasy and other "Dance Drugs" at the Raves themselves (Fromberg, 1993).

We need to know more about who uses MDMA. The recency of its popularization must also be taken into account in attempting to understand its spread to new populations and contexts. Since MDMA use has been occurring for less than two decades, we simply have not had time to perform adequate assessments of its diffusion patterns or abuse potential. But since it *is* so new, we are in the unique position of being able to "chart" such patterns almost from the beginning. As Kaplan and colleagues conclude from their analysis of the Dutch "Acid House" scene: "MDMA provides a case where more attention is needed on the characteristics of cultural networks and transmission of information in defining both risk groups and true abuse potentials" (Kaplan et al., 1989:9).

In addition to assessing the reliability of our own findings regarding MDMA's potential for abuse, research is urgently needed on patterns and problems associated with the Rave scene both here and abroad. Continued naturalistic research is necessary to determine the impact of MDMA's spread to potentially higher-risk populations and contexts. Although qualitative research often lays the groundwork for more quantitative studies of etiology and epidemiology, we think it is essential to avoid overreliance on such efforts. Attempts to obtain representative samples and meaningful data will continue to be hampered by intractable problems related to MDMA's illegality and relatively small (compared with that of other illicit drugs) user population. In addition to these difficulties, it is important to realize that well-constructed naturalistic studies often provide the most comprehensive and valid way of understanding illicit-drug-using populations. The findings derived from such research are often invaluable in developing and implementing promising harm reduction strategies.

Research on MDMA's Therapeutic Potential

Most of our respondents strongly believed in the therapeutic potential of MDMA. Even recreationally oriented users, though rarely taking Ecstasy for such purposes, felt that MDMA's properties could make it a useful adjunct in helping others. Many of their perceptions were similar to those of various therapists (Adamson and Metzner, 1988; Downing, 1985; Grinspoon, 1985; Greer and

Tolbert, 1986, 1990; Lynch, 1985; Wolfson, 1986). Testimony at the administrative hearings provided compelling arguments for MDMA's therapeutic promise (Young, 1986). One prominent government witness argued that formal, well-controlled studies be conducted to assess what he viewed as a potentially valuable compound for psychotherapy (Docherty, 1985a). The World Health Organization (WHO) Expert Committee on Drug Dependence urged nations to "facilitate research on this interesting substance" (WHO, 1985:8). Psychiatrist George Greer, acknowledging the necessity for such research, expressed confidence in favorable outcomes: "Because every therapist I know who has given MDMA to a patient has found it to be of significant value, I am convinced that it can be shown scientifically to be efficacious" (1985:6).

Support for Greer's contention comes from psychologist Deborah Harlow's in-depth interviews with twenty therapists whose combined experience with MDMA-assisted psychotherapy totaled over eight thousand sessions. The fifteen American therapists who had used MDMA before its criminalization and the five Swiss psychiatrists currently permitted to use MDMA generally concurred on its unique value as a therapeutic adjunct for a number of conditions (Harlow and Beck, 1990).

Obstacles to Research   Assuming that MDMA does possess both significant therapeutic value and relative safety at prescribed doses, what would it take to convince the FDA of its *efficacy* and *safety* for research on human subjects? An adequate answer must address the formidable legal, economic, scientific, and moral obstacles which confront such an assessment. One must look at the roles played by particular branches of government (DEA and FDA) and medicine (psychiatry and the pharmaceutical industry) in inhibiting research with MDMA.

Our findings clearly suggest the need to reexamine the criteria for scheduling various drugs, particularly those substances with potential value for insight enhancement. The MDMA hearings called into question many of the basic precepts underlying the Controlled Substances Act. The DEA administrative law judge himself was frustrated by the limitations of the five available schedules and the vagaries of the criteria used to place drugs in them.[3]

Unfortunately, governmental response toward substances such as MDMA, and the way they are scheduled, continue to be dominated by uncompromising social control concerns. The rigid-ity of this approach comes at the expense of therapeutic and/or public health considerations. Smith, Wesson, and Buffum echo the concerns expressed by many of the respondents in our study:

> Moving a drug to Schedule I does not stop illicit availability. The whole notion of controlled drugs is a misnomer. Nothing is so out of control as those drugs the DEA and FDA have appropriated to Schedule I. Moving a drug to Schedule I does, however, have consequences. Price generally increases, the quality control of licit manufacture is destroyed, and responsible research becomes almost impossible. MDMA, a drug with low abuse potential and possible therapeutic use, is the latest victim of our misguided drug control policies. (1985:3).

Ultimately, Rick Seymour contends that "what is being called into question is not just the control of one drug that may or may not have a high abuse potential. The core issue is one of scientific inquiry and medical progress and how these are to be balanced against public safety and integrity" (1986:102).

Researchers currently find themselves thwarted by the inability of accepted scientific methodology to adequately assess substances employed for insight enhancement. For example, although numerous studies strongly suggested LSD's therapeutic value, the inability of such research to conclusively demonstrate efficacy contributed to its placement into Schedule I (Grinspoon and Bakalar, 1979; Neill, 1987; Yensen, 1985). Considerable skepticism over the therapeutic efficacy of psychedelic drugs arises in part from the empirical difficulties that plague any attempt at conducting well-controlled, double-blind studies with insight-oriented techniques (Bakalar and Grinspoon, 1990; Seymour, Wesson, and Smith, 1986). As psychiatrist Sidney Cohen succinctly pointed out with regard to LSD research: "No method of using LSD therapeutically has as yet met rigid scientific requirements, . . . but, in truth, no other type of psychotherapy has been fully tested by these exacting methods either" (1965:71).

The large pharmaceutical houses play an important role in the determination of which drugs will or will not be investigated. Psychiatrist Lester Grinspoon asserts that the current system "is not set up to magnify the scientific and intellectual interest in the drug. It's set up for the drug companies, and the purpose is profit" (quoted in *Psychiatric News*, 1992). Such companies have no interest in MDMA, since it was already patented in 1914, putting it in the "public domain." This means that *any* company could produce and market it for approved conditions. But in order to obtain FDA approval for marketing, a pharmaceutical company would have to invest millions of dollars in research. Why should a company do so, when any *other* firm could also market it with minimal investment (Doblin, 1988)?

An additional problem inhibiting pharmaceutical interest is the probable lack of profit associated with the marketing of MDMA or similar substances employed as adjuncts to psychotherapy. Since patients are usually prescribed only a few doses, profits would be minimal compared with those garnered from currently prescribed psychotropic medications (such as tranquilizers or antidepressants) that are often intended for use on a daily basis.[4]

In general, psychiatry is limited by the lack of accepted pharmaceutical options in treating the gamut of mental problems. Most medications are pharmacological depressants prescribed primarily for symptomatic relief. Nichols decries this lack of choice, declaring that "it is a harsh reality indeed that tells patients with emotional pain to suffer quietly, that they will not be helped except with drugs that dull the mind" (1987:35).

Neurotoxicity Concerns   Since the DEA administrative law hearings, MDMA research has centered primarily on various *animal* studies conducted to assess concerns about potential neurotoxicity. There is now a considerable body of animal research associating MDMA with varied degrees of serotonin nerve terminal degeneration in particular areas of the brain (Battaglia, Zaczek, and De Souza, 1990; McKenna and Peroutka, 1990; Ricaurte et al., 1988; Schmidt, 1987). The significance of this apparent neurotoxicity, however, continues to remain unknown. Also uncertain is whether it occurs (and at what dosage levels) in humans and, if so, whether it is permanent or transient in nature.

Manifestations of serotonergic neurotoxicity have yet to be clearly identified among *human* MDMA users (Fitzgerald, 1991; Grob et al., 1992). Nevertheless, disorders or problems associated with other neurotoxic substances (such as MPTP) have not always been immediately apparent in users (Barnes, 1988; Peroutka, 1990a). As Dr. Charles Schuster, co-author of the original MDA neurotoxicity study (and former director of the National Institute on Drug Abuse) cautions: "What we don't know is whether twenty or thirty years from now, at the age of 45, they [MDMA users] may begin to be showing central nervous system degenerative signs that ordinarily would not be seen until they get to be 70 or 80" (quoted in Associated Press, 1986).

The government's well-publicized concern about MDMA's neurotoxic dangers has been amply reflected in popular media accounts. Reminiscent of LSD horror stories twenty years before, articles with predictable headings such as "The Agony of Ecstasy" or "Ecstasy to Agony" convey fears of MDMA-induced brain damage (cf. Gertz, 1985; Rae, 1989; Roberts, 1986).

Describing the increasing popularity of "MDMA, the most fashionable of a crop of synthetic 'designer' drugs," in New York nightclubs, a *Mademoiselle* exposé ominously states that it may already be too late for many enthusiasts of the Acid House scene. Noting the nostalgia for the sixties among those too young to remember the antidrug lessons learned from that era, the author concludes that "Acid House may be the latest trend, but as Ecstasy spreads across the country, one can only hope that its users remember what previous generations of drug users have learned the hard way: Trends come and go, but brain damage is forever" (Rae, 1989:210).

The government's vocal fears of MDMA stand in sharp contrast to its silence regarding the prescription drug fenfluramine (Pondimin®). This diet medication has been found by Schuster and others to produce serotonergic changes similar to those of MDMA at dosages only slightly above the usual prescribed dose (Johanson, 1985; Kleven, Schuster, and Seiden, 1988; Molliver and Molliver, 1988; Schuster, Lewis, and Seiden, 1986; Wagner and Peroutka, 1988). Noting the government's expressed fears about MDMA's neurotoxicity, the DEA administrative law judge stated in his findings that

> the drug fenfluramine has been determined to produce the biochemical effects in rats of which MDMA is suspected, but at much lower dosage levels than in the case of MDMA. In fact, the proven dosage levels of fenfluramine causing these effects are merely 1.25 times its ED50 when used for anorexia in humans. Nonetheless, the FDA has approved the daily use of fenfluramine in humans on a chronic basis. (Young, 1986:47)

The 1992 *Physician's Desk Reference* (PDR) reveals that fenfluramine remains in Schedule IV. Most surprising, however, is the continued absence of any mention of neurotoxicity research alerting physicians and other readers to this putative risk *(Physician's Desk Reference, 1992)*. Clearly, the scheduling of many psychoactive drugs has more to do with politics than toxicity concerns.

Fear of Ecstasy   The LSD controversy in the 1960s not only resulted in a pervasive image of psychedelics as frightening substances but also redefined any therapeutic claims as illusory. As a result, much of the medical community increasingly distanced themselves from LSD. The psychiatric profession's increasing closeness to the government at that time made it particularly vulnerable to political pressure (Neill, 1987). The transformation of both public and medical conceptions of LSD resulted in the collapse of once-thriving investigations into its therapeutic potential.

A fear of psychedelic substances continues to permeate both social and medical opinion (Bakalar and Grinspoon, 1990). However, even without its reputation as a psychedelic, MDMA's nickname of "Ecstasy," together with its popularization in the midst of the current drug war, certainly contributed to the government's posture concerning therapeutic use or even research. The government has been reluctant to allow any research into the therapeutic use of Schedule I substances out of apparent fear that such permission would somehow "send the wrong message" or "condone" nonmedical use as well. This has several implications. Psychopharmacologist David Nichols contends that

> as a result of this government-induced stagnation in the field of drug-assisted psychotherapy research, psychiatry has not been offered various types of novel psychoactive drugs to assess what their value might be to medicine. . . . The very nature of the organization of the FDA precludes it from taking any kind of risk—theoretical or actual. Yet risk is an essential part of drug discovery. The paternalistic idea has developed that consumers must be protected from any risk, of any kind, from the cradle to the grave. (1987:36)

Positive Developments in Therapeutic Research   Much can be learned from research in Switzerland, which in June of 1988 became the first country in the world to permit psychiatrists to use MDMA and other insight-enhancing substances in therapy. Currently, five psychiatrists are allowed to use MDMA, LSD, and psilocybin at their discretion in psychotherapy. Each strongly believes that MDMA can provide a "breakthrough" in the psychotherapeutic process, allowing them to reach some patients not helped by other means (Harlow and Beck, 1990; Widmer, 1992). As one Swiss psychiatrist confidently asserted:

> The process which now goes on in Switzerland with LSD and other such drugs in psychotherapy will serve the governments in other countries as a model when they see that this has worked in Switzerland for several years. They will lose their anxiety about giving licenses themselves. (Zanger interview with Baumann, 1989: 10)

Undaunted by impediments to American therapeutic research, psychedelic researcher Rick Doblin formed the Multidisciplinary Association for Psychedelic Studies (MAPS) in 1986 to generate support and financing to investigate therapeutic efficacy and safety. Doblin explained how

> in a very real sense, MAPS would like to act as a non-profit people's pharmaceutical company, whose goal is to bring MDMA into the medical pharmacopoeia. This focus on MDMA does not mean that MDMA is the "best" psychedelic drug, simply that it is extremely remarkable, unique, relatively easy to work with, and likely to become an extremely valuable psychotherapeutic tool. (Doblin, 1990:4)

For the first time in fourteen years, in the summer of 1992 the National Institute on Drug Abuse (NIDA) convened a technical review on "hallucinogens." This was immediately followed by a meeting of the FDA's Drug Abuse Advisory Committee. The FDA committee reviewed general policies regarding "hallucinogenic" research and specific issues concerning the MDMA research protocol. The consensus of the experts at these two meetings was that there were significant scientific benefits to be gained by administering psychedelics to human subjects in order to research the brain's basic physiological mechanisms and their psychological correlates. Most important, the experts believed that these scientific benefits outweighed the estimated risks to subjects and society from conducting the research (Doblin, 1992; Pekkanen, 1992; Yensen, 1992). This sentiment was reflected in an advisory paper submitted to the FDA by Harvard professor Mark Kleiman. From his review of current data, he concluded that "one would have to rank MDMA quite low on the list of potential drug problems. This suggests that great weight should not be given to drug abuse-control considerations in deciding whether to proceed with research or clinical use" (Kleiman, 1992:8).[5]

As a result of the NIDA and FDA meetings, many of the constraints impeding human research with psychedelic drugs have been lifted (Doblin, 1992; Pekkanen, 1992; Yensen, 1992). In particular, the Drug Abuse Advisory Committee recommended that the FDA assist Dr. Charles Grob and colleagues at the University of California, Irvine, in designing two studies. The first is a safety and tolerance study to determine the psychological and analgesic threshold level for MDMA. Toxicity concerns will also be addressed by providing MDMA to a group of healthy subjects—psychiatrists informed of potential risks (Doblin, 1992). It is anticipated that what is learned will help in preparing and gaining approval for subsequent research. The second study will assess the safety and efficacy of MDMA-assisted psychotherapy in reducing the pain and distress of patients suffering from end-stage pancreatic cancer (Doblin, 1992; Grob et al., 1991).

FINAL REMARKS

Media accounts and professionals in the drug field have often dismissed MDMA as a short-term fad. Such observations may seem sound considering significant reduction in the use of most illicit drugs in the 1980s, particularly among those groups commonly associated with MDMA use. However, there are a number of enduring reasons for MDMA's continued popularity among respondents in our study.

We believe the therapeutic and euphoric qualities ascribed to MDMA, combined with the relative ease of the experience, will continue to attract new users in spite of the current antidrug climate. However, the implementation of harm reduction strategies, to help ensure its safer use, and investigation of MDMA's therapeutic potential will depend largely upon revamping the governmental policies that continue to stymie such efforts.

We still have much to learn about MDMA and its users. The direction of further sociological inquiry should bear in mind Norman Zinberg's closing remarks in his seminal work *Drug, Set and Setting*:

> Certainly, if our understanding of drug use is to improve, we must obtain more information about the social context of use, including a knowledge of how group customs and norms operate to shape different styles of use, how these customs (controls)

arise, and how new users acquire them. Further research can discover ways to strengthen these informal social controls (sanctions and rituals) that encourage abstinence, promote safer use, and discourage misuse.

A final caveat. Throughout the duration of my project my subjects continued to make one point clear: at certain times, if not during the whole of their using careers, they experienced benefits from their intoxicant use and from different patterns of use. Thus, despite the reigning cultural morality, future studies of intoxicant use should take into account not only the liabilities but also the benefits of drug use itself and also of the differing patterns of use. (1984:217)

Our respondents' accounts of what they valued in MDMA contained a message, tacit but telling, about the nature of modern society. It mattered little which social world they were part of when introduced to MDMA. The therapeutic types, the dancers, and the professionals on the beach described the benefits of MDMA in similar terms. Regardless of how calloused or flippant they might have been at the outset, they shared in common an experience of Ecstasy as total acceptance (others of them, themselves of others), tolerance, and love as fears and defenses melted away. These were feelings derived from few other settings. Since our respondents generally had considerable life options, this Ecstasy-filled void is particularly revealing. In the modern developed world there is a genuine paucity of "time-outs" from the stresses of work, family, and urban life. There is too little love and too much intolerance.

Despite the diversity of social worlds, respondents shared a common vocabulary of positive effects that were seen by many as almost inherent attributes of the MDMA experience. However, the relative value placed on such feelings often differed in a manner consistent with user motivations and contexts. For example, respondents frequently described the common and highly desired experience of "bonding" while on Ecstasy. Along with the few who reported bonding with themselves, the feeling of bonding with others ranged from couples or small groups of intimate friends to ravers and deadheads trance-dancing with several thousand "intimate strangers." As with other facets of the MDMA experience, to understand the meaning of bonding requires a deep appreciation of drug, set, and setting.

A primary interest guiding our research in the "Exploring

Ecstasy" study was to examine the influential roles played by contextual factors in creating the varieties of the MDMA experience. Minimal availability and publicity about MDMA in most parts of the country continue to ensure that both interest and access to Ecstasy are largely determined by the company one keeps. User social world(s) are extremely influential in shaping expectations, motivations, and interpretations of MDMA as therapeutic tool, spiritual guide, or good-time high.

Our responents left us with a healthy respect for the multiplicity of interactive factors that shape their MDMA experiences. Much more needs to be learned about the potential problems and therapeutic promise of this unique substance. In assessing the MDMA phenomenon, researchers need to be observant of the interactive and ever-changing nature of various pharmacological, psychological, and sociological factors. The continual challenge is one of making sense of this dynamic interplay which exists among drug, set, and setting.

Appendixes

APPENDIX A
THEORY AND METHODOLOGY

THEORETICAL PERSPECTIVES

From the beginning, our research was guided by the premise that, in order to comprehend individual experience, one must understand the actor's perspective (Becker, 1970; Geertz, 1973; Schutz, 1967). We subscribed to the theoretical perspectives of phenomenology and symbolic interactionism (Mead, 1939; Blumer, 1969). The philosophy of phenomenology maintains that the individual's perspective about his or her social world is central. Therefore, the definitions, meanings, and categories used by actors themselves are important factors in structuring their activities.

Phenomenological approaches attempt to avoid preconceived assumptions and thus tend to elicit responses that are meaningful to the subject and helpful in understanding his or her contextual environment. As sociologist John Lofland notes:

> The commitment to get close, to be factual, descriptive and quotive, constitutes a significant commitment to represent the participants in their own terms. . . . A major methodological consequence of these commitments is that the qualitative study of people in situ is a process of discovery. It is of necessity a process of learning what is happening. Since a major part of what is happening is provided by people in their own terms, one must find out about those terms rather than impose upon them a preconceived or outsider's scheme of what they are about. (1971:4)

A theoretical framework of symbolic interactionism maintains that humans interact with their environment and other individuals through symbolic means such as language. According to Blumer (1969), three primary principles form the basis of symbolic interactionist thought: (1) people act on the basis of the *meaning* that things have for them; (2) this meaning grows out of *interaction* with others—especially intimate others; and (3) this meaning is continually modified by *interpretation*. From the symbolic inter-actionist point of view, then, people are not simply "products" of their upbringing or environment, but arrive at what they think, feel, and do through dynamic and creative processes. Meanings are conferred upon social events by interacting individuals, who must first interpret what is going on from the social context in which these events occur. Consequently, the effectiveness of vari-ous "sociology of the inside" approaches largely depends on their ability to gain reliable access to the actor's point of view.

METHODOLOGICAL APPROACHES

The "Exploring Ecstasy" study was the first federally funded soci-ological examination of MDMA users. The paucity of epidemio-logical data on MDMA use necessitated a "discovery" phase of research rather than traditional hypothesis testing (Sellitz, 1961). The study primarily relied on qualitative methodologies widely regarded as essential in explorations of poorly understood phe-nomena. Before one can properly study the etiology of drug use, McBride and Clayton claim that "there is no substitute for begin-ning with the subject and his or her context of development and behavior. Such an approach must be open, without the imposition of preconceived etiological cause, but rather allowing the etiolog-ical variables to emerge from intense observation" (1985:526).

Grounded Theory

In deciding how to best carry out this study, we were guided by both the little-known nature of the phenomenon and a commit-ment to understanding the user's perspective. We relied primarily on a "grounded theory" methodology operating within a symbolic interactionist framework. This combination is not unusual. As with symbolic interactionism, Mullen explains that "the general perspective adopted for purposes of a grounded theory study looks to the person's social and interpersonal context and to the meaning he or she attributes to a given situation" (1985–1986:182).

Grounded theory is centered on the "discovery" of theory from data systematically obtained from social research. To accomplish this task, this approach offers a rigorous, orderly guide to theory development that at each stage is closely integrated with particular methods of analysis. In this way, ongoing data analysis allows the basic social, psychological, and structural processes to emerge naturally (Glaser and Strauss, 1967).

In the initial phases of data collection, the researcher begins with a few preconceived ideas about the phenomenon under study. The research proceeds by exploring these "hunches," and through this examination, other areas emerge which had not been initially apparent, and they are pursued. Basically, the researcher discovers a social or social-psychological process in the data and seeks to understand it by examining if and how it occurs in different settings and among different actors. Glaser and Strauss (1967) refer to this as the "constant comparative method."

The next process in the analysis is "theoretical sampling," in which one tests emergent ideas or hunches on different sociodemographic groups. Theoretical sampling is possible because data collection and analysis occur simultaneously; data are not analyzed only after they are all collected. Several studies have demonstrated the efficacy of this process of concurrent data collection and analysis in understanding little-known illicit-drug-using populations (cf. Rosenbaum, 1981; Waldorf et al., 1989, 1991).

Glaser and Strauss (1967) argue that the inductively developed theory of their approach offers many advantages over more common "logico-deductive" strategies. Generating theory and conducting social research are seen as two parts of the same process. In this manner, the full continuum of processes underlying the generation of theory and research are all guided and integrated by the emerging theory.

Grounded theory stands in sharp contrast to most methodological approaches, which ostensibly seek to verify preexisting theories or hypotheses. A major problem with such preconceived hypothesis testing is that data which cannot be forced into a questionnaire or selectively picked are often discarded. To overcome this narrow focus, grounded theory places a high emphasis on theory as process. The theory is viewed as an ever-developing entity determined by the emerging data, rather than a finished product (Glaser and Strauss, 1967).

Glaser (1978) argues that a major problem with sociological research is that it commonly attempts to apply preconceived formal theories to a substantive area, thus supplying almost all of the necessary concepts and hypotheses. As a result, data are often forced into preconceived categories, and relevant concepts and hypotheses that might emerge are neglected. Grounded theory, on the other hand, allows substantive theories to emerge from the data. Such an approach is particularly well suited for researching poorly understood phenomena such as MDMA use.

Ethnographic and Other Observational Methodologies

In our "Exploring Ecstasy" study we utilized various types of observational fieldwork to better understand differing patterns and perspectives among various MDMA-using populations. In general, ethnographic approaches involve studying a group from within, attempting through field observation to record how individuals "perceive, construct, and interact within their social and economic environments" (James, 1977:180).

Observational research works from the premise that there are a variety of interpretations of any phenomenon which must be learned in the field rather than assumed in the office. Such approaches allow assumptions to be checked out against actual user interpretations as they are learned from the users themselves. Rather than seeking "objective data" in attempting to explain etiology, ethnography emphasizes interpretation.

Many studies have found the assumptions of professionals and researchers to be quite different from those of users themselves (Agar, 1985; Weppner, 1977). Such findings often have profound implications for both understanding and successfully addressing various drug problems. This is prominently illustrated in the many ethnographic studies which challenged long-standing addict stereotypes supported by earlier clinical research with incarcerated populations (cf. Agar, 1973; Coombs, 1981; Preble and Casey, 1969; Waldorf, 1973).

Having first encountered MDMA while employed at the University of Oregon Drug Information Center in 1976, Beck found himself on the ground floor in researching use of this substance. Through his capacity as a drug educator, counselor, and researcher in Oregon and later in the San Francisco Bay Area, he relied on observational fieldwork and informal interviewing to sketch a profile of MDMA use in two locations where MDMA had enjoyed early popularity (Beck, 1986, 1987; Beck and Morgan, 1986).

Ethnographic fieldwork was also an important component of the "Exploring Ecstasy" study. This included observing the current nightclub scene in Dallas and attending local gatherings and events associated with MDMA use (such as Grateful Dead concerts, Acid House nights in local nightclubs, Raves and accompanying users on Ecstasy "trips"). This fieldwork provided a useful complement to the interviews and enabled us to better understand the similarities and differences between various user groups as well as the MDMA experience itself.

We have strived to stay abreast of MDMA trends through continued fieldwork and literature review. In particular, we have closely followed the rapidly expanding Rave scene in Britain and elsewhere. Prompted by the explosive growth of this scene in San Francisco and Los Angeles in late 1991, we conducted a number of informal interviews with participants in both cities and attended Rave gatherings. The data garnered from this additional research as well as other recent studies are included for purposes of comparing or updating the findings of the "Exploring Ecstasy" study.

DATA COLLECTION

In addition to ethnographic fieldwork and informal interviewing, project staff conducted one hundred formal interviews between 1987 and 1989. Two basic concerns were repeatedly addressed throughout the study: (1) Who should be interviewed and how best to locate them? (2) What should we ask these respondents? Our tasks were roughly divided between subject procurement and information gathering. Ongoing data analysis and flexibility allowed us to continually refine our answers to these questions. The following discussion describes the rationales underlying these procedures.

Procurement of the Study Population

Our own previous fieldwork and media accounts identified initial target populations of MDMA users. We deliberately hired a diverse staff of interviewers for the study, which greatly aided the search for respondents from different social worlds. A variety of referral sources (MDMA "experts") enabled us to easily locate large numbers of respondents from targeted social worlds. We also used various fieldwork techniques to procure subjects from seemingly undersampled populations (such as racial minorities).

To be considered for a formal interview, a potential respondent had to have used MDMA at least three times. Although we informally interviewed many individuals who had tried MDMA only once or twice, we felt that respondents should have a broader number of experiences as a base for an often lengthy formal interview.

Initially, we also felt that at least one experience should have taken place in the last six months in order to avoid some of the problems inherent in retrospective accounts (faulty or selective memory). Ultimately, we did make some exceptions to the six-month criterion, having come to realize that even those who greatly enjoyed MDMA often used it infrequently for a number of reasons (such as lack of availability, time constraints). We also wanted to interview respondents who might have been regular users at one point but who had discontinued use for various reasons.

Our sampling procedure relied on a "chain-referral" strategy (Biernacki and Waldorf, 1981) guided by "theoretical sampling" (Glaser and Strauss, 1967). We began by interviewing associates we knew who had used MDMA. The chain-referral method worked in the following way: a respondent who had been interviewed would inform a friend or acquaintance (typically within his or her social world) about the study. The friend would call and be interviewed, and subsequently refer other friends, forming chains of respondents.

We made decisions as to whether a particular chain had been exhausted and when and where a new chain should be started using "theoretical sampling." When we felt that a particular population (such as Jewish professionals, "New Age seekers") had been saturated, we would stop interviewing its members. On the other hand, when we learned through interviews of previously unknown groups who were using MDMA (such as "postpunk New Wavers"), we attempted to procure subjects from that group.

In contrast to many studies of illicit drug users, it was exceptionally easy to procure willing, articulate respondents. We attribute this ease to the effects of MDMA itself, the composition of our research team, and the nature of the subject population. A surprisingly difficult part of this phase of research was having to turn people away. Users were often not only willing but anxious to express their opinions and feelings about MDMA.

Sampling Problems

Having such a large population to choose from, there was a natural tendency to choose users who were easiest to interview. In general, our respondents were probably much more enthusiastic about their MDMA use than the "average" individual who had tried the drug. Most likely to request an interview were those who strongly believed in the therapeutic value of MDMA and other enthusiastic users who wanted to tell their story. Less likely candidates included infrequent users or discontinuers (particularly those who had equivocal experiences), and those with something to lose and little to gain by being interviewed (for example, individuals in sensitive positions whose jobs or relationships could be affected by a revelation of their MDMA use).

In general, when we were contacted, it was more likely by potential respondents who felt that MDMA had "changed their lives" than by individuals who "didn't get off" or were not particularly enthusiastic about the drug. However, we did take field notes when screening all callers or referrals. Through field research, we were frequently able to talk with user populations who might be underrepresented in the formal interviews. A conscientious effort was made to carefully examine each of the many user groups found through our investigations. We are confident, therefore, that the study population provided a good cross-section of MDMA users at that time, particularly in the San Francisco Bay Area, where most of the formal interviewing was conducted.

The Study Population

Of the one hundred subjects formally interviewed for our study, sixty-two were male and thirty-eight female. Their average age was 35, with an overall range of 16 to 73 years of age. Largely white (95 percent) and heterosexual (84 percent), the majority of respondents were single (59 percent) and had no children (67 percent). This was a well-educated population with an average of 16.3 years of schooling. Although some were still students at various levels, 30 percent had Master's degrees and 12 percent had earned a Ph.D. or M.D. Most were middle class or upper middle class, with nearly one in three reporting annual incomes of $35,000 or more.[1]

The Interview

In the initial stages of interviewing and data collection, we assembled data collection instruments (interview guides) which would tap "hunches" derived from anecdotal reports in the media, staff perceptions, and earlier research (Beck, 1986, 1987; Beck and

Morgan, 1986). In order to formulate this instrument, we began with a set of sensitizing concepts: preliminary notions about the categories, relationships, and problems we found to be significant in drug use. We wanted to explore these ideas without precluding the possibility that other important issues would arise as we collected the data. Thus our qualitative interview guide was both semistructured and open-ended. Sociologist John Lofland's words guided us in developing our instrument:

> Its [the instrument] object is not to elicit choices between alternative answers to pre-formed questions but, rather, to elicit from the interviewee what he considers to be important questions relative to a given topic, his descriptions of some situations being explored. Its object is to carry on a guided conversation and to elicit rich detailed materials that can be used in qualitative analysis. Its object is to find out what kinds of things are happening, rather than to determine the frequency of predetermined kinds of things that the researcher already believes can happen. (1971: 76)

Since we were interested in process and career, the interview followed a "life history" format. We also administered a quantitative component which covered demographics, drug use history, use patterns, and perceived benefits and problems of MDMA and other drug use.

The interviews themselves began with the initial contact. After being informed of the study through fieldwork or by an individual in the chain-referral network, the potential respondents were screened to determine eligibility. If the respondent met the criteria for inclusion in the study (having used MDMA three times, once in the previous six months), an interview appointment was arranged. Most interviews were conducted in respondent homes. We provided information about the nature of the study, as well as about confidentiality and other relevant concerns. This was followed by a taped interview ranging from two to four hours in length. Following completion, the interviewer wrote a summary statement and "instant impressions" about the respondent. The interview tapes were then transcribed for detailed analysis.

DATA ANALYSIS

We began to analyze our data almost simultaneously with its collection. Summary statements and theoretical, observational and methodological notes were written shortly after completion of the interview. Concurrent data collection and analysis allowed the flexibility needed to pursue new areas for exploration as they appeared in the data. As a consequence, we were able to correct mistaken hunches and continually test new ones prior to completion of the study.

Following transcription, we would proof the text and "memo" it, making theoretical and methodological notes based on the transcribed document. The memos were unstructured and served as the initial building blocks of the analysis. They varied in length, often containing direct quotes. The memos were used to create as well as add to categories of information, which eventually shaped our substantive theoretical analysis. For example, many respondents told us that they thought MDMA was a drug which increased "self-awareness." Although this was initially conceived of as a therapeutic property, one of the analysts noted in a memo that self-awareness did not necessarily always mean "therapeutic" (as we had defined the term). Therefore, we began to look more closely at the reasons why people took the drug and were able in later memos to break down definitionally a range of meanings attached to the concept of self-awareness.

As suggested by the above example, memos often acted as flags and suggested ways for us to form the analysis. We were able to capture the salient dimensions which framed our exploratory analyses (Glaser, 1978). This strategy was further strengthened by the diversity of researchers involved in the study who reviewed and memoed transcripts of interviews as they were completed. Because of this diversity, much comparative analysis occurred during regular staff meetings, prompted by the sharing of summary statements, fieldwork experiences, problems, questions, and memos. As a group, the staff would categorize memos in an effort to begin constructing theoretical building blocks. Analyzing the interviews shortly after completion allowed us to follow new leads when sampling new chains of social worlds and also when analyzing new "hunches" as they emerged from our data.

A couple of examples illustrate the benefits of this strategy. At the start of the study, we were unsure of the relative significance of various reasons for beginning to use MDMA and continuing to do so after the first time. Through the constant comparative method, we began to devise a preliminary typology of the process of learning about and using the drug, which we were then able to explore further in subsequent interviews. In another example, we began to find differences in long-term use patterns. Among other things, these differences seemed to be related to the age and profession of respondents and what we began to refer to as "levels of responsibility." Consequently, we expanded our chain to include more "professionals" and found that they had a unique pattern of MDMA and other drug use rarely explored in previous studies of other substances.

In each of these cases, the initial analysis led us to explore new ideas regarding methods, patterns and prevalence of use as well as new user groups. As we continued interviewing, particular patterns and categories began to emerge. These categories formed the basis of our analysis. Eventually, these categories reached "theoretical saturation," when no new information about a particular phenomenon came out of the data. For example, although many respondents reported using MDMA on the spur of the moment the first time, subsequent use was generally planned and use tended to taper off over time. When we found this to be the case for all the different user groups, we assumed theoretical saturation.

Validity and Reliability

In the exploratory research of this study we attempted to provide an accurate description and analysis of a social environment and/or phenomenon. To that end, our methods will have to stand the test of validity and reliability.

Simply stated, validity is the extent to which a study produces a "correct" result. In qualitative research such as this, validity concerns the ability to correctly reproduce and understand the phenomenon under study (for example, social worlds of MDMA users). Kirk and Miller (1986) argue that naturalistic research is particularly well suited in this regard:

> This "method" is unusually sensitive to discrepancies between the meanings presumed by investigators and those understood by the target population. Indeed this is one reason that qualitative research has been such a dominant method in the anthropological study of exotic populations, where it is quite apparent that the investigator makes assumptions about meanings, situations and attributions at his or her own risk. Because of this built-in sensitivity, field research intrinsically possesses certain kinds of validities not ordinarily possessed by non-qualitative methods. (1986:30–31)

We consistently tested or questioned assumptions about meaning, context, and attributions in several ways. Probably the most common type of validity error is "asking the wrong questions" (Kirk and Miller, 1986). In this study, the focus was not on asking specific questions but rather on allowing respondents to describe their experiences in their own words. Past research has demonstrated that, given the assurance of confidentiality, illicit drug users can be relied upon to provide valid information when interviewed (Ball, 1967; Bonito, Nurco, and Shaffer, 1976; Maddux and Desmond, 1975; Stephens, 1972). When we did find inconsistencies in the accounts of a singular respondent, we would zero in and ask for the information in different ways. If still unresolved, we would ask the respondent about the inconsistency.

The detailed nature of the research endeavor itself strengthened its validity. According to Marshall and Rossman: "An in-depth description showing the complexities of variables and interactions will be so embedded with data derived from the setting that it cannot help but be valid" (1989:145). Utilizing comparisons, we continually tested assumptions over a period of months, often relying on ethnographic fieldwork for further validation.

A larger problem with qualitative research concerns reliability, which is essentially a problem of consistency. Would other researchers, using similar data-gathering and analytical techniques, come up with the same findings? Given the exploratory nature of this research, external reliability is impossible to accurately assess. We hope that this research will set the stage for studies better designed for sampling representativeness.

We were able to address at least some concerns regarding validity and reliability through the triangulation of multiple sources of data. Past social science inquiry has shown this to be an effective strategy (Denzin, 1978; Jick, 1979; Kirk and Miller, 1986; Rossman and Wilson, 1985). We sought to increase reliability through utilization of three primary data-gathering techniques in the study: ethnographic fieldwork, in-depth qualitative interviews and quantitative self-reports. Fieldwork and informal interviews were particularly valuable in counteracting previously described sampling problems, thus providing a more accurate description of the MDMA-using population.

APPENDIX B

Respondent Demographics*

No.	Sex	Age	Ed	Inc	SO	Occupation
001	M	31	16	6	Ht	Insurance
002	M	32	18	3	Ht	Writer
003	M	39	12	7	Ht	Insurance
004	F	34	16	6	Ht	Facialist
005	M	35	20	7	Ht	Psychiatrist
006	M	32	18	3	Ht	Chemist/FormrManuf
007	M	33	16	3	Ht	Student
008	M	49	16	1	Ht	Researcher
009	M	29	16	6	Ht	Computers
010	M	41	22	8	Ht	Teacher
011	M	39	22	7	Ht	Sociologist
012	F	57	17	6	Ht	Writer/Student
013	M	58	22	7	Ht	Professor
014	F	24	18	3	Bi	Computers
015	M	46	14	5	Ht	Filmmaker
016	M	65	14	5	Hm	Postal Wkr
017	M	38	18	6	Ht	Therapist
018	F	23	14	4	Ht	Paralegal
019	F	38	18	5	Ht	Sociologist
020	F	33	16	2	Ht	Writer
021	M	33	16	5	Ht	Elect Eng
022	F	26	16	4	Ht	Computers
023	M	30	16	6	Ht	Computers
024	F	25	16	5	Ht	Fin Analyst
025	M	30	18	5	Ht	Civil Eng
026	F	30	17	4	Bi	Artist
027	F	27	18	3	Ht	Student
028	F	41	15	4	Ht	Food Svc
029	M	36	18	8	Ht	Finance
030	M	24	16	4	Ht	Composer/Mus
031	M	24	6	2	Ht	Jewelry Des
032	F	26	16	4	Ht	Secty/Admin

No.	Sex	Age	Ed	Inc	SO	Occupation
033	M	37	16	3	Bi	Contractor
034	F	43	16	4	Ht	Jwlry/fashn
035	M	41	13	4	Ht	Artist
036	M	39	14	2	Ht	Bus/Designr
037	F	70	16	4	Ht	Artist
038	M	40	22	8	Ht	Psych/Composer
039	F	40	16	6	Ht	Consultant
040	M	47	19	6	Ht	Insurance
041	M	21	13	2	Ht	Waitr/Student
042	M	39	21	4	Bi	Psychologist
043	M	26	18	2	Ht	Student
044	F	24	16	4	Ht	Crm Jus Adv
045	M	22	16	2	Ht	Student
046	M	26	12	2	Hm	FormrDealer
047	M	31	17	4	Ht	Wine Sales
048	F	46	22	4	Ht	Sociologist
049	F	30	19	5	Ht	R.N.
050	M	40	22	7	Ht	Computers
051	M	29	16	4	Ht	Psych Tech
052	F	23	17	3	Hm	Student
053	F	18	12	2	Bi	Student
054	F	39	15	3	Ht	FormrDealer
055	M	38	18	4	Hm	Thrpst/Wrtr
056	M	18	13	1	Ht	Coll Studnt
057	M	36	18	5	Ht	Psysiolo
058	M	29	16	4	Ht	Cook
059	M	20	14	2	Ht	Student
060	M	23	16	4	Ht	Paralegal/Stdnt
061	F	26	16	3	Bi	Grad Studnt
062	M	18	18	2	Ht	Student
063	M	35	16	8	Ht	Advertising
064	M	32	15	6	Ht	Restrnt Mgr
065	F	25	16	7	Ht	Pub Rel
066	M	37	18	8	Ht	Real Estate
067	F	30	16	5	Ht	Secretary
068	M	36	16	8	Ht	Advertising
069	F	30	16	6	Ht	Unempl Dsnr
070	F	60	22	8	Ht	Writer
071	F	40	22	8	Ht	Physician
072	M	51	16	8	Ht	Airline Pilot
073	M	43	16	3	Ht	FormrDealer
074	M	35	19	7	Ht	Attorney

No.	Sex	Age	Ed	Inc	SO	Occupation
075	F	73	14	3	Ht	Retired Salesclerk
076	M	50	17	1	Ht	Writer
077	F	57	14	3	Ht	Counselor
078	M	72	16	2	Ht	Owner/Mgr
079	M	64	22	7	Ht	Psychiatrist
080	M	45	15	5	Ht	FormrDealer
081	M	35	22	6	Ht	Rsrch Chmst
082	F	32	16	5	Ht	ProjManager
083	M	25	16	4	Hm	Clerical
084	M	21	15	1	Ht	Student
085	M	34	16	3	Ht	Insulator
086	F	34	18	3	Ht	Hlth Instr
087	M	33	13	5	Ht	Carpenter
088	M	34	18	7	Ht	Manager
089	M	16	10	1	Ht	HS Student
090	F	26	16	4	Bi	Store Mgr
091	M	42	22	8	Ht	Physician
092	M	30	16	5	Ht	ComputrTech/Mus
093	F	31	16	5	Ht	Journalist
094	F	35	14	2	Ht	Counselor
095	F	34	16	2	Ht	Coll Stdnt
096	F	30	16	1	Ht	Therapist/Grad Stdnt
097	F	24	16	5	Ht	Teacher
098	M	21	14	1	Hm	Student
099	F	27	15	1	Bi	Dancer
100	M	44	12	5	Hm	Businessman

*CODES: No. = respondent's I.D. #; Ed = years of education; Inc = yearly income level: 1. 0–5,000, 2. 5–10,000, 3. 10–15,000, 4. 15–20,000, 5. 20–35,000, 6. 34–50,000, 7. 50–75,000, 8. 75,000+; SO = sexual orientation.

APPENDIX C

Respondent Drug Use: Lifetime and Current Use

Drug	Never	Once	Number of Lifetime Uses				Quit Use? Yes/No
			2–10x	11–100x	101–1000x	1000+x	
MDMA	—	—	30	56	14	—	9/91
MDA	58	17	17	6	—	—	23/18
MDE	78	8	11	1	—	—	10/11
MMDA/MDOH	92	3	2	—	—	—	5/5
2-CB	73	11	10	3	1	—	7/17
LSD	17	5	30	37	10	—	33/48
Psilocybin	13	8	42	31	4	1	24/58
Mescaline	42	15	31	9	2	—	23/34
Marijuana	1	2	11	9	29	48	15/81
Cocaine	14	3	24	33	20	6	37/47
Methamphet	52	8	18	17	4	1	24/24
Speed pills	35	8	26	20	9	1	48/18

| Drug | Never | Once | Number of Lifetime Uses | | | | Quit Use? |
			2–10x	11–100x	101–1000x	1000+x	Yes/No
PCP	74	14	10	1	—	—	21/6
Barbituates	68	9	13	5	3	1	21/11
Quaaludes	47	14	18	14	6	—	30/22
Heroin	73	13	8	4	1	—	20/9
Other opiate	41	12	29	10	7	—	20/37
Minor tranqs	42	10	22	19	6	—	23/32
Major tranqs	87	7	4	1	—	—	9/5
Antidepress	890	2	2	3	2	1	8/7
Alcohol	2	—	1	9	24	62	10/78
Caffeine	3	3	3	10	—	79	9/80
Tobacco	28	5	8	12	6	40	40/27

APPENDIX D

Respondent Drug Preference and Changes in Use

Drug	Drug Preference*					Mean	Use in Past Year Compared to Previous Year†			
	1	2	3	4	5		1	2	3	4
MDMA	74	19	5	5	2	1.36	20	45	23	12
MDA	12	13	5	4	6	2.47	2	3	1	36
MDE	4	6	3	6	—	2.58	2	4	1	15
MMDA/MDOH	1	—	1	3	—	3.20	—	2	1	8
2-CB	7	8	4	3	2	2.38	4	5	5	17
LSD	34	25	10	8	6	2.12	13	17	11	40
Psilocybin	38	31	9	8	1	1.89	16	25	13	30
Mescaline	22	22	6	5	1	1.95	1	6	4	44
Marijuana	38	33	12	11	5	2.11	21	43	23	10
Cocaine	12	30	11	20	12	2.88	14	30	11	29
Methamphet	10	9	11	10	6	2.85	10	5	5	28
Speed pills	5	12	17	18	13	3.34	3	6	1	55
PCP	2	3	4	2	13	3.87	3	1	1	22
Quaaludes	10	20	9	10	3	2.54	3	4	2	46

Drug	Drug Preference*					Mean	Use in Past Year Compared to Previous Year†			
	1	2	3	4	5		1	2	3	4
Barbituates	1	5	10	8	5	3.38	3	5	23	1
Heroin	6	5	10	1	3	2.60	3	—	—	27
Other opiate	15	28	14	—	1	2.03	10	5	4	39
Minor tranqs	9	16	16	12	3	2.71	5	11	7	33
Antidepress	2	3	2	2	1	3.80	3	1	—	11
Alcohol	13	53	15	5	1	2.17	16	34	32	6
Caffeine	27	40	18	5	1	2.04	12	25	47	7
Tobacco	10	11	12	9	24	3.39	9	9	16	35

*1 = strongly like; 2 = moderately like; 3 = neutral; 4 = moderately dislike; 5 = strongly dislike.

†1 = increased; 2 = decreased; 3 = stayed same; 4 = did not use.

APPENDIX E
NATIONAL INSTITUTE
ON DRUG ABUSE
CAPSULE ON MDMA

MDMA

MDMA, called "Adam," "Ecstacy," or "X-T-C" on the street, is a synthetic, psychoactive (mind-altering) drug with hallucinogenic and amphetamine-like properties. Its chemical structure (3-4-methylenedioxymethamphetamine) is very similar to two other synthetic drugs: MDA and methamphetamine, which are known to cause brain damage. MDMA is a so-called "designer drug," which, according to the Drug Enforcement Administration (DEA), has become a nationwide problem as well as a serious health threat. It has been known to be the cause of at least two deaths.

Beliefs about Ecstasy are reminiscent of similar claims made about LSD in the 1950s and 1960s, which proved to be untrue. According to its proponents, MDMA can make people trust one another and break down barriers between therapists and patients, lovers, and family members.

Many of the problems users encounter with MDMA are similar to those found with the use of amphetamines and cocaine. They are:

Psychological difficulties, including confusion, depression, sleep problems, drug craving, severe anxiety and paranoia—during and sometimes weeks after taking MDMA. Even psychotic episodes have been reported.

Physical symptoms such as muscle tension, involuntary teeth clenching, nausea, blurred vision, rapid eye movements, faintness and chills, or sweating

Increases in heart rate and blood pressure, a special risk for people with circulatory or heart disease.

The National Institute on Drug Abuse (NIDA) has arranged to have MDMA synthesized so qualified researchers can conduct studies on the drug's long-term neurotoxicity and abuse potential. It is believed that this research will indicate that it causes brain damage, just as MDA and methamphetamine do.

MDA, the parent drug of MDMA, is an amphetamine-like drug with has also been abused and is very similar in chemical structure to MDMA. According to NIDA-supported researchers Drs. L. S. Seiden and C. R. Schuster of the University of Chicago, MDA destroys serotonin-producing neurons, which play a direct role in regulating aggression, mood, sexual activity, sleep, and sensitivity to pain. It is probably this action on the serotonin system which gives MDA its purported properties of heightened sexual experience, tranquility, and conviviality.

MDMA is also related in structure and effects to methamphetamine. Methamphetamine has been shown by the Chicago researchers to cause degeneration of neurons containing the neurotransmitter dopamine. Damage to these neurons is the underlying cause of the motor disturbances seen in Parkinson's disease.

In laboratory experiments, a single exposure to methamphetamine at high doses or prolonged use at low doses destroys up to 50 percent of the brain cells which use dopamine. Although this damage may not be immediately apparent, scientists feel that with aging or exposure to other toxic agents, Parkinsonian symptoms may eventually emerge. These symptoms begin with lack of coordination and tremors and may eventually result in a form of paralysis.

DEA officials have said that the drug is available in at least 21 states and Canada and is especially popular with college students and young professionals. Areas of concentrated use include California, Texas, Florida, New York, and New England. Treatment authorities in California report at least 3–4 MDMA related cases per month in 1985.

In June, 1985, DEA banned MDMA, placing the drug in the Schedule 1 classification based on the Controlled Substances Act. The emergency scheduling was effective July 1, 1985. Schedule 1 drugs are generally dangerous narcotics that have a high potential for abuse and no medical usefulness. Other drugs in Schedule 1 include heroin, LSD, and MDA. Manufacturers and sellers of Schedule 1 drugs are subject to fines of up to $125,000 and 15-year prison terms. The scheduling will be effective for one year, during which time authorities will decide how best to classify MDMA based on hearings and scientific research. Until it became illegal, MDMA was used by some psychiatrists and therapists as an aid in psychotherapy.

The Justice Department has proposed legislation to combat designer drugs such as MDMA. "Designer drug" is a term used to refer to a substance that appears in the illicit drug market that is a chemical composition of illegal drugs so that they are technically legal. In many cases, the new designer drugs are more dangerous and more potent than the original drug. Legislation would call for a 15-year prison sentence and $250,000 fine for those convicted of producing such drugs.

Source: NIDA (National Institute on Drug Abuse) Capsules. Issued by the Press Office of the National Institute on Drug Abuse, 5600 Fishers Lane, Rockville, Maryland 20857, 1985.

FLIGHT INSTRUCTIONS FOR A FRIEND USING XTC

From what you said, you mostly did everything correctly except the most important part, which is the absolute necessity of sharing the same setting and space with another person—one you are fond of.

This is *not* a "mind altering" trip. This is an enhancement of the tactile senses in a giving and receiving way. It does not blow your mind out of your body or isolate your body from your mind or cancel out one or the other.

The operative words are empathy, gentleness, and joy of life, body and mind. If you want to groove only on yourself, this is not the way to go.

1. Be in a pleasant setting.
2. Rested.
3. No food, drugs, or alcohol in your system.
4. A companion you care about (wife/husband, lover, friend).
5. Ingest the entire amount you plan to take at one time. If you want it to come on a little faster, dissolve it in about $1/4$ glass of beer (the bitterness of beer helps to mask the bitter taste of XTC) and drink it down.
6. You will feel a gentle warmth flooding your body and your mind becoming peacefully alert. There is no rushing or hurtling toward the uncontrollable unknown.

    This is happiness. Security. Peace. Freedom. Your body feeling life, kissing in your veins. Your mind agile. No nuclear explosions, but a blooming sensuality. Each sense enhancing the others. A big smile, the easing of tensions in mind, body and soul!

7. After an hour or so to get used to the sensations you might want to go for a walk and enjoy the surroundings - or you might find yourself perfectly contented to simply enjoy being where you are.

8. You will experience a certain lassitude the next day. We prefer to consider this an after-glow and like to take the time to bask in one another's company and discuss the experience of the previous day.

However, everyone does not always have the luxury of times available and sometimes we all simply relate to this lassitude as tiredness. The following combinations of vitamins (available from most any health food store) will dispell the tiredness and re-invigorate you almost immediately.

Mix and Ingest Each Combination Separately in Water

A. 1.   L-phenylalanine
   2.   Vitamin B6
   3.   Vitamin C powder

B. 1.   colein chloride
   2.   Vitamin B5

P.S. We have discovered that the colein chloride also helps to re-energize male sexual vitality. Try taking it before retiring for a couple of nights before taking the XTC as well as the day after.

HOW TO PREPARE FOR AN *ECSTASY* EXPERIENCE

1. Just in case you may have a calcium deficiency, you should take a calcium supplement of some kind prior to taking ECSTASY. You should take calcium with a meal (1 with breakfast and 1 with lunch) but not on an empty stomach.

2. About an hour prior to taking ECSTASY, you might want to prepare a snack tray of some sort. Example: cheese and crackers or fresh fruit. Whatever you prepare, make sure it

is something very soft and something that you really like. Also, be sure to cut it up into small bite-size pieces. (You will not want anything to eat until after you start coming down, but caution should be taken in chewing food very well and swallowing very carefully. You will be amazed at how good food tastes.)

3. Things you might want to have on hand: (A) LoSal: antacid tablets (like Rolaids or Tums, but better, and taste good). (B) Peppermint: (Just in case of an upset stomach, chew up 2 LoSal and suck on a small piece of peppermint). (C) A bottle of wine (of your preference); nothing bubbly or carbonated. (Just in case someone cannot relax or starts to feel uptight or nervous, pour them a small glass. Only for such reasons mentioned above should anyone drink the wine. (Alcohol and drugs will lessen the effect of ECSTASY.) (D) A couple of wet cool wash cloths: (If someone starts feeling warm, it is very pleasant to wipe the face, or the neck, or chest, back, or arms.) (E) A couple of blankets and lots of pillows: (Almost everyone goes through a stage when they feel cold or chilled. Just bundle up in a blanket or cuddle with a pillow. The pillows are nice to lay around on also.

4. Do not eat anything at least 3 to 4 hours prior to taking ECSTASY. Do not do any kind of drugs or alcohol at least 8 hours (even better 24 hours) prior to taking ECSTASY.

5. Light some incense and candles and, if you want, turn on some very soft (elevator) music. (It is very important that the music is soft and low [in the beginning] to create a very relaxed and mellow atmosphere. You might even want to unplug the telephones.)

6. Fill an ice bucket, and have a large picture of water and enough glasses for everyone. Keep this in the same room with you (not out of the way).

7. Take out enough ECSTASY for everyone to have 1.

8. Make everyone come together and sit in a circle or group. *Do not* let anyone sit off alone at first. Make each person feel like you really want them there, to experience one of the greatest things you've ever done. It is easy, when you already know just how wonderful they are going to feel in 30 minutes to an hour—and especially easy because they

are your friends. (You have to set the rules. If they don't want to be part of the group, then they don't really want to have a wonderful ECSTASY experience.)

9. For *faster* results, crush each ECSTASY pill up separately and put in a spoon. Or, you can chew it up (Warning: It tastes terrible). If the taste is unbearable, eat a very small piece of peppermint.

10. Refill everyone's glass.

11. Now the wait: Sit around and talk about what you might expect, or what you want to expect, or read the ECSTASY booklet out loud so everyone knows what it is all about. If you like, you could make your snack tray now, to kill the time. (You could do steps 2 through 6 now, if you wanted.) You will be amazed at how quickly the time goes by. It is very common for someone experiencing ECSTASY for the first time to say (or at least think) "When is it going to *Hit* me?" First of all, it isn't going to *Hit* you. It will come on very gradual and smooth. Secondly, the effect it has on you depends on your state of mind. You can make it come on by just laying back, closing your eyes, and being quiet. However, you can shut it off instantly. Example: the phone rings or someone knocks on the door, you become straight, automatically. Always keep everyone in sight or at least know what state of mind they are in. If they are off alone, in another room, check on them. They may need someone to talk to, but they don't want to burden someone else with their problems.

It is not unusual for someone on their first ECSTASY trip to go through an emotional stage. These stages never last long, and in each person's own way they find (or become) their "Real Self." As for the different emotional stages you may go through, remember, they will pass. However, if there are any bad emotions that you have held in, they will usually surface first. Give in to them, let them surface, and get them out of your system and then the rest of your ECSTASY experience will be for all of your emotions to surface.

12. So, kick back, relax, and be prepared to experience the Ultimate High.

Your Friend

REFLECTIONS ON THE NATURE AND USE OF XTC, PART II

XTC has enormous potential as a tool for connecting and unifying groups of people. Although there are endless possibilities for application of this tool within a group setting, the following guidelines have proven invaluable in terms of creating productive sessions. People seem to get higher if the sessions are directed and organized. We see these guidelines as a point of possible departure, open to change and interpretation but of enough importance to pass this information along. Create your own ritual.

A session is organized as the result of one person's decision to host the event. The host invites friends over and prepares a space for the session that is clean, attractive, warm and safe.

The participants begin by expressing their hopes, reservations and expectations for the session.

As the effect unfolds, all participants are encouraged to share their experience and insights with the group as an entity.

Private conversations tend to disconnect the group, and should be minimized.

Shared silence is exquisite.

Having pencils and papers on hand at all times allows people to retrieve information for use at a later time.

Getting together the following day for a de-briefing after the experience has dissipated is helpful to bind the things learned during the session into normal operating consciousness. We recommend doing this.

If the session is successful and the group wishes to get together again, a new host volunteers to provide the space for the next one, and sets a date.

This procedure seems to work best if the majority of the participants are already familiar with the XTC experience, and first-timers are held to a few.

Provision of the XTC itself works well if all participants bring their own supply to the session as much as possible. This relieves the host or any one person from the burden of providing for all, and tends to make the experience more collective and easier to get together for repeats.

As mentioned in Reflections, Part I, it is possible for people to have very difficult trips on XTC, although this occurrence is rare. Individuals most likely to react in this fashion are people with strongly suppressed negative emotions who act as if they aren't hurting when they are hurting badly. People with rigid personalities and belief systems can also have difficulties when their operational foundations dissolve.

Should a negative reaction occur in a group setting, the participants can best handle the situation by extending love and compassion to their brother or sister who is in trouble. What does this mean? It means supporting them in feeling whatever they're feeling, even if it's negative. On the other side of all negative emotions is love. Experience has shown that these people often stand to gain the most from these experiences. The act of releasing themselves allows them to be reborn as more sensitive and understanding people, infused with new vigor for life. If possible, try to initiate these people in a small, private session rather than a group session, if the potential for difficulty can be recognized ahead of time. This occurrence is rare, but does happen and should be considered. It can be very intense.

XTC is a tool for reaching out and touching others in soul and spirit. If responsibly used, strong bonds of unity and love can be forged that strengthen everyone involved.

Celebrate in life,
choose to evolve,
create peace.

POSITIVE AND THERAPEUTIC USE
OF ADAM OR ECSTASY

I Benefits:	improved human relational capacity, self-esteem, mood, insight, and recovery from drug abuse.
II Mood:	generally positive: heartful, truthful, thankful, forgiving, empathetic, warm, loving, present. In some cases a difficult experience may occur, especially if dosage, set, or setting are inappropriate.
III Intensity:	generally mild to subtle though profound. In some cases, may be more dramatic, especially in women.

IV	Most Common Side Effects	(not always, and usually mild). Jaw tension or shaking or teeth clenching, which can be controlled by consciously relaxing jaw, or by taking 1–2 grams of calcium mineral (preferably chelated). Mild fatigue, occasional nausea.
V	Contra-indications:	hypertension, heart disease, hyperthyroidism, diabetes mellitus, hypoglycemia, seizure disorder, glaucoma, diminished liver function, pregnancy or possible pregnancy. For safety, consult doctor, have sitter, use half dose.
VI	Dosage:	50 to 150 mg. (depending upon body weight) orally. Compute one milligram per pound of body weight. Use lower doses (say one-half to two- thirds) for recreational use or beginner, especially female (tendency for more dramatic effect). Full doses may be used for inner work. A booster dose of 50mg. or less may be taken after one hour (or after onset) to prolong effect.
VII	Food:	Fast or only light meal in previous 6–12 hours. No food in previous 2 hours. No drink in previous half hour. There is no appetite during session. Plenty of water may be taken during, and should be taken after the session to replace fluid and clear the liver and kidneys.

Before and after fasting period, a good quality high protein meal may reduce mild fatigue effect.

Easily assimilable calcium/ magnesium mineral taken with dose and during session may alleviate jaw tension.

VIII   Timing: onset within one hour. Possible
                                  disturbing effect for 5–30 minutes
                                  which can be minimized and used by
                                  relaxing, chanting (any sound that
                                  comes), and trusting the drug
                                  process. Peak effect for one to two
                                  hours. Urge to move about after 4
                                  hours. Return to baseline (eat, drive
                                  carefully) after six hours.

IX   Set and Setting: a safe, comfortable, warm, natural
                                  indoor or outdoor space.

                                  a) lying perfectly relaxed and still
                                  with eyes closed for 4 or more hours,
                                  preferably with a sitter, especially if
                                  the first time. A sitter keeps the space
                                  safe, changes music if used, and
                                  provides reassurance and guidance if
                                  needed. Adopt a gentle, meditative,
                                  watchful mind allowing insight, body
                                  releases, healing, God to come. Just
                                  watch even the urge to move.

                                  b) with a good or intimate friend for
                                  relationship healing or deepening.
                                  Relax and allow the process to move
                                  you. No program.

                                  c) with a few compatible people—a
                                  group healing.

                                  A willingness to tolerate, accept
                                  and surrender to difficult emotions
                                  such as sadness, fear, depression,
                                  agitation as well as much more
                                  common pleasant ones like joy, love,
                                  gratitude.

                                  A willingness to accept changes in
                                  personality, occasionally negative
                                  and persisting until the stimulated
                                  issue has been resolved by further
                                  inner work (ie. in meditation,
                                  another session, therapy).

Best benefit returned by having no social or work obligation on that or next day. Continue to act on insights and practice teachings, even if it may feel a bit unusual or risky. However, defer life-changing decisions or action for 7–10 days.

APPENDIX G
BRITISH HARM REDUCTION PAMPHLETS

chillin...

If you want to make the most of next week-end, slow down. Sleep is vital to re-charge your batteries so you can do the things you like to do - so, get plenty!

Some raves can get very crowded and extremely hot. This can cause you problems like dehydration (loss of body fluids), hyperthermia (overheating) and heat exhaustion - all of which are dangerous. Sweating is how your body keeps cool and stops hyperthermia, so, drink a lot of non-alcoholic drinks to replace lost fluid and avoid dehydration. Wear lightweight clothes, no hat and take a change of clothes with you for when you leave to avoid catching a chill.

There have been deaths associated with Ecstasy. Some of these have been caused by people getting too hot, dehydrated and then overheating. Amphetamine keeps the heat inside your body so you can't cool down. Alcohol dehydrates you.

Forgetting to eat can cause fatigue, cramps and weight loss. It is important to eat properly and regularly - like every day! If you're going out raving, eat early in the day to avoid stomach cramps. Extra salt on your food a few days before will also help to retain body fluids, while multi-vitamins through the week can help to keep you fit and healthy.

...out

If you have taken drugs and start to feel ill, tell someone and ask them to help. If you are going to help someone in this situation or someone gets panicky, take them to a quiet place where you can be on your own (eg a chill out, another room, or go for a walk out of the club) and calm them down by explaining that they are experiencing the effects of a drug which will wear off within a short while and by reassuring them that they are quite safe.

Do not give them tea, coffee or alcohol to drink, or any other drugs to take (if they smoke, a cigarette may help to calm them) and don't let them have anything to eat. Sips of fruit juice or water can be given if needed.

If someone is breathing rapidly, help them to breathe slowly and deeply by counting each breath slowly in and out with them. Quite soon they will begin to calm down. However, if they get more panicky and you cannot cope, phone an ambulance or take them to a hospital casualty department. When you get there, don't mess about, explain to a nurse and/or doctor what your friend has taken and how long ago.

If someone faints, it may be because of heat, exhaustion or drugs - or a combination of all three. Make sure they are getting enough air, give them space, and check they aren't hurt if they fell. When they come round and are OK, take them somewhere cool, sit them down with their head between their knees. They'll soon feel better, but don't let them get up too soon, give it 10-15 minutes.

If someone collapses (eyes rolled back, erratic breathing, skin cold and clammy), CALL AN AMBULANCE IMMEDIATELY - if anyone has first aid experience, get them to help. Lie the person on their side with head turned to one side (the recovery position), and keep an eye on their breathing and pulse. When the ambulance arrives, tell the medics what the person has taken and how much - don't be afraid, this could save their life.

Using any drug involves risks, taking more or mixing drugs increases the risks. Remember, no drugs means no risks

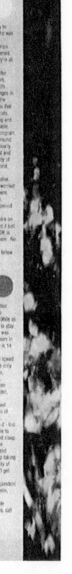

- What are the facts?
- What does it do for the Mind, Body and Soul?
- What does the law say?
- Your career as a user?

**HERE ARE SOME OF THE QUESTIONS
ANSWERS COMING SOON!
WATCH THIS SPACE**

STOP PRESS
FOR SNEAK PREVIEW
RING

 'E': THE FACTS

- Ecstasy has become popular as a dance drug. Other dance drugs are Amphetamine sulphate powder, low dosages of L.S.D. and sometimes Cocaine.

- Of the dance drugs proper 'E' is most closely related to Amphetamine sulphate powder (whizz) and low dosage L.S.D.

- One of the main problems with Ecstasy is buying a real one.

- Recently in the North West the following drugs have been sold as Ecstasy.

  i)   L.S.D and Amphetamine Sulphate
  ii) Methamphetamine
  iii) Heroin and Amphetamine
  iv) Ketamine - an anaesthetic drug used in surgery with very unpleasant side effects.

- Little is known about how proper 'E' affects the brain, but there is growing evidence that too much, too often could cause problems. For a much more detailed picture, in confidence, contact

entactogenic

"Something for your Mind, Body and Soul . . . . . .
an Entactogen, perhaps?"

● In the chemical jargon; proper 'E' is an Entactogen.
Drugs with an Entactogenic effect break down barriers
and put you more in touch both with yourself and other
people.

● This is why proper 'E' has become a favourite party
drug.

● Proper 'E' can have both good and bad effects on your
Mind, Body and Soul. Examples:

MIND   good effects include: Sensual rush and
                               spacey sense of well-being.
        bad effects include: Feelings of anxiety and
                               depression.

BODY   good effects include: Increased energy.
        bad effects include: Fatigue and weight loss.

SOUL   good effects include: Confidence, trust and
                               openness.

● It has to be said that the only way of totally avoiding the
bad is not to do 'E".

● If you are going to do 'E', the best way of minimizing the
bad and maximising the good is to use small amounts on
an occasional basis.

Remember the Golden 'E' Rule: Less is More.
For more information on 'E' and MBS contact

INCARCERATION

● E is a category 'A' drug - it's the same as heroin in the eyes of the law!

● Most people caught with E are charged with:-

   a.   possession for personal use only.
or b.   possession with intent to supply others.

● People with small amounts of E have been charged with supply - even
though they only intended to supply friends.

● Those found guilty on supply charges run a strong risk of going to jail.

For free confidential advice about E and the law ring

APPENDIX H
RAVE FLYERS

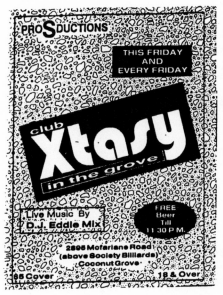

E 10 PM - ?

E
L
E
V
A
T
I
O
N

21 ID E

L
E
V
A
T
I
O
N

WELL NOW I KNOW. AND NOW I DO. I WISH I DIDN'T. BUT IF I DIDN'T, I'D HAVE NEVER. SO IN THE LONG RUN, I'M GLAD I DO. BETTER THAN NOT. BUT SOME OF YOU KNEW THAT, DIDN'T YOU. THE ONES THAT DIDN'T RUSH STRAIGHT TO ELEVATION DIDN'T. NOW YOU COULD KNOW. OH YES IT'S THE BIGGEST NEWS ON THURSDAYS. SO IT'S. AND DO YOU WANT TO KNOW WHAT IT'S? YOU DO? NOBIL, ERIC L, SCOTT & ERIC HAVE A THURSDAY NIGHT. GO ON,!!! RACE YA. WHO'S DJ SCOTT D'IMPORT AND DJ CORLOS, THAT'S WHAT WE WANT TO BLOODY WELL KNOW. ANYWAY...

300 DE HARO ST. @ 16TH ST.

RAVE IV PEACE

SUNDAY FEB. 23RD. 4 P.M. UNTIL

INTENSE MUSIC
3 1 6 0   1 6 S T.   S.F.

NOTES

CHAPTER 1. INTRODUCTION:
VARIETIES OF THE MDMA EXPERIENCE

1. National Institute on Drug Abuse (NIDA) Grant 1 R01 DA 04408, "Exploring Ecstasy: A Descriptive Study of MDMA Users," Marsha Rosenbaum, principal investigator; Patricia Morgan, co-principal investigator; Jerome Beck, project director; Beatrice Rouse, NIDA project officer.

2. To quote from Hammersley and Atkinson:

For us ethnography (or participant observation, a cognate term) is simply one social research method, albeit a somewhat unusual one, drawing as it does on a wide range of sources of information. The ethnographer participates, overtly or covertly, in people's daily lives for an extended period of time, watching what happens, listening to what is said, asking questions; in fact collecting whatever data are available to throw light on the issues with which he or she is concerned.

In many respects ethnography is the most basic form of social research. Not only does it have a very long history (Wax, 1971), but it also bears a close resemblance to the routine ways in which people make sense of the world in everyday life. (1983)

3. For a detailed discussion of the study methodology, see Appendix A.

4. Our background, like many others in federally funded research, was in the study of illegal drugs such as heroin, used primarily by financially disadvantaged populations.

CHAPTER 2. EMERGENCE OF ADAM AND ECSTASY:
DISTRIBUTION AND CRIMINALIZATION OF MDMA

1. MDMA and MDA are both semisynthetic drugs related to volatile oils found in a number of plants, most notably sassafras and nutmeg. Described in the *Ayurveda* of ancient India as *made shaunda* ("narcotic fruit"), nutmeg has a long history of use in various cultures

which has continued into this century. However, the frequent nausea, dizziness, and other unpleasant side effects which detract from the sought-after positive qualities have limited nutmeg use to only the most desperate drug-seeking populations such as prison inmates (Stafford, 1992). Although many accounts describe MDMA being developed and tried as an appetite suppressant, it appears that MDA was the sole subject of this early research (Shulgin, 1990). Confusion between the two substances is responsible for other inaccuracies commonly observed as well (cf. Kirsch, 1986; Roberts, 1992).

2. Deborah Harlow made significant contributions to this section.

3. We relied on a number of sources in attempting to assess the extent as well as history of MDMA use. In particular, eight large-scale distributors were interviewed for the study (four granted formal interviews, and the other four allowed shorter "supplementary" discussions). Some of these individuals had been actively dealing since MDMA's emergence in the mid-1970s. Consequently, they were able to supply valuable data regarding the history and early use of MDMA. To supplement their information, the research team also talked with longtime users and smaller-scale dealers, as well as chemists, researchers, and therapists who were knowledgeable about MDMA use over the past two decades. By cross-checking their information with government data and media reports, we were able to construct a fairly accurate, albeit incomplete, picture regarding the history and evolution of MDMA distribution and use.

4. Thirty-seven percent of our respondents reported introducing ten or more people, with 8 percent claiming to have initiated at least one hundred new users to MDMA.

5. The numbers cited in the text refer to formal interviews and the page number(s) of the quote from the transcription. Selected demographic information for these respondents can be found in Appendix B.

6. According to Eisner, the distributor who coined the term "Ecstasy" told him "he chose that name 'because it would sell better than "Empathy." "Empathy" might be more appropriate, but how many people know what it means?'" (Eisner, 1989:6).

7. Of the five schedules provided by the 1970 Controlled Substances Act (CSA), Schedule I is reserved for those drugs determined to lack currently accepted medical use and safety as well as possessing a high potential for abuse (such as LSD, heroin). The other four schedules contain legally prescribed drugs which are placed according to abuse potential. Whereas Schedule II is for drugs possessing a high potential for abuse, Schedule V is for little-abused substances at the other end of the spectrum.

8. This amendment to the Controlled Substances Act provides the attorney general with authority to place any substance posing "an imminent hazard to public safety" into Schedule I for a period of one year (plus an additional six months, if necessary) while the final scheduling process is under way (Beck and Rosenbaum, 1990).

9. For a more detailed discussion of the Administrative Law Hearings and subsequent appellate court decisions, see Beck and Rosenbaum, 1990.

10. The "designer drug" label has been applied to the intentional process of chemically engineering existing controlled substances to create drugs that are not currently illegal. As Wesson defines them, these are "substances wherein the psychoactive properties of a scheduled drug have been retained, but the molecular structure has been altered in order to avoid prosecution under the Controlled Substances Act" (Quoted in Smith and Seymour, 1985:1). Although MDMA is often referred to as a designer drug, this designation is debatable, since it was first synthesized in 1912 and patented in 1914, long before passage of the Controlled Substances Act of 1970 (Beck and Morgan, 1986).

CHAPTER 3. WORLDS OF ECSTASY: WHO USES MDMA?

1. By "convenience" we mean study samples that are not random. Instead the researcher polls whoever is willing.

2. Lynne Watson contributed significantly to this section. For further discussion of MDMA use among New Agers and as an adjunct for spiritual explorations, see Watson and Beck, 1991.

3. Additional evidence of MDMA's enduring popularity in Texas is provided by the findings of the 1990 Texas School Survey. Randomly sampling over thirty thousand students, this survey found that a surprising 9.1 percent of high school seniors had tried Ecstasy, with 2.5 percent having used it in the past month. As with adults, white students were the primary users, with 14.7 percent of white seniors having tried Ecstasy and 4.1 percent having used it in the past month (Fredlund et al., 1990). These figures vastly exceed those of young adults in the 1990 "Monitoring the Future" study, which found that only 4.7 percent of individuals in their early 20s had ever tried MDMA (Johnston et al., 1991).

4. Tom Wolfe, *The Electric Kool-Aid Acid Test* (1968).

5. Typical of such visits to shows in the mid-1980s, groups of MDMA users were often recognizable by such commonly observed behaviors as mass hugging and excessive verbosity while the rest of the crowd was reverently listening to a Jerry Garcia guitar solo.

CHAPTER 5. LIMITS TO USE:
WHY PEOPLE MODERATE OR QUIT ECSTASY

1. Although only 9 percent had actually discontinued use, 80 percent reported using MDMA less than once a month during the past year. Although almost three-fourths of the respondents described themselves as "strongly liking" MDMA, well over half (57 percent) had taken it less than four times during the past year.

2. See Appendix D for declining use patterns.

3. What she found there was "Eve," an analogue of MDMA, which she bought for $25 a tablet. As described in Chapter 2, attempts to market the still licit MDE (Eve) following MDMA's criminalization were largely unsuccessful. As a former Dallas user remarked: "Eve was a mutant of X. I wouldn't go near that. I used to get upset at my friends that did it, 'cause it was still legal. I said, 'Yeah, but you don't know what you're taking here.' . . . And when people started stepping on it and messing with it, I didn't want to deal with it anymore" (067:30).
Of the 20 percent of respondents who had reportedly tried MDE, all preferred MDMA. Eve was seen as "too laid back and analytical" as well as lacking the intensity and "heartfelt qualities" of MDMA. One respondent described scoring some Eve when he could no longer find MDMA after it was scheduled. Referring to the MDE as "fake Ecstasy," he only took it once and didn't care for the experience: "It was totally funky" (056:44).

4. The European Ecstasy scene has been increasingly plagued by the aforementioned problems. Unlike in America, where lack of availability is often the problem, the Manchester Raver is often confronted with a plethora of brands ("Love Doves," "Disco Biscuits," "New Yorkers," "Californian Sunrise") offered at Rave venues (Pearson et al., 1991). The choice is important given the considerable amounts of "fake Ecstasy" circulating through the dance club scenes. The high cost of MDMA explains the frequent substitution of less expensive amphetamine in Holland (Korf, Blanken, and Nabben, 1991). The same is true for Britain, where various combinations of amphetamine, LSD, and other drugs are often passed off as Ecstasy (Dorn et al., 1991; DrugLink, 1992; James, 1991; Sawyer, 1992).

5. Conversations with nonusers suggest that media reports of the research have undoubtedly discouraged many would-be experimenters. Reflecting media headlines, variations of the following were often heard by researchers asking individuals about Ecstasy: "Isn't that the stuff that causes brain damage?"

6. An amusing commentary on this myth was provided by Dr. George Ricaurte, who was conducting spinal tap studies on a small number of MDMA users to detect serotonin metabolites. He responded to the misconception by noting that "it's not MDMA but MDMA *researchers* that will drain your spinal fluid" (Ricaurte, 1989). A more likely explanation is the neck and backaches that occasionally follow MDMA use for some individuals. Nevertheless, it is likely that publicity accompanying the spinal tap research provided additional support in spreading the myth. Responding to its recent arrival in Europe, Dutch MDMA researcher Arno Adelaars asserts that "all this stuff about Ecstasy draining your spinal fluid is a myth, though—it's dancing which makes you ache the next day, or your kidneys trying to deal with the other chemicals which you have ingested" (Adelaars, quoted in James, 1991).

CHAPTER 6. ADVERSE REACTIONS AND ABUSE: WHEN ECSTASY BECOMES AGONY

1. Given the implications of these findings, they are further examined in the discussion of harm reduction strategies found in the concluding chapter.

2. In contrast to these reported health problems, a few respondents described positive reactions which suggest that MDMA's effect on the immune system may be twofold. They believed that MDMA may exert some type of immune-enhancing effect—at least during the duration of the high. A small number of respondents strongly believed in MDMA's value or potential in dealing with a range of physical ailments. A few regularly took MDMA to combat incipient colds or flu. One longtime user asserted: "Colds go away when you take it—allergies—for most everybody. . . . Lots of people have reported that to me. I think it does enhance the immune system while you're doing it. G. worked with a cancer patient. It took away pain" (007:96).

A few individuals noted how various allergies almost magically disappeared while under the influence of MDMA. While coming on to MDMA, one respondent (052) described how he was stung several times inside the mouth by a yellowjacket which had flown into a can of soda he was drinking. Temporarily concerned about the implications, he soon forgot about it and surprisingly experienced no swelling or pain during or after the MDMA trip. Similar observations were noted by Weil (1976), who found that MDA also appears to exert an anti-allergenic response.

3. Although Winstock (1991) provides some evidence of more chronic heavy use patterns, only five respondents had reportedly used

MDMA over one hundred times (Winstock, 1991). Though sketchy as to duration and changing patterns of use, this appears to concur with our findings regarding to the apparent rarity of veteran abusers.

4. At the time of the hearings, there were only eight mentions for MDMA in the Drug Abuse Warning Network (DAWN), a figure all the more remarkable if one accepted the high estimates of use provided by the DEA (Beck, 1986; Seymour, 1986).

5. The marked contrast in number of uses between Peroutka's survey and our study can be largely attributed to our intentional oversampling of frequent and binge users. In addition, our respondents tended to be much older and to have had longer use histories than Peroutka's undergraduates.

6. We've consistently included a question about Ecstasy use in our studies of methadone and cocaine. In Rosenbaum and Britton's current study of methadone maintenance, only 2 out of 233 respondents (less than 1 percent) had tried it (1990–1993). In Murphy and Rosenbaum's recent study of women and crack, only 5 percent had tried MDMA (1989–1992).

CHAPTER 7. WHAT SHOULD BE DONE ABOUT ECSTASY? FINDINGS AND RECOMMENDATIONS

1. This was best exemplified by Bennett's denunciation of *Nation* reporter Jefferson Morley as a "defector in the war on drugs," following an article in the *New Republic* describing his personal experience with crack (Giordano, 1990).

2. As an example, in 1983, Dr. Andrew Weil and Winifred Rosen published *Chocolate to Morphine*, a book written for the purpose of educating young people about legal and illegal drugs (Weil and Rosen, 1983). The authors took no position about drug use, but simply described various popular substances, telling readers about the harms and benefits of drugs, and stressing that there were no good or bad drugs, simply good or bad relationships with drugs. After an initial positive response to the book, it was increasingly attacked by politicians and parent groups for not taking a strong antidrug stand. Claiming the book advocated drug use, many libraries subsequently took it off their shelves.

3. Judge Young concluded that MDMA did not meet any of the three criteria necessary for a Schedule I placement, presenting a significant challenge to his agency's interpretation of the scheduling process (Young, 1986).

4. Whereas the pharmaceutical industry may not see the value of reduced ingestion of (their) drugs (therefore fewer profits), our current efforts to scale down health care costs indicate that Americans support this change. If one or two MDMA-assisted sessions could help at least some individuals avoid many years of chronic and costly use of other psychotropic medications, a strong case could be made for its cost-effectiveness.

5. Interestingly, Kleiman notes that favorable publicity accompanying therapeutic research and use of MDMA may indeed pique public curiosity. However, he goes on to suggest why this should not be simply perceived as only "sending the *wrong* message":

> On balance, it seems likely that the eventual approval of MDMA for clinical use will tend to foster non-medical use as well, or at least to speed the pace at which knowledge of the drug's effects, and interest in experiencing them also spreads. Yet this very dissemination of knowledge about the medical use of MDMA may also help to create a more educated and responsible set of social norms concerning appropriate use patterns, thereby reducing the harms of non-medical use though perhaps increasing the quantity of non-medical use. But it also seems likely that non-medical use will be present whether or not clinical use is approved, and the eventual size of the illicit market may depend very little on the decision to approve or disapprove the use of MDMA in therapy. (1992:7)

APPENDIX A. THEORY AND METHODOLOGY

1. Appendix B provides selected demographic information for individual respondents. Appendices C and D provide data on respondents' lifetime drug use, preference, and changes in use from the previous year.

REFERENCES

Accola, J. (1988) "MDMA: Studies of Popular Illicit Drug Raise Questions about Effects," *Rocky Mountain News*, p. 72, March 4.

Adamson, S., and Metzner, R. (1988) "The Nature of the MDMA Experience and Its Role in Healing, Psychotherapy, and Spiritual Practice," *Revision*, 10(4):59–72.

Adler, J. (1985) "Getting High on 'Ecstasy,'" *Newsweek*, p. 96, April 15.

Agar, M. (1973) *Ripping and Running*, New York: Academic Press.

Agar, M. (1985) "Folks and Professionals: Different Models for the Interpretation of Drug Use," *International Journal of the Addictions*, 20(1):173-182.

Associated Press. (1986) "Researchers Say 'Ecstasy' Is Dangerous," January 16.

Bakalar, J. B., and Grinspoon, L. (1990) "Testing Psychotherapies and Drug Therapies: The Case of Psychedelic Drugs." In S. J. Peroutka (Ed.), *Ecstasy: The Clinical, Pharmacological and Neurotoxicological Effects of the Drug MDMA*, Norwell, MA: Kluwer Academic Publications.

Baldinger, S. (1992) "Ecstasy: A Decade on the Rave," *Out Magazine*, pp. 47–53, Summer.

Ball, J. (1967) "The Reliability and Validity of Interview Data Obtained from 59 Narcotics Addicts," *American Journal of Sociology*, 72:650–654.

Barnes, D. M. (1988) "New Data Intensify the Agony Over Ecstasy," *Science*, 239:864–866.

Battaglia, G., Zaczek, R., and De Souza, E. B. (1990) "MDMA Effects in Brain: Pharmacologic Profile and Evidence of Neurotoxicity from Neurochemical and Autoradiographic Studies." In S. J. Peroutka (Ed.), *Ecstasy: The Clinical, Pharmacological and Neurotoxicological Effects of the Drug MDMA*, Norwell, MA: Kluwer Academic Publishers.

Baumeister, R. F. (1984) "Acid Rock: A Critical Reappraisal and Psychological Commentary," *Journal of Psychoactive Drugs*, 16(4):339–345.

Beck, J. (1986) "MDMA: The Popularization and Resultant Implications of a Recently Controlled Psychoactive Substance," *Contemporary Drug Problems*, 13(1):305–313.

Beck, J. (1987) *MDMA*, White Paper for State of California Drug Abuse Information and Monitoring Project, Sacramento, CA: Department of Alcohol and Drug Programs.

Beck, J. (1990a) "The MDMA Controversy: Contexts of Use and Social Control," Doctoral Dissertation, School of Public Health, University of California, Berkeley.

Beck, J. (1990b) "The Public Health Implications of MDMA Use." In S. J. Peroutka (Ed.), *Ecstasy: The Clinical, Pharmacological and Neurotoxicological Effects of the Drug MDMA*, Norwell, MA: Kluwer Academic Publishers.

Beck, J., Harlow, D., McDonnell, D., Morgan, P. A., Rosenbaum, M., and Watson, L. (1989) *Exploring Ecstasy: A Description of MDMA Users*, Final Report to the National Institute on Drug Abuse, Grant 1 R01 DA04408.

Beck, J., and Morgan, P. A. (1986) "Designer Drug Confusion: A Focus on MDMA," *Journal of Drug Education*, 16(3):287–302.

Beck, J., and Rosenbaum, M. (1990) "The Scheduling of MDMA ('Ecstasy')." In J. Inciardi (Ed.), *The Handbook of Drug Control in the United States*, Westport, CT: Greenwood Press.

Becker, H. (1967) "History, Culture and Subjective Experience: An Exploration of the Social Bases of Drug-Induced Experiences," *Journal of Health and Social Behavior*, 8:162–176.

Becker, H. (1970) *Sociological Work*, Chicago: Aldine Press.

Becker, H. S. (1974) "Consciousness, Power and Drug Effects," *Journal of Psychedelic Drugs*, 6(1):67–76.

Bennett, W. (1989) Office of National Drug Control Policy, *National Drug Control Strategy*, Washington, D.C.: U.S. Government Printing Office, September.

Biernacki, P., and Waldorf, D. (1981) "Snowball Sampling: Problems, Techniques and Chain Referral Sampling," *Sociological Methods and Research*, 10(2):141–163.

Blum, R., and Associates. (1964) *Utopiates: The Use and Users of LSD-25*, New York: Atherton Press.

Blum, R., and Associates. (1972) *The Dream Sellers*, San Francisco, CA: Jossey-Bass, Inc.

Blumer, H. (1969) *Symbolic Interactionism*, Englewood Cliffs, NJ: Prentice-Hall.

Bonito, A., Nurco, D., and Shaffer, J. (1976) "The Verdicality of Addicts' Self Reports in Social Research," *International Journal of the Addictions*, 11(5):719–724.

Brecher, E. M. (1972) *Licit and Illicit Drugs*, Boston: Little Brown Publishers.

Buffum, J., and Moser, C. (1986) "MDMA and Human Sexual Function," *Journal of Psychoactive Drugs*, 18:355–359.

Cahr, D., and Bashara, S. (1989) "Acid House Reaches America," *The National College Newspaper*, September.

Calvert, C. (1987) "Psychedelic Drug Use Up on Farm," *Stanford Daily*, March 3.

Cohen, S. (1965) "LSD and the Anguish of Dying," *Harper's Magazine*, 231:69–72, 77–78, September.

Coombs, R. (1981) "Drug Abuse as Career," *Journal of Drug Issues*, 11(4):369–387.

Creighton, F., Black, D., and Hyde, C. (1991) "Ecstasy Psychosis and Flashbacks," *British Journal of Psychiatry*, 159:713–715.

Denzin, N. (1978) *The Research Act: A Theoretical Introduction to Sociological Methods*, New York: McGraw-Hill.

Doblin, R. (1988) *A Proposal for Orphan Pharmaceuticals, Inc.*, Self-published manuscript.

Doblin, R. (1990) "Psychedelics in the 1990s: A Thousand Points of Light," Self-published manuscript.

Doblin, R. (1992) *Multidisciplinary Association for Psychedelic Studies, Inc.*, (MAPS) Newsletter, 3(2), Spring.

Docherty, J. P. (1985a) Oral Testimony Submitted on Behalf of Drug Enforcement Administration, United States Department of Justice, Drug Enforcement Administration Law Hearings, Docket No. 84-48.

Docherty, J. P. (1985b) Written Testimony Submitted on Behalf of Drug Enforcement Administration, United States Department of Justice, Drug Enforcement Administration Law Hearings, Docket No. 84-48.

Dorn, N., Murji, K., and South, N. (1991) "Abby, the Ecstasy Dealer," *Druglink*, 6(6):14–15, November/December.

Dowling, C. (1985) "The Trouble with Ecstasy," *Life Magazine*, 88–94, August.

Dowling, G. (1990) "Human Deaths and Toxic Reactions Attributed to MDMA and MDEA." In S. J. Peroutka (Ed.), *Ecstasy: The Clinical, Pharmacological and Neurotoxicological Effects of the Drug MDMA*, Norwell, MA: Kluwer Academic Publishers.

Dowling, G., McDonough, E., and Bost, R. (1987) "Eve and Ecstasy: A Report of Five Deaths Associated with the Use of MDEA and MDMA," *JAMA*, 257:1615–1617.

Downing, J. (1985) Written Testimony Submitted on Behalf of Drs. Grinspoon and Greer, Professors Bakalar and Roberts, United States Department of Justice, Drug Enforcement Administration Law Hearings, Docket No. 84-48.

Downing, J. (1986) "The Psychological and Physiological Effects of MDMA on Normal Volunteers," *Journal of Psychoactive Drugs*, 18:335–340.

Drug Abuse Warning Network (DAWN). (1986) Series 1, No. 5., Rockville, MD: National Institute on Drug Abuse, pp. 24–25.

Drug Abuse Warning Network (DAWN). (1987) Series 1, No. 6, Rockville, MD: National Institute on Drug Abuse.

Drug Abuse Warning Network (DAWN). (1988) Series 1, No. 7, Rockville, MD: National Institute on Drug Abuse, p. 26.

Druglink. (1992) "Agencies Face Wave of Ecstasy Problems," January/February.

Duster, T. (1970) *The Legislation of Morality: Laws, Drugs, and Moral Judgment,* New York: The Free Press.

Dye, C. (1982) "XTC: The Chemical Pursuit of Pleasure," *Drug Survival News,* 10(5):8–9.

Eisner, B. (1989) *Ecstasy: The MDMA Story,* Berkeley: Ronin.

Fagan, J., and Chin, K. (1991) "Social Processes of Initiation into Crack," *Journal of Drug Issues,* 21(2):313–344.

Farrell, M. (1989) "Ecstasy and the Oxygen of Publicity," *British Journal of Addiction,* 84:943.

Ferguson, M. (1980) *The Aquarian Conspiracy,* Los Angeles: J. P. Tarcher.

Fitzgerald, J. (1991) "MDMA and Harm," *International Journal of Drug Policy,* 2(4):22–24, January/February.

Fitzgerald, J., and Reid, J. (1992) "MDMA Use in Melbourne, Preliminary Results from a Qualitative Analysis." Paper presented at Reduction of Drug Related Harm Conference in Melbourne, Australia, March.

Foderaro, L. W. (1988) "A Drug Called 'Ecstasy' Emerges in Nightclubs," *New York Times,* p. 26, December 11.

Fong-Torres, B. (1988) "Journey into the New Age," *San Francisco Chronicle,* April 28.

Fredlund, E., Kavinsky, M., Dyer, J., and Carmichael, D. (1990) *The 1990 Texas School Survey of Substance Abuse,* Austin: Texas Commission on Alcohol and Drug Abuse.

Fromberg, E. (1992). Personal Communication.

Gay, G., Newmeyer, J., Perry, M., Johnson, G., and Kurland, M. (1982) "Love and Haight: The Sensuous Hippie Revisited. Drug/Sex Practices in San Francisco, 1980-1981," *Journal of Psychoactive Drugs,* 14(1-2):111–123.

Geertz, C. (1973) *The Interpretations of Cultures,* New York: Basic Books.

Gertz, K. R. (1985) "'Hug Drug' Alert: The Agony of Ecstasy," *Harper's Bazaar,* p. 48, November.

Gilman, M. (1991) Beyond Opiates—And into the '90s, *Druglink,* 6(6):16–18, November/December.

Giordano, A. (1990) "Who Drafted the Press?" *Washington Journalism Review,* pp. 20–24, January/February.

Glaser, B. (1978) *Theoretical Sensitivity,* Mill Valley, CA: The Sociology Press.

Glaser, B., and Strauss, A. (1967) *The Discovery of Grounded Theory: Strategies for Qualitative Research*, Chicago: Aldine.

Goodman, F. (1990) The End of The Road? *Rolling Stone*, August 23.

Greer, G. (1983) "MDMA: A New Psychotropic Compound and Its Effects in Humans," Self-published manuscript.

Greer, G. (1985) Written Testimony Submitted on Behalf of Drs. Grinspoon and Greer, Professors Bakalar and Roberts, United States Department of Justice, Drug Enforcement Administration Law Hearings, Docket No. 84-48.

Greer, G., and Tolbert, R. (1986) "Subjective Reports of the Effects of MDMA in a Clinical Setting," *Journal of Psychoactive Drugs*, 18:319–327.

Greer, G., and Tolbert, R. (1990) "The Therapeutic Use of MDMA." In S. J. Peroutka (Ed.), *Ecstasy: The Clinical, Pharmacological and Neurotoxicological Effects of the Drug MDMA*, Norwell, MA: Kluwer Academic Publishers.

Grinspoon, L. (1985) Written Testimony Submitted on Behalf of Drs. Grinspoon and Greer, Professors Bakalar and Roberts, United States Department of Justice, Drug Enforcement Administration Law Hearings, Docket No. 84-48.

Grinspoon, L., and Bakalar, J. (1979) *Psychedelic Drugs Reconsidered*, New York: Basic Books.

Grinspoon, L., and Bakalar, J. (1987) "Medical Uses of Illicit Drugs." In R. Hamowy (Ed.), *Dealing With Drugs: Consequences of Government Control*, Lexington, MA: Lexington Books.

Grob, C., Bravo, G., McQuade, J., and Doblin, R. (1991) "Analgesic Efficacy of 3,4-Methylenedioxymethamphetamine (MDMA) in Modification of Pain and Distress of End-Stage Cancer," FDA IND Application.

Grob, C., and Dobkin de Rios, M. (1992) "Adolescent Drug Use in Cross-Cultural Perspective," *Journal of Drug Issues*, 22(1):121–138.

Haafkens, J. (1989) Personal communication.

Hammersley, M., and Atkinson, P. (1983) *Ethnography: Principles and Practice*, London and New York: Tavistock Publications.

Harbin, H. (1988) "MDMA. Narcotics, Forfeiture and Money-Laundering Update," United States Department of Justice, Criminal Division 2(1):14–19.

Harding, W., and Zinberg, N. (1977) "The Effectiveness of the Subculture in Developing Rituals and Social Sanctions for Controlled Use." In B. M. du Toit (Ed.), *Drugs, Rituals and Altered States of Consciousness*, Rotterdam, Netherlands: Balkema.

Harlow, D., and Beck, J. (1990) "Survey of the Clinical Use of MDMA." Paper presented at Multidisciplinary Association for Psychedelic Studies, Inc. (MAPS) International Conference on Psycholytic Psychotherapy, Bern, Switzerland, November 29.

Hayner, G. N., and McKinney, H. (1986) "MDMA: The Dark Side of Ecstasy," *Journal of Psychoactive Drugs*, 18:341–347.

Heley, Mark. (1991) "House Music: The Best Techno-Shamanic Cultural Virus So Far," *Mondo 2000*, Issue #3, pp. 125–126.

Helmer, J. (1975) *Drugs and Minority Oppression*, New York: Seabury Press.

Henry, J. (1992) "Ecstasy and the Dance of Death," *British Medical Journal*, 305:5–6, July, 4.

Henry, J., Jeffreys, K., and Dawling, S. (1992) "Toxicity and Deaths from 3,4-Methylenedioxymethamphetamine ('Ecstasy')," *Lancet*, 340:384–387, August 15.

Holsten, D., and Scheister, D. (1985) "Controls over the Manufacture of MDMA," *California Society for the Treatment of Alcoholism and Other Drug Dependencies News*, 12(2):14–15.

The Illustrated London News. (1988) "The Hyping of Ecstasy," pp. 29–30, 32, October.

International Journal on Drug Policy. (1989) 1(3):9.

Irwin, J. (1977) *Scenes*, Beverly Hills: Sage.

James, J. (1977) "Ethnography and Social Problems." In R. S. Weppner (Ed.), *Street Ethnography*, Beverly Hills: Sage.

James, M. "Ecstasy." (1991) *The Face*, 38, November.

Jick, T. (1979) "Mixing Qualitative and Quantitative Methods: Triangulation in Action," *Administrative Science Quarterly*, 24:602–661.

Johanson, C. (1985) "Report for the University of Chicago Drug Abuse Research Center." In L. Harris (Ed.), *Problems of Drug Dependence, 1984: Proceedings of the 46th Annual Scientific Meeting*, NIDA Research Monograph 55:78–85, Rockville, MD: National Institute on Drug Abuse.

Johnston, L., Bachman, J., and O'Malley, P. (1991) *Monitoring the Future: Drug Use Among American High School Seniors, College Students and Young Adults, 1975–1990: Volume II*, Rockville, MD: National Institute on Drug Abuse.

Jones, C., and Dickinson, P. (1992) "From Ecstasy to Agony," *Nursing Times*, 88(13):28–30, March 25.

Jones, G. (1991) *The Times*, September 9.

Jones, G., *The Times*, September 27, 1989, as cited in *International Journal on Drug Policy*, Vol. 1, No. 3, p. 9, Nov.–Dec. 1989.

Kamiya, G. (1991) "Night of the Living Dead," *Image*, January 27.

Kaplan, C., Grund, J-P. C., Dzolijic, M., and Barendregt, C. (1989) "Ecstasy in Europe: Reflections on the Epidemiology of MDMA," *Community Epidemiology Work Group Proceedings*, Rockville, MD: National Institute on Drug Abuse.

Kaye, E. (1986) "Drugless in L.A.: The New Trend Is Sobriety," *New Age Journal*, May.

Kirk, J., and Miller, M. (1986) *Reliability and Validity in Qualitative Research*, Beverly Hills: Sage.

Kirsch, M. M. (1986) *Designer Drugs*, Minneapolis, MN: CompCare Publications.

Klein, J. (1985) "The New Drug They Call Ecstasy," *New York*, pp. 38–43, May 20.

Kleiman, M. (1992) "Considerations about MDMA Research," Paper prepared for FDA Drug Abuse Advisory Committee, July 7.

Kleinman, J. (1985) Rebuttal Testimony Submitted on Behalf of Drug Enforcement Administration, United States Department of Justice, Drug Enforcement Administration Law Hearings, Docket No. 84-48.

Kleven, M., Schuster, C., and Seiden, L. (1988) "Effect of Depletion of Brain Serotonin by Repeated Fenfluramine on Neurochemical and Anorectic Effects of Acute Fenfluramine," *Journal of Pharmacology and Experimental Therapeutics*, 246:822–828.

Korf, D., Blanken, P., and Nabben, T. (1991) *Een Nieuwe Wonderpil? Verspreiding, Effecten en Risico's van Ecstasvgebruik in Amsterdan*, Amsterdam: Jellinek Centrum.

Lawn, J. C. (1985) "Schedules of Controlled Substances: Temporary Placement of 3,4-Methylenedioxymethamphetamine (MDMA) into Schedule I," *Federal Register* 50(105):23118–23120, May 31.

Lawn, J. C. (1986) "Schedules of Controlled Substances: Scheduling of 3,4-Methylenedioxymethamphetamine (MDMA) into Schedule I of the Controlled Substances Act," *Federal Register* 51(198):36552–36560, October 14.

Lawn, J. C. (1988) "Schedules of Controlled Substances: Scheduling of 3,4-Methylenedioxymethamphetamine (MDMA) into Schedule I of the Controlled Substances Act," *Federal Register* 53(5156): February 22.

Leary, T. (1985) "XTC: The Drug of the '80s," *Chic*, pp. 75–76, July.

Leavy, J. (1985) "Ecstasy: The Lure and the Peril," *Washington Post*, pp. 1, 4, June 1.

Lee, M., and Shlain, B. (1985) *Acid Dreams: The CIA, LSD, and the Sixties Rebellion*, New York: Grove Press.

Leuw, E. (1991) "Dutch Penal Law and Policy: Notes on Criminological Research from the Research and Documentation Centre," Ministry of Justice, The Hague, The Netherlands, November 4.

Lewis, L., and Ross, M. (1991) "Sex on Ice (d-Methamphetamine Hydrocholoride) in Sydney: A Qualitative Analysis." National Centre for Social and Behavioural Research into Human Immunodeficiency Virus, Sydney, Australia.

Lindesmith, A., Strauss, A., and Denzin, N. (1977) *Social Psychology* (5th Edition), Hinsdale, IL: Dryden Press.

Lofland, J. (1971) *Analyzing Social Settings: A Guide to Qualitative Observation and Analysis*, Belmont, CA: Wadsworth.

Lynch, R. (1985) Written Testimony Submitted on Behalf of Drs. Grinspoon and Greer, Professors Bakalar and Roberts, United States Department of Justice, Drug Enforcement Administration Law Hearings, Docket No. 84-48.

Lyttle, T. (1988) "Drug Based Religions and Contemporary Drug Taking," *Journal of Drug Issues*, 18(2):271–284.

Maddux, J., and Desmond, D. (1975) "Reliability and Validity of Information from Chronic Heroin Users," *Journal of Psychiatric Research*, 12:87–95.

Maloff, D., Becker, H.S., Fonaroff, A., and Rodin, J. (1982) "Informal Social Controls and Their Influence on Substance Use." In N. E. Zinberg and W. M. Harding (Eds.), *Control over Intoxicant Use: Pharmacological, Psychological and Social Considerations.* New York: Human Sciences Press.

Mandel, B. (1984) "The Yuppie Psychedelic," *San Francisco Examiner*, A–2, June 10.

Marshall, C., and Rossman, G. (1989) *Designing Qualitative Research*, Newbury Park, CA: Sage.

Marshall, W., and Taylor, G. (1967) *The Art of Ecstasy*, Toronto: Burns and MacEachern.

McBride, D., and Clayton, R. (1985) "Methodological Issues in the Etiology of Drug Abuse," *Journal of Drug Issues*, 15:4.

McDermott, P., Matthews, A. and Bennett, A. (1992) Responding to Recreational Drug Use, *Druglink*, January/February. Vol. 7, No. 1, pp. 12–13.

McDonnell, E. (1992) "One World, One Party," *San Francisco Weekly*, January 29.

McGuire, P., and Fahy, T. (1991) "Chronic Paranoid Psychosis after Misuse of MDMA ('Ecstasy')," *British Medical Journal*, 302:697, March 23.

McKenna, D., and Peroutka, S. (1990) "Neurochemistry and Neurotoxicity of 3,4-Methylenedioxymethamphetamine (MDMA, 'Ecstasy')," *Journal of Neurochemistry*, 54(1):14–22.

Mead, G. (1939) *Mind, Self and Society*, Chicago: University of Chicago Press.

Meyers, F., Rose, A., and Smith, D. (1967–1968) "Incidents Involving the Haight-Ashbury Population and Some Uncommonly Used Drugs," *Journal of Psychedelic Drugs*, 1(1):140–146.

Molliver, D., and Molliver, M. (1988) "Selective Neurotoxic Effects of (+/-) Fenfluramine upon 5-HT Axons in Rat Brain: Immunocytochemical Evidence," Abstract, *Society for Neuroscience*, Annual Meeting.

Morgan, P. (1978) "The Legislation of Drug Law: Economic Crisis and Social Control." In J. Weissman and R. DuPont (Eds.), *Criminal Justice and Drugs: The Unresolved Connection*, Port Washington, NY:

Kennikat Press, 1982, Reprinted from *Journal of Drug Issues* 8(1), Winter.

Morgan P. (1991) "Agenda for Action," *Council on Illicit Drug Policy*, Newsletter, Spring, 1(1).

Morley, J. (1989) "What Crack Is Like," *The New Republic*, pp.12–13, October 2.

Mullen, F. (1984) "Schedules of Controlled Substances: Placement of 3,4-Methylenedioxymethamphetamine into Schedule I," *Federal Register* 49(146):30210–30211, July 27.

Mullen, P. D., "Generating Grounded Theory: Two Case Studies," *International Quarterly of Community Health Education,* vol. 6, No. 3, pp. 177–214, 1985–1986.

Murphy, S., and Rosenbaum, M. (1992) "Women and Cocaine," NIDA Grant 1 R01 DA05332.

Musto, D. F. (1973) *The American Disease*, New Haven, CT: Yale University Press.

Naranjo, C. (1973) *The Healing Journey: New Approaches to Consciousness*, New York: Random House.

Naranjo, C., Shulgin, A., and Sargent, T. (1967) "Evaluation of 3,4-Methylenedioxyamphetamine (MDA) as an Adjunct to Psychotherapy," *Medicine et Pharmacologia Experimentalis*, 17:359–364.

Nasmyth, P. (1986) "The Agony and The Ecstasy," *The Face*, pp. 52–55, October.

Neill, J. (1987) "'More than Medical Significance': LSD and American Psychiatry—1953–1966," *Journal of Psychedelic Drugs*, 19(1):39–46, 1987.

Newcombe, R. (1988) "'Ecstasy': New Drug Same Panic," *Mersey Drug Journal* 2(4):12–13.

Newcombe, R. (1992) "A Researcher Reports from the Rave," *Druglink*, pp. 14–15, January/February. Vol. 7, No. 1.

Newmeyer, J. (1986) "Some Considerations on the Prevalence of MDMA Use," *Journal of Psychoactive Drugs*, 18(4):361–362.

Newmeyer, J. A., and Johnson, G. (1979) "Drug Emergencies in Crowds: An Analysis of 'Rock Medicine' 1973–1979," *Journal of Drug Issues*, 9:235–245.

Nichols, D. (1986) "Differences Between the Mechanism of Action of MDMA, MBDB, and the Classic Hallucinogens, Identification of a New Therapeutic Class: Entactogens," *Journal of Psychoactive Drugs*, 18:305–313.

Nichols, D. (1987) "Discovery of Novel Psychoactive Drugs: Has It Ended?" *Journal of Psychoactive Drugs*, 19(1):33–38.

NIDA Press Office. (1985) "MDMA," *NIDA Capsules*, Rockville, MD: National Institute on Drug Abuse.

O'Hagan, S. (1989) "Acid House," *Spin Magazine*, January.

Pearson, G., Ditton, J., Newcombe, R., and Gilman, M. (1991) Everything Starts with an "E," *Druglink*, 6(6):10–11, November/December.

Pekkanen, S. (1992) "FDA Gives Approval to Testing of Ecstasy," *San Francisco Examiner*, November 12.

Peroutka, S. (1988) "Incidence of Recreational Use of 3,4-Methylenedioxymethamphetamine (MDMA, 'Ecstasy') on an Undergraduate Campus," *New England Journal of Medicine*, 317:1542–1543.

Peroutka S. (1990a) "Preface." In S. J. Peroutka (Ed.), *Ecstasy: The Clinical, Pharmacological and Neurotoxicological Effects of the Drug MDMA*, Norwell, MA: Kluwer Academic Publishers.

Peroutka, S. (1990b) "Recreational Use of MDMA." In S. J. Peroutka (Ed.), *Ecstasy: The Clinical, Pharmacological and Neurotoxicological Effects of the Drug MDMA*, Norwell, MA: Kluwer Academic Publishers.

Peroutka, S., Pascoe, N., and Faull, K. (1987) "Monoamine Metabolites in the Cerebrospinal Fluid of Recreational Users of 3,4-Methylenedioxymethamphetamine (MDMA, 'Ecstasy')," *Research in Community Substance Abuse*, 8:125–138.

Physician's Desk Reference. (1992) Oradell, NJ: Medical Economics Company, Inc., pp.1694–1695.

Prangnell, M. (1988) "The Hyping of Ecstacy," *The Illustrated London News*, pp. 29–32, October.

Preble, E., and Casey, J. (1969) "Taking Care of Business: The Heroin User's Life on the Street," *International Journal of the Addictions*, 4:1–24.

Prentice, T. (1992) "The Enigma and the Ecstasy," *The London Times*, January 2.

Psychiatric News. (1992) "Drug Policies, Laws Said to Stymie Care," February 7.

Rae, S. (1989) "The Agony of Ecstasy," *Mademoiselle*, pp. 158–161, 206, 210, June.

Ray, L. (1985) "Problems of Substance Abuse: Exploitation and Control," *Social Science Medicine*, 20(12):1225–1233.

Randall, T. (1992) "Ecstasy-Fueled 'Rave' Parties Become Dances of Death for English Youths," *Journal of the American Medical Association*, 268(12):1505–1506, September 23/30.

Reinarman, C., and Levine, H. (1989) "The Crack Attack: Politics and Media in America's Latest Drug Scare." In Joel Best (Ed.), *Images of Issues*, New York: Aldine de Gruyer, pp. 115–135.

Renfroe, C. (1986) "MDMA on the Street: Analysis Annonymous," *Journal of Psychoactive Drugs*, 18:363–369.

Ricaurte, G. (1989) Personal communication.

Ricaurte, G., Bryan, G., Strauss, L., Seiden, L., and Schuster, C. (1985) "Hallucinogenic Amphetamine Selectively Destroys Brain Serotonin Nerve Terminals," *Science* 229:986–988.

Ricaurte, G., Finnegan, K., Irwin, I., and Langston, J. (1990) "Aminergic Metabolites in Cerebrospinal Fluid of Humans Previously Exposed to MDMA: Preliminary Observations," *Annals of New York Academy of Science*, 600:699–710.

Ricaurte, G., Forno, L. S., Wilson, M. A., DeLanney, L. E., Irwin, I., Molliver, M. E., and Langston, J. W. (1988) "3,4-Methylenedioxymethamphetamine Selectively Damages Central Serotonergic Neurons in Nonhuman Primates," *JAMA*, 260(1):51–55.

Riedlinger, T. and Riedlinger, J. (1989) "The Seven Deadly Sins of Media Hype Considered in Light of the MDMA Controversy," *Psychedelic Monographs and Essays*, 4:22–43.

Roberts, M. (1986) "MDMA: Madness, Not Ecstasy," *Psychology Today*, pp. 14–15, June.

Roberts, T. (1992) "Psycho-Dope! Into the Hallucinogenic Zone—Too," *URB Magazine*, pp. 36–39, March.

Robins, C. (1992) "The Ecstatic Cybernetic Amino Acid Test," *San Francisco Examiner*, Image, February 16.

Room, R. (1975) "Normative Perspectives on Alcohol Use and Problems," *Journal of Drug Issues*, 5(4): 358–368.

Rosenbaum, M. (1981) *Women on Heroin*, New Brunswick, NJ: Rutgers University Press.

Rosenbaum, M. (1990–1993) "I. V. Drug Use, Methadone Maintenance and AIDS," NIDA Grant 1 R01 DA05277.

Rosenbaum, M., and Doblin, R. (1991) "Why MDMA Should Not Have Been Made Illegal." In J. Inciardi (Ed.), *The Drug Legalization Debate*, Newbury Park, CA: Sage.

Rosenbaum, M., Morgan, P., and Beck, J. (1989) "Ethnographic Notes on Ecstasy Use among Professionals," *International Journal on Drug Policy*, 1(2):16–19.

Rossman, G., and Wilson, B. (1985) "Numbers and Words: Combining Quantitative and Qualitative Methods in a Single Large-Scale Evaluation Study," *Evaluation Review*, 9(5):627–643.

Sager, R. (1989) Personal communication.

Sapienza, F. (1985) Written Testimony Submitted on Behalf of Drug Enforcement Administration, United States Department of Justice, Drug Enforcement Administration Hearings, Docket No. 84-48.

Sapienza, F. (1986) "MDMA and the Controlled Substances Act," Paper presented at MDMA: A Multidisciplinary Conference, San Francisco, CA, May.

Satin, M. (1974) *New Age Politics*, West Vancouver, British Columbia: Whitecaps Books Ltd.

Sawyer, M. (1992) "Ecstasy," *Select Magazine*, pp. 56–61, July.

Schifano, F. (1991) "Chronic Atypical Psychosis Associated with MDMA ('Ecstasy') Abuse," *Lancet*, 338:1335.

Schmidt, C. J. (1987) "Neurotoxicity of the Psychedelic Amphetamine, Methylenedisoxymethamphetamine," *Journal of Pharmacology and Experimental Therapeutics*, 240:1–7.

Schuster, C., Lewis, M., and Seiden, L. (1986) "Fenfluramine: Neurotoxicity," *Psychopharmacology Bulletin*, 22(1):148–151.

Schutz, A. (1967) "Common Sense and Scientific Interpretations of Human Action." In *Collected Papers I: The Problem of Social Reality*, The Hague, Netherlands: Martinus Nijoff.

Seiden, L. S. (1985) Written Testimony Submitted on Behalf of Drug Enforcement Administration, United States Department of Justice, Drug Enforcement Administration Law Hearings, Docket No. 84-48.

Sellitz, C. (1961) *Research Methods in Social Relations*, New York: Holt, Rinehart and Winston.

Selvin, J. (1989) "London Fad Hits the Local Clubs," *San Francisco Chronicle*, p. E1, February 15.

Seymour, R. (1986) *MDMA*, San Francisco: Haight Ashbury Publications.

Seymour, R., Wesson, D., and Smith, D. (1986) "Editor's Introduction, MDMA: Proceedings of the Conference," *Journal of Psychoactive Drugs*, 18(4).

Shafer, J. (1985) "MDMA: Psychedelic Drug Faces Regulation," *Psychology Today*, pp. 68–69, May.

Shannon, H. E. (1985) Rebuttal Testimony Submitted on Behalf of Drug Enforcement Administration, United States Department of Justice, Drug Enforcement Administration Law Hearings, Docket No. 84-48.

Sheldrake, R. (1983) *A New Science of Life*, Los Angeles: J. P. Tarcher.

Shibutani, T. (1955) "Reference Groups as Perspectives," *American Journal of Sociology*, 60: 562–569.

Shibutani, T. (1961) *Society and Personality*, Englewood Cliffs, NJ: Prentice-Hall.

Shulgin, A. (1985) "What Is MDMA?" *PharmChem Newsletter*, 14(3):3–5, 10–11.

Shulgin, A. (1990) "History of MDMA." In S. J. Peroutka (Ed.), *Ecstasy: The Clinical, Pharmacological and Neurotoxic Effects of the Drug MDMA*, Norwell, MA: Kluwar Academic Publishers.

Shulgin, A., and Nichols, D. (1978) "Characterization of Three New Psychotomimetics." In Stillman and Willette (Eds.), *The Psychopharmacology of Hallucinogens*, New York: Pergamon Press.

Shulgin, A., and Shulgin, A. (1991) *Pihkal: A Chemical Love Story*, Berkeley, CA: Transform Press.

Siegel, R. (1985a) "Chemical Ecstasies," *Omni*, p. 29, August.

Siegel, R. (1985b) Written Testimony Submitted on Behalf of Drug Enforcement Administration, United States Department of Justice, Drug Enforcement Administration Law Hearings, Docket No. 84-48.

Siegel, R. (1986) "MDMA: Nonmedical Use and Intoxication," *Journal of Psychoactive Drugs*, 18:349–354.

Smith, D., and Seymour, R. (1985) "How the Federal Government Classifies Drugs: From Medical Use to Abuse Potential," *High Times*, August 30.

Smith, D., Wesson, D., and Buffum, J. (1985) "MDMA: 'Ecstasy' as an Adjunct to Psychotherapy and a Street Drug of Abuse," *California Society for the Treatment of Alcoholism and Other Drug Dependencies News*, 12(2):1–3.

Smith, E. (1988) "Evolving Ethics in Psychedelic Drug Taking," *Journal of Drug Issues*, 18(2):201–214.

Smith, G. (1985) "Junior Chemists Concoct Potent Mindblowers," *Tallahassee Flambeau*, pp. 1, 5, 7, August 29.

Solowij, N., Hall, W., and Lee, N. (1992) "Recreational MDMA Use in Sydney: A Profile of 'Ecstasy' Users and Their Experiences with the Drug," *British Journal of Addiction*, 87:1161–1172.

Solowij, N., and Lee, N. (1991) "Survey of Ecstasy (MDMA) Users in Sydney," New South Wales Health Department Research Grant Report Series DAD 91–69, Rozelle, NSW.

Stafford, P. (1992) *Psychedelics Encyclopedia* Third Expanded Edition, Berkeley, CA: Ronin.

Stephens, R. C. (1972) "The Truthfulness of Addict Respondents in Research Projects," *The International Journal of the Addictions* 7(3):549–558.

Stevens, J. (1987) *Storming Heaven: LSD and the American Dream*, New York: Basic Books.

Strang, J., and Farrell, M. (1992) "Harm Minimization for Drug Misusers," *British Medical Journal*, 304:1127–1128, May 2.

Strassman, R. J. (1985) Written Testimony Submitted on Behalf of Drs. Grinspoon and Greer, Professors Bakalar and Roberts, United States Department of Justice, Drug Enforcement Administration Law Hearings, Docket No. 84-48.

Street, L. (1986) "The Outlawed Aphrodisiac," *Forum*, pp. 49–52, October.

Sullivan, A. (1992) "Provincetown Diarist," *The New Republic*, p. 45, September 28.

Texas Commission on Alcohol and Drug Abuse. (1991) Current Substance Abuse Trends in Texas, July.

Tocus, E. C. (1985) Written Testimony Submitted on Behalf of Drug Enforcement Administration, United States Department of Justice, Drug Enforcement Administration Law Hearings, Docket No. 84-48.

Toufexis, A. (1985) "A Crackdown on Ecstasy," *Time*, p. 64, June 10.

Trebach, A. S. (1987) *The Great Drug War: And Radical Proposals That*

Could Make America Safe Again, New York: Macmillan Publishing Company.

Turek, I. S., Soskin, R. A., and Kurland, A. A. (1974) "Methylenedioxy-Amphetamine (MDA) Subjective Effects," *Journal of Psychedelic Drugs*, 6(1):7–13.

United States Department of Justice. (1985) Drug Enforcement Administration Fact Sheet.

Wagner, J. A., and Peroutka, S. J. (1988) "Comparative Neurotoxicity of Fenfluramine and 3,4-Methylenedioxymethamphetamine (MDMA)," *Soc. Neurosci. Abst.*, 14:327.

Waldorf, D. (1973) *Careers in Dope*, Englewood Cliffs, NJ: Prentice-Hall.

Waldorf, D., Murphy, S., Marotta, T., and Lauderback, D. (1989) "Gay Prostitution, IV Drug Use and AIDS." Final Report to the National Institute on Drug Abuse, Grant R01 DA04535.

Waldorf, D., Reinarman, C., and Murphy, S. (1991) *Cocaine Changes*, Philadelphia: Temple University Press.

Watson, L., and Beck, J. (1991) "New Age Seekers: MDMA Use as an Adjunct to Spiritual Pursuit," *Journal of Psychoactive Drugs*, 23(3):261–270.

Watson, M. (1991) "Harm Reduction—Why Do It?" *The International Journal on Drug Policy*, 2(5):13–15, March/April.

Wax, R. (1971) *Doing Fieldwork: Warnings and Advice*, Chicago: University of Chicago Press.

Weil, A. (1972) *The Natural Mind: A New Way of Looking at Drugs and the Higher Consciousness*, Boston: Houghton Mifflin.

Weil, A. (1976) "The Love Drug," *Journal of Psychedelic Drugs* 8(4):335.

Weil, A., and Rosen, W. (1983) *Chocolate to Morphine: Understanding Mind Active Drugs*, Boston: Houghton-Mifflin.

Weppner, R. S., "Street Ethnography: Problems and Prospects," In R. S. Weppner, *Street Ethnography*. Beverly Hills, CA: Sage, 1977.

Whitaker-Azmitia, P. A., and Aronson, T. (1989) "'Ecstasy' (MDMA)-Induced Panic," *American Journal of Psychiatry*, 146:119.

Widmer, S. (1992) "Clinical Work Using MDMA in Switzerland Since 1985," *Multidisciplinary Association for Psychedelic Studies, Inc.*, (MAPS) Newsletter, Summer, 3(3).

Winstock, A. (1991) "Chronic Paranoid Psychosis after Misuse of MDMA," *British Medical Journal*, 302:6785.

Wolfe, T. (1968) *The Electric Kool-Aid Acid Test*, New York: Bantam.

Wolfson, P. E. (1985) Written Testimony Submitted on Behalf of Drs. Grinspoon and Greer, Professors Bakalar and Roberts, United States Department of Justice, Drug Enforcement Administration Law Hearings, Docket No. 84-48.

Wolfson, P. E. (1986) "Meetings at the Edge with Adam: A Man for All Seasons?" *Journal of Psychoactive Drugs* 18(4):329–333.

World Health Organization. (1985) "Excerpt from the Report of the Twenty-Second WHO Expert Committee on Drug Dependence," Annex II, May 20: 8.

Yensen, R. (1985) "LSD and Psychotherapy," *Journal of Psychoactive Drugs*, 17(4): 267–277.

Yensen, R. (1992) "U.S. Government Reconsiders Hallucinogen Research," *The Albert Hofmann Foundation Bulletin*, 2(4):18–19, Fall.

Yensen, R., DiLeo, F., Rhead, J., Richards, W., Soskin, R., Turek, I., and Kurland, A. (1976) "MDA-assisted Psychotherapy with Neurotic Outpatients: A Pilot Study," *Journal of Nervous and Mental Disease*, 163(4): 233–245.

Young, F. (1986) Opinion and Recommended Ruling, Findings of Fact, Conclusions of Law and Decision of Administrative Law Judge. Submitted in the Matter of MDMA Scheduling, Docket No. 84-48, May 22.

Zanger, R. (1989) "Dr. Peter Baumann: LSD Therapy in Switzerland," Interview, *The Albert Hofmann Foundation Newsletter* 1(2):3, 8–11.

Zinberg, N. (1976) "Observations on the Phenomenology of Consciousness Change," *Journal of Psychoactive Drugs* 8(1):59–76.

Zinberg, N. (1984) *Drug, Set, and Setting*, New Haven: Yale University Press.

Zinberg, N., and Robertson, J. (1972) *Drugs and the Public*, New York: Simon and Schuster.

INDEX